The World Island

The World Island

*Eurasian Geopolitics and
the Fate of the West*

ALEXANDROS PETERSEN

Praeger Security International

 PRAEGER

AN IMPRINT OF ABC-CLIO, LLC
Santa Barbara, California • Denver, Colorado • Oxford, England

Library of Congress Cataloging-in-Publication Data

Petersen, Alexandros.
  The World Island : Eurasian geopolitics and the fate of the West / Alexandros Petersen.
    p. cm.
  Includes bibliographical references and index.
  ISBN 978-0-313-39137-8 (hard copy : alk. paper) — ISBN 978-0-313-39138-5 (ebook)
1. Eurasia–Politics and government. 2. Geopolitics–Eurasia. 3. Eurasia–Foreign relations–Western countries. 4. Western countries–Foreign relations–Eurasia. 5. Russia (Federation)–Foreign relations–Western countries. 6. Western countries–Foreign relations–Russia (Federation) 7. China–Foreign relations–Western countries. 8. Western countries–Foreign relations–China. 9. Eurasia–Strategic aspects. 10. Security, International. I. Title.
DS33.3.P44   2011
327.5—dc22   2010053258

ISBN: 978–0–313–39137–8
EISBN: 978–0–313–39138–5

15 14 13 12 11   2 3 4 5

This book is also available on the World Wide Web as an eBook.
Visit www.abc-clio.com for details.

Praeger
An Imprint of ABC-CLIO, LLC

ABC-CLIO, LLC
130 Cremona Drive, P.O. Box 1911
Santa Barbara, California 93116-1911

This book is printed on acid-free paper ∞

Manufactured in the United States of America

To Eigil

I would rather excel others in the knowledge of what is excellent than in the extent of my powers and dominion.

—Alexander the Great

With Heaven's aid I have conquered for you a huge empire. But my life was too short to achieve the conquest of the world. That task is left for you.

—Genghis Khan

Contents

Acknowledgments

The creation of this book would not have been possible were it not for the hard work of my gifted, globe-trotting research assistant and friend Richard Cashman. His deep interest in the ideas discussed herein and intimate knowledge of the countries, cultures, and customs of Eurasia were invaluable as we crafted this work together. I thank Paul Hughes for his research support when this project was just a twinkle in my eye and of course Steve Catalano, my intrepid editor at Praeger, who immediately became inspired by the book's concept in a phone call from Kabul.

Finally, I would like to thank all those kind enough to review this book when it was still a manuscript: Ambassador Richard Burt, Dr. Samuel Charap, Dr. Ariel Cohen, The Honorable Dr. John Hillen, The Right Honourable Dr. Liam Fox MP, Professor Charles King, Edward Lucas and General Charles "Chuck" F. Wald.

Any errors of fact or interpretation are my responsibility.

Alexandros Petersen
Ashgabat, Turkmenistan
September 2010

CHAPTER 1

Introduction: Ideas and Geopolitics

The erstwhile position of the Western powers as the unmatched exemplars of progressive political organization, prosperity, and power projection is rapidly threatening to become an historical memory. While for a time the rise of the major Eastern powers had proceeded in parallel with continued betterment in the West, the dominant trend of global power politics since the end of the 1990s seems to point to a developing East-West divergence along zero-sum lines. The 1990s now looks to have represented an ahistorical geopolitical bubble, characterized by the default unipolarity of Western preponderance following Russia's imperial implosion and occurring at a time before most onlookers had been struck by the full brilliance of the Asian ascendency. As the glare of that sun has loomed into proper view it has become clear that the light at its center—China—seeks to challenge the institutionalized setting of Western power as it exists beyond the borders of the Euro-Atlantic community. Added to this is the Russian recovery, which, although replete at every level with questions about its sustainability, is nonetheless a fact in the Eurasian space in the early twenty-first century. The watchword is authoritarianism, and while the Russian and Chinese stars may not be aligned in the long term, Moscow and Beijing do find themselves sharing a common short- to medium-term goal of banishing Western political and economic influence from the larger part of the Eurasian space and undermining it in its peninsular stronghold of Western Europe.

Of the two, Moscow is the more pugnacious in this enterprise, but Beijing's effort carries with it the greater momentum. Russia's reexpansion into the post-Soviet space is characterized by geostrategic prudence,

China's move into the same area and elsewhere by a spiritual quest to displace what it considers is its natural weight in world affairs. The unfolding struggle will be typified less by open use of force, or even the threat of it, than by economic leverage and political subterfuge. In that way we should not be thinking in Cold War terms even though great power confrontation is what is being discussed. Yet there remains a strong current of ideological competition, which is in many ways a truer representation of East-West digress than the capitalist-Communist struggle that characterized the Cold War. It is today's increasingly conspicuous free nation-authoritarianism struggle that goes to the heart of the East-West schism. Moscow and Beijing want to preserve their political culture, and the areas it has spread into, free from the Western institutional arrangements that have proven so attractive almost everywhere else in the world. The diplomatic score to this modern geopolitical opera are the soothsayings of multipolarity and equality of political and economic ideology. It is a sound to which Western ears need to be attuned, for it portends a reversal of the advance Western institutions have made, a reduced ability for Western actors to compete fairly for resources, and the possible demise of Western power altogether.

A preoccupied introversion in Europe and something of an identity crisis in the United States means that vacuum conditions are being created in many regions around the world, but particularly in the fissiparous climate of Eurasia. A process of long-term Western decline, perhaps leading to eventual dominance by some form of Chinese informal hegemony, is a distinct possibility. As the manifestations of this reality become increasingly abundant the dynamics of the West's important power relations and their focus need to be reassessed. The Eurasian landmass ought to be the focal point of the West's strategic exertions. The best explanation underlining this imperative remains the Heartland-World Island concept of the early twentieth-century British geostrategist Sir Halford Mackinder. Mackinder argued that a power able to dominate the vast landmass, resources, and peoples of Eurasia would in turn be able to dominate the globe. Therein lay the great problem for the West, which he identified and which will stand as a warning through the ages. Today Russia remains the power exercising the greatest influence throughout Eurasia, but much of that is historical and is becoming increasingly redundant in its existing guise. The power best placed to exploit that reality is China. While the countries of the Caucasus, Central, Inner, and South Asia generally want to escape Russia's grip, they are seeking too to emerge from China's ever increasing shadow. That, however, is hard to do when Moscow and Beijing have resolved to act in concord so far as it means denying to those smaller states the option of engagement with the West. If the nascent process of Western decline is to be arrested and reversed, a better understanding of the geopolitical relevance of Eurasia, and the struggle therein, and a concerted effort there, is crucial.

That dynamic understood, it is useful to look at the works of two other twentieth-century geostrategists for instructive examples of how best to formulate a Western strategy for the twenty-first century. George Kennan and Josef Pilsudski, though working independently, both proffered solutions to the essential challenge Mackinder identified. Kennan's "containment" and Pilsudski's "Prometheism-Intermarum" go far in helping to explain why, where, and how still-preponderant Western influence can and must be brought to bear to ensure its survival in the future. The conclusion is that a Twenty-First-Century Geopolitical Strategy for Eurasia (21CGSE) must employ the methodical and determined spread of Western institutions and good governance as the West's own greatest defense. In detail the strategy advocates a new realization of Mackinder's warning, prevention of Russian-Chinese condominium, and the expansion of Western institutions into the heart of Eurasia to anchor the West geopolitically, benefit those smaller states politically, and realize the potential of the old East-West trade corridor for the benefit of all powers concerned, including Russia and China.

The Twenty-First-Century Geopolitical Strategy for Eurasia reestablishes fundamental Western strategic objectives, the clarity of which has all too often become muddied by anxiety over short-term considerations. It sets out and communicates what is at stake for the West in the Eurasian theater and urges a robust forward strategy to further and protect essential Western values. With its focus on the "West." the strategy provides a joint framework for trans-Atlantic cooperation. Its most important policy implication is the restoration of geopolitical purpose to Western institutions such as the North Atlantic Treaty Organization (NATO), the European Union (EU), and the Organization for Security and Co-operation in Europe (OSCE), among others, by arguing forcefully that their activities and expansion be refocused on Eurasia. A central facet the strategy promotes is the diffusion of good governance to ensure that the struggle for the fundamental theater in world politics is resolved in favor of Western democratic governance and market-based systems, without the domination of Eurasia by autocratic powers. However, although this idea-driven initiative is employed to rationalize the strategy, it is couched firmly in terms of its functionality in furthering an intrinsically realist project.

THE WORLD ISLAND

To understand the formative geopolitical trends that have shaped societies through the ages is to picture the world in its unconstrained whole. The dominant feature is the one mega-continent of Eurasia and Africa, popularly divided into Europe, the Middle East, East and South Asia, and Africa, but which really constitutes one land surrounded by one giant interconnected ocean. This is the World Island—the single Great Continent, as distinct from Australasia, Antarctica, and the Americas, or more colloquially, the Old World as distinct from the New. To fully appreciate it is to view the world from above and imagine the absence of the north polar ice so as to make it possible to sail right around the Giant Continent of the World Island. This could be done on the interconnected oceans of the Atlantic, Indian, and Pacific, which together make up the Great Ocean enveloping the World Island. The peripheral nations of the World Island include Germany, Austria, Turkey, and India, together forming an inner or marginal crescent. At varying distances from the World Island in the Great Ocean are the islands of Britain, Japan, the Americas, and Australasia, which together form an outer or insular crescent. Though numerous and large in some cases, these lands yet pale into insignificance next to the vastness and population of the World Island.

Come the beginning of the twentieth century man had explored and laid claim to all the land of the World Island together with what lay over the oceans in the so-called New World. All that remained unclaimed was at the poles, but even that was known if not owned. Thus it was not so long ago that the world finally became a closed political system in which territorial expansion could only be achieved in a zero-sum struggle among the great powers. Such was the distribution of those great powers and antipathy between them that one could point to a particular region at which the fulcrum of world power was and had historically been poised. This was the Heartland, that closed land space, inaccessible to ships, that began in Eastern Europe and stretched eastwards almost but not quite to the Pacific forests of the Far East. From north to south the region extended from the Arctic Circle to the South Asian deserts and mountain ranges. Thus together with the core area occupied for the most part by Russia, at its greatest extent the Heartland took in the Baltic and Black seas, as well as the navigable Middle and Lower Danube, Asia Minor, Armenia, northern Persia, Tibet, and Mongolia. At the western boundary was the crucial 800-mile isthmus between the Black and Baltic seas, which constituted the eastern approach to European civilization.

Mighty Europe thus occupied only a slight proportion in an isolated peninsula of the vast Eurasian continent and was dwarfed by the size of the Heartland to the east. Yet Europeans from the Renaissance onwards had typically claimed for "their" continent the land all the way up to the rather arbitrary boundary of the Ural Mountains, deep in the Heartland. As set against one another, the relationship between the real Europe in its peninsular area and the Heartland was characterized by the precariously indefensible eastern approach to the former through that broad gap between the seas—and through which for centuries the nomadic peoples of the Heartland had surged, wreaking havoc amongst the civilizations there, in contrast to which all European advances in the opposite direction had faded and retreated. Around the world the Europeans had been able to make their will felt by shipborne coercion, but the Heartland was inaccessible to this phenomenon. This meant that the power or combination of powers occupying the essential territory of the Heartland could marshal its resources without harassment from outside. It would therefore be a priority for any Heartland power or powers to secure access to the seas in order to deploy resources there. Herein lay the crux of Mackinder's warning:

If the whole World Island, or the larger part of it, were to become a single united base of seapower, then would not the insular nations be out-built as regards ships and out-manned as regards seamen?

Mackinder's underlying assumption was that "the grouping of lands and seas, and of fertility and natural pathways, is such as to lend itself to the growth of empires, and in the end of a single world-empire." This was Mackinder's fear at the beginning of the twentieth century. Yet the utility of Mackinder's analysis has not been lost over that century. Today his reasoning is as valid as ever, though we might adapt it for a world of submajor state violence for the time being. Zbigniew Brzezinski acknowledged the worth of Mackinder's geography-based approach to understanding international relations in his seminal work *The Grand Chessboard*. Colin S. Gray, former defense and security adviser to both the British and American governments, has similarly acknowledged Mackinder as a conceptual starting point for much of his strategizing and policy prescriptions. Most recently, Gerry Kearns in his book *Geopolitics and Empire: The Legacy of Halford Mackinder*, as well as Robert Kaplan in *Foreign Policy* magazine, have been vocal in reminding readers that they neglect the geographical paradigm rendered to us by Mackinder at their peril when trying to understand international relations past, present, and in the future. Gray and Kearns were recent participants in a BBC radio program that described the impact of Mackinder's thinking through the twentieth century and into the twenty-first. The conclusion was that Heartland Theory has been nothing short of the preeminent concept underpinning Western foreign policy since Mackinder's time. The irony, however, is that later generations of policy makers, commentators, and the interested public have lost focus of how the foreign policy precepts they have inherited have originated with Mackinder. In this way nonreasons have been crafted to explain things we have always known we "should" do, and a true understanding of Mackinder's message has been lost to many. Today, Mackinder needs to be rediscovered before a sensible forward strategy for the West can be formulated.

Although these pages should not be read as portending major interstate violence in the near future, the economic struggle to develop the World

Island, and the geopolitical boost afforded to the powers that can do that, is very real. Today the smaller states of Eurasia sit astride the world's fastest growing trade corridor, with a vibrant demographic base and in possession of huge, but largely unexploited, energy and mineral reserves. Transit through this space along the ancient trade routes known to the classical world has the potential to connect disparate and voluminous markets on a giant east-west axis at a price that in many instances will undercut the corresponding route by sea. Authoritarianism and economic backwardness over centuries have allowed the sinews of this once vibrant transport network to atrophy and the region to become an obscurity despite its glaring size and functionality. Russia is concerned first and foremost that no Western actors succeed in revivifying this region that Moscow has maintained in a state of developmental stasis to be plundered at will. China has more constructive designs economically, but ones which similarly entail the retardation of good governance as it certainly has the potential to be adopted in those states. In this climate, Western actors need first to appreciate the full importance and potentialities of the World Island as described by Mackinder; to understand the motivations of the major powers there and the vulnerability of the weaker ones; and then to address to that situation a prudent, dynamic forward strategy for the West in the twenty first century.

KENNAN AND PILSUDSKI

George Kennan and Josef Pilsudski each developed a concept implicit in which was an understanding of the geopolitics of Eurasia as described by Mackinder. Pilsudski's focus was on Russia as the preeminent Heartland power undefeatable in the guise of its vast Czarist then Soviet Empire, but only to the extent that it was able to disperse into and create so many march lands out of its feebler neighbors in order to protect it from its strong ones. Pilsudski's Poland was one of Russia's weaker neighbors after the disintegration of the Polish-Lithuanian Commonwealth. Not only that, but Poland sat between Russia and its strongest neighbor, Germany. For Pilsudski, the process whereby Russia had descended on the weak Eastern Europe nations in order to defend itself in depth from the strong Western ones, was plain. So too were the results: authoritarianism and economic stagnation. Pilsudski's response was therefore to foment discord amongst Russia's subject peoples as a prelude to splintering the empire and reducing it to its isolated Heartland stronghold, against which the small states could be allied in defense for the future. George Kennan similarly understood the process whereby the Russian geopolitical dilemma underpinned the Soviet Union's desire to fully mobilize the resources of its vast empire and expand throughout the World Island and across the seas. Kennan's response was to fence in

Russian (but also Communist Chinese) ambitions to a perimeter within which they could not tip the geopolitical balance decisively against the West. Containment was the policy that emerged as the best way to defend the West when it faced a powerful foe in an age that could contemplate seriously if not with equanimity the prospect of world war once more. In the more subtle climate of today's East-West struggle, Pilsudski can update Kennan in the fashioning of a twenty-first-century strategy to preserve and promote Western interests in the wider world.

WHY WESTERN?

Defining the "West" or "Western" is not something the 21CGSE attempts on an exhaustive basis. Rather, it uses the received understanding of those general norms of governance associated with the broader Euro-Atlantic community and which set that community apart historically and still today from many other quarters of the world. The Euro-Atlantic community is that grouping of states from Western Europe and North America whose institutions have dispersed widely and work now for the most part towards the complementary objectives of democratic governance, rule of law, free trade, and the protection of civil and human rights. In outline we might characterize the Western value set as elevating the importance of the individual above that of the state; this in contrast to the multifarious forms of authoritarianism to which Western ideals stand in opposition. The term "Western" has long been used and clearly understood in popular discourse. Although since the end of the Cold War the formal division between "Eastern" and "Western" military-oriented blocs has softened considerably, the essential dialectic between Western individualism as the basis for government and the authoritarian alternative remains. Indeed, some, such as Samuel Huntington, have argued that the label "Western" has in fact gained greater meaning in that time. That said, the 21CGSE does not subscribe to the stark categorization of civilizations for which Huntington argued. Although Huntington addressed the dynamic of Western integration in the Black Sea region in his *Clash of Civilizations*, his framework for understanding geopolitics—in which, for example, he distinguishes between "Western" and "Orthodox" civilizations, thereby dividing Central Europe—is wont to misunderstand not only the history of the greater Black Sea region but also the contemporary Western integrative dynamics at play in this area.

A better paradigm through which to understand the concept of the "West," and one that informs the 21CGSE, is Arnold J. Toynbee's more inclusive and self-critical analysis of the way in which history has seen the politics and economics of much of the world suffused with Western ideas and practice, whether for good or bad. Toynbee's analysis still traces the idea of "Westernism" from its Hellenic origins, through Roman and

Byzantine to Renaissance, Colonial, and modern Europe and the fissures of the Cold War. However, it does this with a healthy appreciation of the historically fluid nature of what it means to be Western. Toynbee's understanding does not focus exclusively on the geopolitical, but neither is it preoccupied with culture, nor brittle in its defense of "Western" values and traditions in a way that would limit any program for integration if applied too rigorously. Rather, it emphasizes the practical application of ideas based on reason and humanism. In the early twenty-first century it can be convincingly argued that these essential Western values are now universally recognized principles adopted by global institutions such as the United Nations and the World Bank, to which nearly all states subscribe at least in outline. It is precisely these principles that require protection where they are truly established and promotion in the areas where their writ runs only in principle, not in practice. The most effective way of ensuring those goals is the implementation of a Western integrative process in the smaller states of Eurasia, a process that, although not an inherently confrontational or anti-Eastern dynamic, must be clear about its opposition to authoritarianism.

IDEAS AND GEOPOLITICS

Viewing the world in staunchly geopolitical terms has long been considered a trait of autocratic regimes themselves—the practice of realpolitik, overly concerned with the control of territory and resources, generally to the exclusion of values and ideas. The chief criticism says that geopolitics is a prism unable to account for the full range of motivations impelling action at the international level, perhaps because it fails to acknowledge much of what happens at the substate level. That said, the lens of geopolitics has provided an accurate enough explanation of the great structural trends in the international system of the twentieth century, and it has much to teach us about those which are unfolding in the twenty-first. Pioneering institutions such as the European Union have tempted some in the West into thinking they perceive the decline of international relations as we know it, specifically, the exercise of power by the powerful to leverage their relations with the weak—or what might be thought of as the democratization of international relations. However, the European nations are unique in being so many in such a compact space, and yet with such a proximate and interwoven experience of history as to be independent but practice nearly identical forms of government and economic organization. Elsewhere in the world that cohesion does not exist, and the lack of familiarity, through either violent or peaceful experience, means that suspicions run much higher and the costs of potential conflict are more readily accepted for the benefits the results or threat thereof might beget. In this climate, Western democracies will forever be at a disadvantage if they do not see the world in the terms so clearly dictating the strategies of many powers, specifically the great Eastern ones of Eurasia. Yet geopolitics does not make the power of ideas redundant. The 21CGSE is fundamentally not concerned with promoting the narrow interests of any one state nor simply those of an elite group of states. Rather, it is concerned with the preservation and promotion of a set of values, albeit by realist means, best delineated in geopolitical terms. Geopolitics here is not therefore in conflict with the pivotal role of ideas in world politics, but rather it furnishes the tools with which to achieve the victory of ideas over authoritarianism—an idealess form of regressive order.

The bureaucrat and professional pessimist may dismiss the recommendations of the 21CGSE as inconsistent with the spirit of foreign relations as pursued by the West since the dissolution of the Soviet Union. That trend has been marked by the avoidance of great power confrontation and the abandonment of the smaller states of the world to recalibrate themselves, even when many of their fundamental problems derive from the actions of the great powers in the first place. In the round, it has been a period guided more by vague hope than concrete calculation. Should Western policy makers in North America and Europe not now begin to think more geopolitically, to view geopolitics in terms of the paramount importance of the World Island, and in the coming years not make every effort to implement the policy imperatives which the 21CGSE is intended to address, the preeminence and power of the West will diminish far more rapidly than many might expect. Whether, and how, to engage in Eurasia is therefore the West's existential question.

CHAPTER 2

Sir Halford Mackinder
and the World Island

THE INFLUENCE OF ALFRED T. MAHAN UPON HISTORY

At the opening of the twentieth century most statesmen from the great powers were avowed big ship men, believers in the status of battleships and their attendant navies as the final word in international affairs. It was generally assumed that mobility on the ocean would always in the end subdue a land position. The decisive battle as emphasized by Carl von Clausewitz had been extruded, foremost by the American naval officer and strategist Alfred T. Mahan, into a naval strategy that stressed control of the commercial sea lanes in peacetime and the ability to meet and defeat one's enemies in conclusive battle in time of war. This idea assumed that mobility was the sine qua non of an effective war-fighting strategy. If naval forces could be deployed to safeguard trade and therefore supplies, that would in turn ensure that the fruits of that trade would be available to prosecute the main struggle to a close. As such, seapower was self-sustaining.

The corollary was control of strategic bases and choke points, the attainment of which, Mahan argued, was just as much a matter of strategy in time of peace as in time of war. Mahan believed that even a well-supplied army could have its efficacy decisively reduced by a strong naval blockade. However, tactical considerations as influenced by technological development played a more secondary role in his thinking, which instead sought to identify enduring strategic truths. It was Mahan's primary contention that immutable principles, and only slightly less robust precedents, could and must be learned from history, for it was warranted that they would repeat themselves in the future. One of Mahan's central conclusions was that peaceful, gain-loving nations generally did not display great powers of foresight. Consequently, policy in such states had often been determined less by the vision of governments than by the natural conditions of geographic position; topography; territorial extent (by which he primarily meant usable coastline); population; and the character of the people, in particular whether or not they were inclined to trade and innovation. In addition there were the nonnatural conditions of the government's character and that of its institutions, with the most desirable being those that allowed for initiative, wealth creation, and innovation and were underlain by democracy and meritocracy. It was in this way that Mahan drew the sting from Napoleon's remark about Britain being a nation of "boutiquers," arguing that the insult was in fact indicative of the real wealth creation afforded by the beneficial nonnatural conditions of that country's social and political fabric, which in turn had allowed for the fullest exploitation of her natural conditions.

The benefits wrought by mobility on the ocean throughout the preceding four centuries had been clear to see. The voyages of the Iberian pioneers had brought treasure but also introduced to Europe a multitude of previously unknown materials and foodstuffs, demand for which had further stimulated naval exploration and innovation. Later, colonies had been established, usually at the chief extraction points for these articles, and more varied and sophisticated forms of wealth creation developed by incorporating the local populaces. Mahan summarized the attitude of the home European governments towards their colonies as being essentially selfish, in that once their value had been recognized they became so many cows to milk. Crucially it was dominance of the element that gave to Britain its island character that was the clear reason for that country having the most cows to milk. The United States had also grown wealthy as Britain, for its own ends, had calculated to employ its seapower to underwrite the Monroe Doctrine in the western hemisphere, thereby facilitating the United States' ascent, unmolested by the other European powers. In the last quarter of the nineteenth century Mahan, together with contemporaries like Theodore Roosevelt, felt confident enough in the United States' consolidation of its mainland expansion to begin making the case for expansion overseas. Indeed, 1898, a year that began with the annexation of lands from the surrounding counties to create the five existing boroughs of New York, ended with the United States' annexation of an entire archipelago in the Far East.

Mahan had been able to point to the dominance of the European powers over the rest of the world, and to British dominance over the rest of the European powers, as evidence of the efficacy of a seapower-focused strategical framework. By 1906, in a well-circulated government memorandum, Eyre Crowe of the British Foreign Office had resolutely declared seapower more potent than landpower.[1] As apropos this view Britain at the time, from the western to the eastern hemisphere, held the key strategic stations of Bermuda, the Falklands, Gibraltar, Malta, the Cape, Suez, Aden, and Singapore. In his 1900 book *The Problem of Asia*, Mahan elaborated on his geostrategy and from this can be understood some of the reasoning underpinning British strategy choices. Mahan stratified the world into the Northern, Southern, and "Debated and Debatable" zones. The Northern was that above the 40th parallel, distinguished by cold and dominated by landpower. The Southern was that below the 30th parallel, lying in the tropics and controlled for the most part by European and American seapower. The middle stratum, lying between the 30th and 40th parallels, he defined as "debated and debatable" on account of its inherent instability, compromised as it was by both land- and seapower. Mahan anticipated Mackinder and Kennan by reasoning that it must be the policy of the seapower-democracies to "contain" Russia's northern landpower by rebuffing her attempts to acquire warm water sea bases giving access to the Debated and Debatable and Southern zones. Mahan further advocated the development of the Panama Canal as a critical U.S.-controlled choke point to complement its British-controlled counterpart at Suez. Fundamentally, Mahan argued that Western seapower must be capable of controlling not just those critical bottlenecks but others such as at the entrances to the Black and Baltic seas. It was this received wisdom of seapower superiority that made what Mackinder was about to say so radical.

HEARTLAND THEORY AND THE WORLD ISLAND CONCEPT

Mackinder acknowledged the evolution of seapower and much of the logic of Mahan's analysis as it addressed the Columbian age of European seafaring. However, Mackinder was working from a lengthier time line and from that spectacle thought he foresaw the demise of the relative advantage that seapower had recently enjoyed over landpower and on which Britain's power wholly rested. Over the course of the nineteenth century Britain had been able to ensure the safe passage of raw materials and manufactures between its colonies, dominions, and trading partners. In times of tension it had generally avoided crisis by drawing on its great credit at the bank of world power,[2] as represented by its incomparable navy, the mere allusion to which had so often sufficed it to see London have its way in international disputes. But how much longer could this regime be maintained, as powers to which the sea had played so little part in their growth came into their maturity? And what if the land those emerging powers occupied was so replete in riches as to ensure that when they did take to the sea their will would be irresistible?

The title of Mackinder's 1943 article "The Round World and the Winning of the Peace" is the best example we have demonstrating the imperative nature of the way he urged his audience to picture the world in its unconstrained whole. Mackinder acknowledged the pre-dominance of seapower at various junctures in history, but he always sought to explain it in terms emphasizing landpower. He was able to convincingly show how seapower was fundamentally a matter of appropriate bases, kept productive and secure. To illustrate this point he gave a brief history of the "closed seas," where in numerous instances the foundation of dominance on the water had been the action of landpower to exclude rival sea bases. He described the Ptolemaic era, when the navigable length of the Nile, although not a sea, had yet been closed to enemy vessels and rival trade by controlling its banks. Then how the Mediterranean had been successfully closed in the same manner by Rome after its victory in the Punic Wars, whereby it gained control of the shores and ushered in the empire's greatest period of expansion. By the time of the British Raj the Indian Ocean too had effectively been closed to rival powers by denying them significant sea bases around the region. Closed seas implied closed political systems or, in other words, empires. Indeed, it was in this way that the Pax Romana and Britannica had been able to hold sway over the known worlds of their respective times.[3]

In 1904, citing the expeditions of Scott and Nansen in the Antarctic, Mackinder asserted that there were now no great discoveries to be made or claims to be laid out. The world had become a closed political system, meaning there was unity of world politics. From thence forward only relative gain by one or an alliance of the Great Powers was possible, meaning that one empire's gain could only be made at the expense of the others. It was the zero-sum game of the post-Columbian age. The immediate background to the concept Mackinder enunciated beginning in 1904 centered on the Boer and Russo-Japanese wars. It was the tremen-dous feats of power projection, by sea in the case of the British in South Africa, and by land in the case of the Russians in Manchuria, that led Mackinder to compare the two forms of mobility. His historical analysis was pregnant with caution. The power that would ultimately control the seas, he predicted, would be the one based on the greater resources of landpower.

Clearly drawing from Mahan Mackinder had characterized the great campaigns of the classical world as representative of the overarching struggle between landfaring and seafaring, or "peninsular" and "insu-lar," peoples. The preeminence of the European and American insular peoples in the late Columbian era had, he suggested, distorted the true relationship between land- and seapower, and the outcome of the Boer and Russo-Japanese wars had only contributed to that process. This was at a time before the Dardanelles campaign of the First World War had shown, contrary to Mahan's assumptions, that seapower could quite easily be prevented from penetrating critical strategic areas, such as the Black and Baltic seas. In the Boer War British seapower had been able to envelop South Africa and maintain delivery of troops and supplies at a rate vastly outstripping anything the Boers could match with their own resources. Similarly, although the Russians had employed the recently built Trans-Siberian Railway to deploy tens of thousands of troops over 5,000 miles to the front lines in Manchuria, the greater Russian effort was ultimately devastated in sea battles with the Imperial Japanese Navy, culminating in the decisive victory by the latter at Tsushima. Before that defeat it might have been expected that the Russian navy would steam halfway around the world to finish with seapower what could not be achieved with landpower.

It was rather going against the grain, then, when in the 1904 Pivot statement Mackinder posed this question:

Is not the pivot region of the world's politics that vast area of Euro-Asia, which is inaccessible to ships, but in antiquity lay open to the horse-riding nomads, and is today about to be covered by a network of railways?[4]

Mackinder pointed out how those railways were transmuting the conditions that had once constrained landpower and that nowhere could they have such effect as in the closed heartland of Eurasia. At the turn of the twentieth century two railways in particular were engendering grave misgivings amongst British strategists—the Russian Trans-Siberian and the proposed German Berlin to Baghdad. Yet the preceding half century had seen rampant railway construction across the globe, so what was it about the supposed effect of these two examples that was the cause for such concern? The Trans-Siberian would allow Russia for the first time to deploy serious military force at almost any point along her massive southern border, which increasingly encroached onto British-controlled South Asia. The German innovation would enable her to simultaneously close the Black and Baltic seas, as well as threaten Britain's lifeline to India through Suez. After all, a military power in control of Arabia, Mackinder had argued, could take easy possession of the crossways of the world at Suez.[5] It would thus be a case of landpower having strangled seapower, in contradistinction to Mahan's theory. The implications were equally ominous with respect to peacetime trading. Mackinder explained how transport by rail from producer to consumer was often more cost-effective than that by sea, cutting out as it did the need for time-consuming loading and offloading at the docks and transfer to trains. In order to convey the full import of Eurasia being transited by these iron roads, Mackinder set about detailing in its full dimensions the concept that would occupy the consciousnesses of statesmen and strategists through generations to come.

THE HEARTLAND

The Heartland was the closed land space, inaccessible to ships, that began in Eastern Europe and stretched eastwards as far as the eastern boundary of modern Siberia. North to south the Heartland extended from the Arctic Circle to the South Asian deserts. The western border was the 800-mile isthmus between the Black and Baltic seas. The southern spur of the Urals, Mackinder said, was therefore in the very pivot of the pivot area, or rather in the very heart of the Heartland, as the pivot came to be renamed in *Democratic Ideals and Reality*. In terms of river drainage the Heartland extended from the Elbe in Germany to the Amur dividing China and the Russian Far East. Other great rivers, some among the greatest on earth, snake across this land, yet crucially none drains to the more accessible seas. The Ob, Yenisei, and Lena run to the frozen wastes of the Arctic. Even the Volga, so central to Russia's development, has only been able to take her traders as far as the landlocked Caspian. Other smaller, but not inconsiderable, streams run south with their ultimate passage to the Indian and Pacific oceans frustrated by the colossal barrier of the Tibetan Plateau and its sister ranges, principally the Tien Shan mountains to the west.

This pattern of river drainage stands in stark contrast to that of the corresponding rivers of the insular regions, which typically drain to oceans or large seas, accessible by large ships of both the trading and the warring varieties. For Mackinder therein lay the key point, that the Heartland was inaccessible to the shipborne coercion of the islanders, the possibility of which had been of such consequence to almost all the other nations of the world. Mahan had pointed out that deep and frequent harbors, especially if also being inlets to navigable streams, were generally sources of strength but became sources of weakness if not properly defended.[6] The Black and Baltic seas, Mackinder argued, were also capable of being closed by landpower occupying the access points of Jutland at the entrance to the Baltic and the Dardanelles at that to the Black Sea. It was fear of landpower closing the Baltic, the only supply and communications route for Britain to its Eastern allies in the Napoleonic Wars, that led Britain to twice attack the Danish fleet at Copenhagen,[7] thereby curtailing the scope of the Heartland. However, for the purposes of strategic thinking the Heartland at its greatest extent includes the Baltic Sea and Black Sea, as well as the navigable Middle and Lower Danube, Asia Minor, Armenia, northern Persia, Tibet, and Mongolia. The evocative defining feature of this area as seen from space is that the whole of it lies under snow in the wintertime.

In the "Round World" Mackinder confirmed that the territory of the Soviet Union was roughly equivalent to the Heartland. In 1904 Mackinder had accurately predicted that social revolution was unlikely to alter

Russia's essential relations to the geographical limits of her existence. The territory of the Soviet Union in fact surpassed in extent that of the Heartland, including as it did the vast region Mackinder termed "Lenaland" around the basin of the mighty but isolated Lena River, dividing what are now the Siberian and Far Eastern Russian federal districts. In the Pivot statement Mackinder arrived more dramatically at the point by contending that, in geostrategic terms, Russia had replaced the Mongol Empire;[8] the crucial distinction was that, unlike the Mongol Empire, the Union of Soviet Socialist Republics (USSR) and its Czarist forebears had sufficient manpower to impart longevity to the imperial enterprise. Again the true significance of this lay in the inaccessible quality of the region. The Heartland was "the greatest natural fortress on earth,"[9] ice-girt in the north and hemmed by desert and mountain to the south and east, with its impenetrable rivers, and only the broad, flat land between the Baltic and Black seas allowing of access. The history of the Heartland was one of violent passage through this space, the flow overwhelmingly being from east to west as successive waves of nomadic warriors from the Turanian descended onto the settled agrarian societies of Europe and Anatolia. Only Alexander, Napoleon, and Hitler had been bold enough to attempt major invasions in the opposite direction, every effort ultimately dissipating in the vast spaces it penetrated.

THE WORLD ISLAND

The Heartland, in Mackinder's theory, was in turn part of the World Island. The World Island encompassed the Eurasian continent in its entirety together with that of Africa. It was the single Great Continent, as distinct from Australasia and the Americas, or more colloquially, it was the Old World as distinct from the New. To fully appreciate it was to view a spinning globe from the top and imagine the absence of the north polar ice covering the Arctic Ocean, instead seeing it as one land, seabound on all sides. From the perspective of the sailor it was simply "the Continent"; a giant promontory capable of being sailed around were it not for the polar ice. The inclusion of Africa as part of the World Island bears little relevance in Mackinder's later strategizing. Only its regions north of the Sahara have physical and cultural connection to the rest of the Eurasian continent. Indeed, Mackinder thought the Sahara rather than the Mediterranean the true boundary of Europe and, by extension, western Eurasia. North Africa's intimate relations with Europe, in people, flora, and fauna, mean it might properly be thought of as European Africa. And apart from its physical detachment, in Mackinder's time as now, sub-Saharan Africa has few people relative to its size and is undeveloped in industry, technology, and civic organization. Mackinder thought that for all intents and purposes the high tableland south of the Sahara was, in fact, capable of being considered a wholly separate Southern Heartland, and none of his later strategizing makes reference to Africa other than the Cape and at Suez.

Around the World Island Mackinder depicted a girdle of wildernesses that included the deserts of the Sahara, Gobi, and Arabia. Outside the girdle to the south of the Tibetan Plateau were the Asiatic monsoon lands of India, China, and South East Asia. These were watered by the Indian and Pacific oceans, themselves in turn part of the Great Ocean, which further included the South Atlantic and enveloped the World Island. Set against the Heartland were the peripheral nations of the World Island, including Germany, Austria, Turkey, and India, which together formed an inner or marginal crescent. At a greater radius were the British Isles, Japan, South Africa, the Americas, and Australasia, forming an outer or insular crescent. Though numerous, these lands paled into insignificance next to the enormity of the World Island, which Mackinder sought to emphasize in his description:

The three so-called new continents are in point of area merely satellites of the old continent. There is one ocean covering nine twelfths of the globe; there is one continent—the World Island—covering two twelfths of the globe; and there are many smaller islands, whereof North America and South America are, for effective purposes, two, which together cover the remaining one twelfth.[10]

The appropriation by various states of all the land constituting that vast expanse of the Old World meant it had become a single, insular unit, a closed space, and incomparably the largest on the globe.

With the lands and seas thus set in their proper relationships to one another, Mackinder extrapolated from his analysis of seapower the hypothesis that if the whole World Island, or the larger part of it, were to become a single united base, then would not the insular nations be out-built as regards ships and out-manned as regards seamen?[11] The underlying assumption said that "the grouping of lands and seas, and of fertility and natural pathways, is such as to lend itself to the growth of empires, and in the end of a single world-empire." Clearly, then, Mackinder was not seeking to deny the importance of seapower. Rather he suggested that in an existential contest that pitted seapower against landpower, it would be the latter that would overwhelm the former. The oversetting for the balance of power in favor of the pivot state, resulting in its expansion over the marginal lands of Eurasia, would permit the use of vast continental resources for fleet-building, so that like would be met with like, but with infinitely superior means. The mechanism by which dominance of Eurasia could come about was distilled into the oft-repeated dictum:

PIVOT AREA

MARGINAL/INNER CRESCENT

INSULAR/OUTER CRESCENT

Mackinder's World Island

> Who rules East Europe commands the Heartland;
> Who rules the Heartland commands the World-Island;
> Who rules the World-Island commands the world.

Of Mackinder's work, the original 1904 statement was the most theoretical and was not designed simply to inveigh against Russia, as a cursory reading might suggest. Czarist Russia occupied the essential territory of the Heartland; however, the manifest weakness of the Russian government, together with Mackinder's appreciation of the transitory nature of all polities, required his theory to leave scope for the possibility that any number of states might occupy the relevant space. Nevertheless, one possibility of ominous proportions did present itself. That was an alliance between Germany and Russia, which, although improbable throughout much of Mackinder's lifetime, did come to pass with the Molotov-von Ribbentrop Pact in 1939 and even today looks more possible than at any time in the last half century. Indeed Mackinder had argued that Germany's position in Europe was analogous to that of Russia in the Heartland. The identity of the Heartland power notwithstanding then, the value of a buffer between Germany and Russia was readily apparent. And it is for that reason that the Heartland's western approaches, through Eastern Europe and the Caucasus, remain the key to gaining or preventing control of the wider Eurasian landmass and all that that entails. Jumping forward to our present day, when Russia remains an anti-Western orientated landpower in control of the substantive part of the Heartland and in increasing cooperation with a rising China, it pays to evoke once more the way the predictions Mackinder made at the turn of the twentieth century have played out until the turn of the twenty-first.

GEOGRAPHY AND HISTORY

If seeking a suitable prism through which to better understand the geopolitics of the last century and beyond, we can do no better than begin with Mackinder's Heartland concept. In Mackinder's Victorian childhood, geography in the schools of Great Britain had been taught alongside and subordinate to history. Physical geography was subsumed in the separate discipline of geology, and discussion of those questions probing political man's relationship with his physical surroundings was confined to an ad hoc timetable dictated according to how and when they appeared to impact upon any particular historical debate. Mackinder's contribution to the discipline of geography was to the very foundation of it as such. He stressed the necessity of a holistic approach to ascertain a correlation between the broader geographical and broader historical generalizations, to perceive geographical causation in universal history. His was the basis of the modern dichotomized approach to teaching geography that includes the physical and human. In the overlapping space lay the geographical realities as they had impact upon the political—the geopolitical. Mackinder stressed the tendencies made inherent in the way states behave by the distribution of their physical features. Physical features of states, then as now, were to Mackinder the most obstinate facts of their makeup. As a didactic exercise for policy makers Mackinder was concerned to see his readers made conversant in geographical reality before they attempted to structure their foreign policy strategies. Policy makers today might similarly benefit from rediscovering geographical reality as Mackinder described it a century ago.

The 1904 Pivot statement began with an examination of history in geographical relief. That examination led Mackinder to conclude that the pivot was of such significance both past, present, and, he said, for the future, as to be considered the essential or pivotal place in global geostrategic terms. The strategic possibilities rendered to the occupier of the area gave Mackinder cause to caution his Edwardian audience about the implications of the pivot being under the control of an authoritarian and aggressively expansionist power, the root of the danger being that such a power could reach out to touch anywhere, while remaining untouchable itself. In 1904 Mackinder's intended audience consisted primarily of British statesmen, many of whom sensed ferment in the European air but were wont to look hopefully to their navy to dispel those fears. In 1919 Mackinder reiterated his warning in *Democratic Ideals and Reality*, reintroducing the Pivot concept as the Heartland thesis. By then his audience had experienced the tumult of the First World War and was consciously restructuring the postwar international security apparatus. At the Royal Geographical Society in December 1914, Mackinder had speculated that the Allies' immediate task should Germany be conquered would be to clip its wings for the future. Four years later that task involved a recalibration of the relations of the victorious great powers to the vanquished, with Mackinder arguing for profound structural changes to safeguard against a repeat of the recent calamity. The policy he advocated was a forward Western strategy for Eurasia. His policies went largely unheeded, however, and 70 years later a similar recalibration was begun upon the dissolution of the Soviet Union, after that power had dominated much of Eurasia but withered in the shadow of Western vitality. Today that process of recalibration remains unresolved, with the Western powers undecided about their level of commitment in Eurasia and in danger of missing the opportunity to prevent the reconquest of Eurasia by authoritarian power.

In formulating his arguments Mackinder spoke not as a liberal or conservative, but from a platform of realism. Most would seek to describe themselves as realists, yet the approach was and is fundamentally characterized by an acceptance that the conceptual must ultimately be subordinated to the empirical. Mackinder was concerned with the transmission of obstinate geographical facts as the proper foundation from which conceptual propositions about Western foreign relations might be put forward. In the aftermath of the First World War, the most trenchant reality, Mackinder argued, was the significance of the Heartland in the relations between the great powers and its foundational relevance to the peace that was being forged. Despite roseate hopes about a new world order, Mackinder could see little evidence of real change in the relations between the great powers, and especially in the relations between the island democracies and the autocratic powers of the Heartland. One of those Eurasian powers, Germany, was organized and her people capable, but she was orientated on an anti-Western axis. While Germany's acquisitive endeavor in the recent war had been abrogated, its aspirations had not. The peoples of Russia, the other major Eurasian power of the day, were similarly robust and ingenious, yet the state's political and social fabric was characterized by disorder and, although the tenant of more territory than it could ever properly diffuse into, it coveted the lands of its poorer neighbors as so many marches against its powerful ones. From this geopolitical tableau Mackinder clearly presaged another degeneration into anarchy should the new system not heed the importance of the realities he had begun warning about in 1904.

MACKINDER'S CENTURY

The years intervening between publication of the Pivot article and the outbreak of the First World War were marked by structural upheaval in the Heartland. Russia's European rivals had taken delight in her humiliation at the hands of the Japanese in 1904–1905 and were pressing against her western flank. In 1908 Austria-Hungary annexed Bosnia and Herzegovina, thereby furthering its influence in the Balkans, which, the declining Ottoman Empire notwithstanding, Russia had hitherto considered a Slavic preserve. At the same time Germany had been expanding with her population and economy both booming. Yet despite its weakness, in 1904 Russia still appeared to Mackinder the most likely organizer of the wider World Island resources. By 1919, however, Mackinder was able, with the benefit of hindsight, to describe German actions leading up to the war in such a way as to represent a deliberate attempt to monopolize the Heartland. "Kultur" had been a defining concept of German geostrategist Friedrich Ratzel, and Mackinder argued that it translated into a society based on materialism. It was a strategic mentality characterized by a ways and means philosophy and a high degree of centralization.[12] At its most basic it was authoritarianism aimed at aggrandizing the state for nationalistic ends. Mackinder contended that the German military colony of Kiauchau (modern Qing Dao) south of Peking in China, along with Germany's East African possessions, were established as the termini of the projected overland routes intended to conquer and control the World Island.[13] An empire terminating at such points would indeed have represented the World Island in its totality. Mackinder contended that had the Germans (by which he meant Germany and Austria) won the war, continental Europe, from St. Vincent to Kazan, and the Asiatic Heartland, would have become the naval base from which they would have fought Britain and America in the next war.

After Russia's withdrawal with the Treaty of Brest-Litovsk in 1918, and following her revolution the year before, the First World War had become a struggle between the Islanders and Continental powers. Not only were the Allies linked by geographical loci according to Mackinder's insular category, but also by their democratic underpinnings. Germany's First World War bid for the Heartland failed, chiefly because the inner and outer insular powers acted in time and with sufficient strength to prevent Germany from securing the sea bases she so coveted. In 1919 the First World War had habitually been referred to as the Great War, with the implication that it would eclipse all that would come after, just as it had done that before. But for Mackinder, history suggested that another attempt on the Heartland would certainly be made. The League of Nations, novel in its universality, had as its sine qua non the mandate to prevent another general conflagration. In that sense it looked a lot like the Congress of Vienna, and many were hoping for a peace comparable in length to that which had followed 1815. The peace of 1815 had ensured against all but localized wars for a hundred years. Yet Mackinder could not foresee a harmonious future with the balance of power set as it was and evidently saw then that the peace of 1918 was specious. Just as Kennan was to do with the United Nations a quarter of a century later, Mackinder bemoaned the blind faith placed in the juridical conceptions of the League of Nations—its constitution and attendant treaties—as a guarantee against future war in the Heartland. "The end of the present disorder," he mused, "may only be a new ruthless organisation."[14] And of course it was. *Democratic Ideals and Reality* was intended to present geopolitical realities in their longest possible historical perspective and, in doing so, to influence the new world order being shaped by the men at Versailles.

In late 1919, after the signing of the Versailles Treaty, and only two years after the Russian Revolution, Mackinder was appointed British ambassador to South Russia, specifically tasked with assisting General Anton Denikin's White Russian force fighting the Russian Civil War.[15] On the way to his post Mackinder stopped in Warsaw, Bucharest, and Sophia, attempting to improve cooperation between the South Russian forces and those of Poland, Romania, and Bulgaria.[16] However, with the legitimizing aim of keeping Russia in the war no longer valid, Bolshevik reversals of Denikin's gains, and increasing war apathy at home, the Allied governments began to pull out their expeditionary forces from Russia, meaning Mackinder's mission was recalled almost as soon as it had begun. On his return in January 1920 Mackinder briefed the British Cabinet on the Russian situation as he saw it. He detailed his vision for Eastern Europe, stressing the fundamental need to institute an arrangement whereby neither Russia, Germany, nor any other pretender could achieve dominance over the World Island. This would require the creation of a tier of independent states stretching from the Baltic to the Adriatic, which would act as the buffer between Russia and Germany. But the new states and alliances he was advocating in Eastern Europe and the Caucasus went much beyond that which had been agreed at Versailles, meaning his proposals were given short shrift in London.[17]

Nevertheless, Poland, together with many other East European states, had become independent for the first time since the seventeenth century. The buffer between Germany and Russia existed, but not in the condition Mackinder thought sufficient. What was lacking was an alliance system between the East European countries directed against Russia and Germany. Instead, fierce nationalism was rife, and East European security was left exposed. The ruthlessness with which the Bolsheviks had consolidated the unlikely success of their coup had by the early 1920s meant their influence was once more pressing westwards. The League was suffering from a lack of credible members, most notably the forced absence of Russia and Germany themselves, but also the voluntary absence of the United States. The League's unanimous voting system, which effectively allowed a veto to all, was early on showing its inherent lack of instrumentality. While its apparatus had some success in arbitrating smaller disputes, it was not designed to achieve the pervasive territorial restructuring Mackinder thought necessary. Germany had been reduced to an embittered debtor nation. The Weimar government was liberal, but unrest was brewing. Centrifugal forces tending to pull the Reich apart vied with ultranationalist sentiment that had been incensed by the incongruity of Germany's condition, as set against the idea of her perceived natural weight within Europe and the world beyond.

KARL HAUSHOFER AND NAZI GRAND STRATEGY IN THE SECOND WORLD WAR

It was in this climate that it appears the leading German geostrategist Karl Haushofer came into contact with Adolf Hitler. Hitler had been imprisoned for his role in organizing the failed 1923 putsch in Munich, which had aimed at wresting power in Bavaria and stemming the flow of the secessionist sentiment that had begun to be acted upon in Germany's southern provinces. He was imprisoned in Landsberg am Lech fortress together with one of his co-agitators, and later deputy,

Rudolph Hess. Hess had previously been a research assistant of Haushofer in the political geography department at Munich University. Haushofer had written a number of influential books amalgamating the work of other geotheorists, among them Mackinder. The similarity between Haushofer's work and some of the expansionist policies outlined in Hitler's *Mein Kampf*, written while incarcerated, and developed by the Nazis once in power, led the American *New Statesman and Nation* magazine to sensationally argue in 1939 that Haushofer and, by extension, Mackinder were the sources of Nazi grand strategy.[18] The autocratic nature of the Nazi-German state meant that many academics, if not producing arguments or work contrary to the Nazi ideology, were necessarily co-opted into the enterprise of aggrandizing the Third Reich. Given that Haushofer had entered academia as Hitler had entered politics to recover German prestige, and given the prominence of each in their respective fields after Hess was to link them, it would be disingenuous to argue that Haushofer exercised no influence on Nazi strategy. However, it is clear that Haushofer's influence would have been at odds with other of Hitler's motivations, the most pronounced of which were his notions concerning race relativity and preparedness to deploy vast resources for cleansing Europe of its Jews. War against the insular powers of France, Britain, and the United States also sat uneasily with Haushofer's theory of Heartland consolidation, something that was to be achieved primarily by strategic alliances, not violent conquest. In this way Hitler and Haushofer's strategies were divergent after Hitler accepted general war in 1939 instead of maneuvering diplomatically to avoid conflict with the West until a later date.

Mackinder's vicarious implication in Nazi aggression becomes diluted when one considers the concept of the Heartland as it appeared to the Heartland powers themselves. The idea of a landlocked fortress-base, control of which rested on control of Eastern Europe, already existed in its essentials in the concept of Mitteleuropa. The sentiment of the Heartland dictum had been voiced before: "Who rules Bohemia rules Europe," was how Bismarck had expressed the theme. Indeed, much of what Mackinder had to say was, to the German, Russian, and East European protagonists (or the landsmen), something approaching axiomatic within the lore of their foreign policy. With the possibility of Russian westward expansion Mackinder was simply giving voice to what at the time was an anxiety among officers of Germany's General Staff.[19] And it was true that Mackinder's precepts did not vary substantially from the "Eurasianist" school of foreign policy decision making in Moscow.[20] What Mackinder brought to the fold, however, was his geographer's appreciation of context. The danger of Eurasia coming under the control of one power many could appreciate, but Mackinder made the clearest statement of the problem and its underlying geographical reasons.[21] By way of illustration Walter A. McDougall has put the case thus, that "we all must learn geography in order to understand history."[22]

Mackinder's anxiety was evidently to educate his Western audience about an idea so well understood on the continent but so dimly perceived at home. It is clear from Haushofer's generous review of *Democratic Ideals and Reality* in the geopolitical magazine *Zeitschrift für Geopolitik* that he jealously admired what he thought had been Mackinder's success in educating a generation of British imperialists.[23] Ironically, however, Mackinder held precisely the converse view, namely that your average Edwardian Briton strategized in a world of comparative geographical ignorance next to his well-versed Prussian counterpart.[24] Whatever the relative levels of British and German geographical understanding, Haushofer's attempt to educate Nazi strategists in the principles understood by Bismarck and described by Mackinder were representative of the importance if not determinative force of Mackinder's work. The impatience that characterized Nazi strategy once war had broken out does not detract from the fact that its primarily land-focused eastward impetus clearly owed a conceptual debt to Mackinder's Heartland concept as publicized in Germany by Haushofer. Had Germany concentrated its efforts on subduing despised Soviet Russia without declaring war on the United States in the wake of Pearl Harbor, it is a moot point whether it would have secured the time to have broken that crucial line between Leningrad and Stalingrad and become the organizer of the Heartland Mackinder so feared.

Mackinder believed that Germany's designs on the Heartland, or its "pivot policy," as he described it, and its concomitant desire for overseas empire evident in the years leading up to the First World War, were policies that pulled at once in different directions. Similarly, during the Nazi period, Germany was wont to pursue strategically antagonistic schemes by provoking its stronger neighbors in the west only to squander the temporal advantage it enjoyed over its weaker ones in the east. The German invasion of Russia was the type of expansion Mackinder had foreseen, and it was in keeping with much of what Haushofer had advocated with respect to German lebensraum. However, instead of the creeping influence of German technical and organizational superiority, which had a long history in Russia, the unbridled expansion into the Slavic lands eventually given free rein to was one of the causes of Haushofer's ultimate disillusionment with and opposition to Hitler. After Hess's desertion and the implication of Haushofer's son Albrecht in the failed July 20th plot to assassinate Hitler, Haushofer fell swiftly out of favor with the Nazi regime and spent the rest of the war in fear for his life and that of his half-Jewish wife.

Ultimately, the discipline of geopolitics as it was then emerging may have been embarrassed by its association with Nazism in the form of German geopolitik. Yet, by its nature, it cannot be specific to a given period, being instead applicable across the entire sweep of history and among the fullest range of actors. In *Democratic Ideals and Reality* Mackinder had predicted and explained the rise of totalitarianism in

Europe in terms of lost communities, centralization, and ultimately dictatorship. Nazism was to some extent condoned by some Anglo-Americans
who, if not sympathetic to its philosophy, at least saw it as a convenient
bulwark against Bolshevism. Yet even though the rise of a fascist organizer
was the antidote to the ultimate threat of a Russo-German alliance he had
warned about, Mackinder was vocal throughout the interwar years in
advocating emasculation of German power, precisely because it represented only one of two evils. It is to Mackinder's credit that the Heartland
theory is such a useful paradigm for describing much of what took place
at the strategic level during the Second World War. As a representative of
the Eurasian mindset, Haushofer's evident acknowledgment of the worth
of Mackinder's thesis only goes to support its validity. It is a strong
indication that Mackinder's view was not simply a Western interpretation
of Eurasian geopolitics, but an accurate understanding of the reality of
power dynamics in the World Island.

In the grand strategic sense the Second World War played out the prescriptions of the Heartland theory. The islanders made a concerted effort
to counter the imbalance in the Heartland's power relations as precipi-
tated by German expansion. In contrast to the First World War one of the
islander nations, Japan, seceded from the alliance, but was still ultimately
intent on expansion into the Heartland, and attacked the United States to
ensure a free hand in achieving that. In the closing stages of the war a
number of events indicated that policy makers were already looking beyond
the peace to the shape of the Heartland to come. Against Eisenhower's
circumspection Churchill was pushing for an Allied advance beyond the
Elbe. The atomic bombs dropped on Hiroshima and Nagasaki were ostensibly aimed at avoiding the Allied deaths it was assumed would be incurred
in an invasion of the Japanese mainland. However, the actual decision to
drop the bombs clearly rested on a number of factors, one of which was
to make redundant the Russian mobilization in preparation for an assault
on the Japanese islands from the north and west, thus ensuring that the
Heartland power continued to labor under its traditional impediment of
having only cold water harbors. Germany demonstrated that it was an
implacable menace to the insular democracies until it was forcefully
split and integrated into the Western institutions of NATO and later the
European Union, which proved to be a less threatening way of ensuring a
credible bastion against Russian expansion.

NICHOLAS SPYKMAN AND RIMLAND THEORY

It would be remiss to neglect mention of another prominent geostrategist and realist here: Nicholas J. Spykman. Spykman was a Dutch-
American teaching at the Institute for International Studies at Yale and
influential for American policy makers throughout the war and after,

despite his early death in 1943. His work reemphasized the central aspect of geography in explaining how nations had come to occupy the positions they had in international affairs and how geographical features would similarly be the key determinants in their future foreign policies. Geography, Spykman concluded, was the most fundamental conditioning factor because of its relative permanence. Spykman began by accepting Mackinder's concepts of unity of world politics in the modern age, and unity of the seas, which had always been the case. Spykman made an important contribution to the Heartland debate, adopting Mackinder's terminology and basic approach, but differing in his conclusions. In *The Geography of the Peace* Spykman set out his concept of the Rimland, which was essentially to rename Mackinder's inner crescent and ascribe to it a greater degree of importance than hitherto afforded it by Mackinder. He further accepted Mackinder's basic definition of the Heartland and of the outer crescent lands, but he renamed the latter the Offshore Islands and Continents.

Spykman agreed with Mackinder that the Heartland afforded an unrivaled defensive fortress base, but he was skeptical about the ability of its chief occupier, Russia, to develop its infrastructure to the extent that it rivaled that of the major seapowers. It was the Rimland region, Spykman argued, that was key to domination of the larger Eurasian landmass. Although the peoples of this region were threatened by assault from both the Heartland and the seapowers, they occupied the most fertile and, for that reason, populous part of the world. In this way Spykman recalled Mahan's "Debated and Debatable" zone. When not in conflict with the Heartland, or if dominant over it for a time, the Rimland nations could secure access to the resources of the interior and also set out upon the oceans to impress their will around in the world. The clear analogy for our own time is with China's superlative rise among the Rimland nations, pressing both northwards against Russia and securing access to ever more resources there, and southwards as far as the Gulf nations, where it has secured access to a string of naval bases to complement its own. Thus Spykman reworked Mackinder's formula to read: "Who controls the Rimland rules Eurasia; who rules Eurasia controls the destinies of the world." Ultimately, then, Spykman, like Mahan, evinced a greater confidence than Mackinder in the capacity of the island democracies to maintain their dominant position in world affairs.

However, Spykman did not assume that that dominance was guaranteed or that the islanders could afford to pursue passive policies in world affairs or opt of them completely. The latter point represented his fear that America would slide back into an isolationist repose. International relations, Spykman contended, was fundamentally the business of states jostling to maximize the margin of power they enjoyed over one another. In *America's Strategy in World Politics* Spykman argued that for the United

States to rely on its geographic isolation between two great oceans was not a viable policy as the conditions of mobility on the ocean and in the air were, just as Mackinder had pointed out with respect to landpower, being transmuted by the day. Such were the conditions of modern technology that the foreign policies of all great powers had a direct effect on the others and could not do otherwise. And such was the potential power of the Rimland nations—Germany was already powerful, but Spykman recognized the potential of China and India too—that those places would necessarily need to be co-opted if containment of the Heartland was ever to be successful.

Spykman's analysis further diverged from that of Mackinder when he argued that history was not primarily a story of seapower contesting landpower, but rather a struggle between mixed seapower/landpower alliances to prevent domination of the Rimland. In Europe at least this assertion seemed to have the ring of truth to it, when one considered the alliances Great Britain had made to prevent the European coastland from coming under the control of alternately Spain, France, Germany, and then Russia. However, to rehabilitate Mackinder in this respect it must be remembered that in three of those contests Britain might equally have been said to have fought against the threat of Eurasia being dominated in its entirety. In this sense Spykman shifted the pivot area of world politics from Eastern Europe to the European littoral. As the balance of power shifted to favor Russia during the Second World War, Spykman argued for the maintenance of a strong Germany to act as a future bulwark against Russian westward expansion. However, he opposed European integration as necessarily destroying the balance of power in the key area of Western Europe and potentially presenting another threat to American interests, depending on which power dominated that integration. The policy of containment that Kennan was later to outline owed an intellectual debt to Spykman's Rimland thesis, concentrating as it did on ensuring that Soviet influence was prevented from penetrating into the Rimland nations that it bordered.

THE COLD WAR: ANTICIPATING CONTAINMENT

While the Soviet advance was halted on the Elbe in the west and the Amur in the east, the reality was that the USSR filled the Heartland space in imitation of the erstwhile Czarist regime. In *Democratic Ideals and Reality* Mackinder had realized that although Russia might be impotent for a time, if it were to be highly organized under Bolshevism it would have the resources and ideological desire to be a powerful contender for supremacy over the World Island. In his sweeping analysis of previous descents by the Heartland powers onto the other peoples of the World Island, Mackinder had ascribed the relative brevity of their conquests to a lack of manpower, with the inevitable result that their thin numbers had tended to be absorbed into the larger populations they assaulted. However, writing in 1919, he acknowledged that in contrast to this historical deficiency the Soviet Union and the Russian Empire before it did have a sufficient base of manpower to maintain the momentum of their expansion. Russian expansion he described as having been carried from its European manpower base by the incorporated Cossacks. It is tempting to criticize Mackinder here by pointing out that the USSR did become a highly organized and, at least in the military-industrial sense, advanced state. Yet with all the resources within its orbit and, broadly speaking, with the technologies to exploit them, it ultimately crumbled in the face of Western resolve and virility. Even in the east Czarist Russia and then the USSR failed to strike south and east against China when that country was in political disarray before 1949. In this sense surely 70 years was a sufficient period to test Mackinder's theory, leading some to criticize Mackinder as at best mistaken, and at worst, plain alarmist. So why was not Russia or its Soviet manifestation the organizer Mackinder had feared? And why, for that very reason, does his theory remain valid?

Precisely because the Heartland was the greatest natural fortress on earth, it stood to reason that if penetration of that area was unlikely (as the Allied governments had discovered during the Russian Civil War), that some form of containment was necessary to prevent the power occupying the area from overspilling into the rest of the World Island. In the "Round World" Mackinder acknowledged the emergence of American military power and said that the real division of east and west was to be found in the Atlantic. In consequence Mackinder described his Midland Ocean concept. This was another distinct geographical area centered on the North Atlantic but which also included its subsidiary seas of the Caribbean, Mediterranean, Baltic, and Arctic, as well as their dependent river basins. Strategically the Midland Ocean incorporated a bridgehead in France, a moated aerodrome in Britain, and a reserve of trained manpower, agriculture, and industries in the eastern United States and Canada.[25] Mackinder suggested that Western Europe and North America constitute "a single community of nations, with a common cause." The resemblance to the NATO concept which was to emerge was clear, and in the years after the formation of that organization in 1949 the chief Midland Ocean powers of Britain, France, the United States, and Canada intervened in Greece, Turkey, Germany, Malaya, Korea, and Vietnam, not to mention numerous places in the Middle East and Africa. Although he did not support the formation of NATO, Kennan's reasoning drew on Mackinder's Heartland thesis for constraining Soviet expansion into the wider Eurasian landmass. It was only by this conscious pressuring of the peripheries of the Heartland and by containing the influence of the Soviet Union therein that the West prevented it from becoming the dangerous organizer Mackinder alerted us to.

CRITICISM

Mackinder held that the ideas which go to form a nation have usually been accepted under the pressure of a common tribulation and under a common necessity of resistance to external force. This is how he saw the formation of European identity, as Europe had withstood successive waves of ruthless and idealess horsemen from the east. In this way Mackinder departed from the classicist mold when he asked his audience to consider European history as subordinate to Asiatic. However, Mackinder's analysis of Eurasian history from the fall of Rome through the medieval period to the Victorian has been criticized as over simplistic, tending as it does to ignore the plethora inter-European wars at the expense of emphasizing civilizational struggle with the Islamic and pagan worlds. Had Mackinder, on the one hand, left out too much in order to delineate a convenient narrative to substantiate his grand theory? And on the other, ascribed events to causes more far reaching than actually existed?

Mackinder had not set out to give a detailed European history. He had set out to distill into the minds of audience the salient structural trend of Heartland powers having for centuries burst from their remote wilderness over the unimpeded steppe and onto the settled peoples to their south and west. Russia, Persia, India, and China were all either made tributary or were incorporated into Mongol dynasties. The Europeans had been spared the full force of the Asiatic blow, but only because it had already stretched for 5,000 miles to reach them. Scythians, beginning at the same Turanian staging post, even wrought havoc in the remoteness of Arabia. Against the broader principle of this momentous pattern the detail of the conflict within Europe paled into insignificance. Clearly few Western policy makers in the twentieth century and in the first decade of the twenty-first have been prepared to ignore Mackinder's interpretation of history, but have actively developed policies established along the lines of his reasoning. To trace a line through the current conflict zones and political hot spots in which the major powers are engaged or threaten to be today—the Caucasus, Iraq, Iran, Afghanistan, Pakistan, and North Korea—is to follow the rough boundary of the Heartland as it meets the extent of Western dominance. The problem is that Western engagement in those regions is lacking in coherent structure.

Overhanging the Boer War in South Africa, which had been the stimulus to Mackinder's theorizing, had been a broader debate about imperial unity within the British Empire. Mackinder was in favor of tariffs against non-Empire goods, and the Pivot statement was clearly a foundation for that argument. For that reason the paper was indeed "a product of its time and a national experience."[26] Yet its very essence was to describe the enduring effects of immutable geographical realities. Critics have sought to dilute the relevance of Mackinder's ideas by pointing out that they were borne of a time of general Russophobia, on the one hand, and were too doctrinaire and indifferent to political and historical subtleties on the other. In 1904 the climate of suspicion that existed in London surrounding Russia's intentions was extreme. Lord Hamilton, as secretary of state for India in 1900, had said that "the Russian advance is like that of a glacier, slow but omnipotent."[27] Lord Curzon, as viceroy of India, was of a more sanguine view, believing that south of a certain line in Asia, Russia's future was much more what Britain chose to make it than what she could make it herself.[28] Nevertheless, the general sentiment to which Mackinder's views can be attributed was clear. In that same year of 1904 a British expedition led by Sir Francis Younghusband had even occupied the Tibetan capital of Lhasa in a paranoid effort to snuff out the influence of Russian embassies there. Yet despite the heady Russian complex, Mackinder insisted that the particular combinations of power brought into balance were immaterial, his contention being that "from a geographical point of view they are likely to rotate around the pivot state, which is always likely to be great, but with limited mobility, as compared with the surrounding marginal and insular powers." Britain's rivalry with Germany and Russia in the nineteenth and twentieth centuries was simply indicative of the truth in the assertion that the pivot area would be at the heart of any struggle for world dominance.[29]

The disconcerted attitude that existed towards Russia in 1904 remains today among the Western powers and has, in fact, been their stock position ever since the Russian state came into its maturity. The peoples of Central and Eastern Europe, the Caucasus, and Central Asia continue to fear Russia for historically understandable reasons, although it seems clear that many of the aggressive moves made by Russia against the Eastern European and Caucasian states in the last century have been, in part, invited by their weakness. At the opposite end of the World Island, China, which Mackinder envisaged as another possible organizer, albeit only if itself first organized by Japan, has grown in stature to become a more likely looking organizer than Russia itself. It therefore pays to address once more the significance of the Heartland, the historical trends of westward expansion that Mackinder identified, and the sound logic of declaring a committed and unswerving intention to build, defend, and maintain strong Western-orientated institutions and enterprises throughout Eurasia, not least by engaging the smaller Eurasian states and supporting progressive new trade and security apparatus where developing states evince an interest in building them.

AIRPOWER AND TECHNOLOGICAL ADVANCE

Another criticism often directed at the Heartland theory is that Mackinder failed to foresee or accommodate the advent and development of airpower as a determinative dimension of grand strategy. Aircraft carriers, nuclear-armed and -powered submarines, intercontinental ballistic missiles, and satellites have become the cornerstones of modern defense planning for the major powers. Yet acknowledgment of the role airpower was likely to play is evident in Mackinder's thinking as early as the Pivot paper itself. At the Royal Geographical Society in 1904 the Conservative parliamentarian Leo Amery put to Mackinder the very suggestion that its development might upset his reasoning. Mackinder's response was reminiscent of Mahan, namely that to become embroiled in the detail of technological advance was to focus on the incidental at the expense of the fundamental. In the Pivot statement, delivered just weeks after the Wright brothers' maiden flight at Kitty Hawk, Mackinder was anticipating the influence of airborne communications at least. Characteristically, however, he was most interested to attempt to guess the constraints placed by geography upon this development.

By the time *Democratic Ideals and Reality* was published, and with the example of the First World War to draw upon, Mackinder had accommodated the nascent appearance of airpower in war into his concept, fundamentally characterizing it as an arm of landpower. Ships, he argued, would only in the future transit the Mediterranean and Red Seas at the sufferance of landpower. Echoing Mahan, the vital point was that technological advance, no matter how apparently radical, invariably settles as it is refined into the basic paradigms of offense and defense. "No proof has yet been presented," wrote Mackinder, "that air fighting will not follow the long history of all kinds of warfare by presenting alternations of offensive and defensive tactical superiority, meanwhile effecting few permanent changes in strategical conditions."[30] Nuclear capabilities have not put paid to the struggle for relative power or even to territorial aspirations; they have simply meant that new ways have been devised to facilitate those elemental urges. A new technology that appears essentially offensive in nature will sooner or later be joined by its defensive counterpart. The first stage of any modern military campaign is neutralization of air defenses, because, other things being equal, the advantage will rest with the ground-based defense. Intercontinental ballistic missiles emerged, followed by "shields" consisting of other missiles to render their threat impotent. Similarly, the contest between sea- and landpower remains. The initially land-based weapon of airpower was soon matched by a sea-based capability in the form of aircraft carriers and cruise missile-equipped submarines. Ultimately both air- and seapower depend on the efficiency of their ground organization, which recalls Mackinder's trenchant description of the World Island and its dimensions relative to the rest of the world—nine twelfths to the remaining three twelfths.

GEOGRAPHICAL DETERMINISM

Mackinder has been criticized by those who have interpreted his work as implying that states have no degree of free agency in their relations but are determined entirely by geographical reality. But the principles Mackinder drew from the perennial physical features he described did not mean his political ideas were shaped to the exclusion of ideas and values. He cautioned that he had spoken as a geographer, but that the real balance of political power was a composite of conditions, both economic and strategic, and of the relative number, virility, equipment, and organization of the competing peoples.[31] One need only look to the industrial revolution era in tiny Britain as evidence of the truth in that statement. Mackinder did warn of the susceptibility of what he called the literary conception of history—"that of concentrating attention upon ideas and the civilisations which are their outcome"—to lose sight of the more elemental movements whose pressure was often the exciting cause of the efforts in which great ideas were nourished.[32] Yet he was clear about how he judged the relative influence of man and geography in the symbiotic relationship to which they belonged when he said that man initiates, but nature controls.[33] With specific reference to the Heartland he said that nature offered all the prerequisites for ultimate dominance of the world, but that it must be for man by his foresight and by the taking of solid guarantees to prevent its attainment.[34] Indeed, he thought the chief lesson of the 1914–1918 war to have been that the unprecedented forces of modern production were in fact capable of control. "Let us recover possession of ourselves lest we become the mere slaves of the world's geography, exploited by materialistic organisers,"[35] was how Mackinder had framed his hope for man's will to triumph over the constraints of his surroundings.

Mackinder was critical of giving free rein to the tendencies of "Going Concerns," by which he meant prospering nations. These were comparable to Lord Salisbury's "Living and Dying Nations," the terms by which the British prime minister and foreign secretary had characterized all nations as essentially moving in either an upwards or downwards trajectory in terms of development, the ones on the upwards turn being the Going Concerns. For Mackinder, one manifestation of this negligent and gratuitous approach to societal development could be found in the economic policy of laissez-faire. This, he argued, tended to produce unbalanced growth between nations, and just as much as the German model was causative of some nations imposing themselves on others or rather of the creation of empires. Balanced growth among nations was therefore the ideal, and the best way of achieving such, Mackinder contended, wasthe maintenance of small but viable units of human organization, such as the states he had envisaged in Eastern Europe. Unbalanced relations and unstable equilibrium were themes to which Mackinder returned to ascribe much disorder. The British example was the chief case in point; it was primarily because of her industrial revolution that she had stolen a march on her rivals in terms of economic and imperial development. By the time of *Democratic Ideals and Reality*, as a cure to the geographical tendency for empires to emerge and compete with one another, Mackinder went as far as to idealize a balanced globe of communities and, by extension, of human beings, brought about by conscious political decisions to achieve such a world.

Thus, from Mackinder's principal writings, one is not confronted by a fatalist but rather a man confident in the ability of mankind to forge a better system of mutual world governance, provided it defer to the geographical realities that had historically and would inevitably in the future encourage polities to act in particular ways. The essence of his work was to stress the tendencies made inherent in the ways various nations and states behave by the distribution of physical features, those obstinate facts. And in doing this Mackinder encouraged a world view. He even spoke of a league of democracies with a common defense policy—a visionary thought during the pugnaciously nationalistic time of the interwar years. Another of his solutions was to internationalize key land-based choke points, such as Palestine, Syria, Mesopotamia (Iraq), the Bosporus, and the Dardanelles, most of which, together with the Panama and Suez canals, would be under Anglo-American control. The fact that many of these notions were brought into being in various guises after the First World War, and that they have generally been considered essential to a robust system of international security, is testament not just to the vision but also to the progressive nature of Mackinder's views.

ENDURING RELEVANCE

In one respect Mackinder certainly was mistaken since, in contrast to his predictions, a maritime alliance had overcome a continental alliance in the three great conflicts of the twentieth century. Yet it cannot be stressed too strongly that although Mackinder backed the wrong side in those battles, he fundamentally understood the nature of the greater, and continued, struggle. As Colin Gray has observed, "From a geographical perspective the twentieth century with the First and Second World Wars, and the Cold War, was a struggle to prevent Mackinder's prediction."[36] The Cold War did not simply end; it was won by the West after the protracted and often painful application of the policy of encirclement and containment. On a longer time line it represented just one victory in the greater and continued struggle for control of the Heartland. Yet it is easy to lose sight of just how ephemeral this security is. It is easy to think of the interaction of peoples and civilizations in static terms and fail to appreciate the powerful latent potential for great dynamic upheaval. Of the World Island under the sway of a single power Mackinder said, "Ought we not to recognise that that is the great ultimate threat to the world's liberty so far as strategy is concerned, and to provide against it in our new political system?"[37] We would do well to bear that advice of 1919 in mind today. With the League of Nations now translated into the United Nations, Mackinder's caution stands, and that body must keep a close eye on the Heartland and its possible organizers in the future.

Of those organizers Mackinder had warned that "they may require a decisive advantage, especially should our people pass into a magnanimous frame of mind." Perhaps that is precisely what has happened in the 20 years since dissolution of the Soviet Union. Mackinder had anticipated China as a possible Heartland organizer with designs to overthrow the Russian Empire. A commonplace Russian joke goes that during the Damansky Island Incident the Chinese military developed three main strategies: the Great Offensive, the Small Retreat, and Infiltration by Small Groups of One to Two Million across the Border. Even if not by overtly violent means to begin with, it seems inconceivable that China's influence, if not its people, will not at some point spill over into the wider World Island. For the moment though, China and Russia's interests are aligned and directed towards the ejection of the West from Asia. The One Baby policy of the 1970s was intended to limit the Chinese population to 750 million by 2050, yet in 2010 it is nearing 1.5 billion. Russia is still a superpower in terms of its nuclear arsenal if nothing else, still in control of the richest resources on earth with the possibility of adding to them in the Arctic, and most importantly with the ruthlessness to make the most of its assets in the geopolitical arena. Imitating Haushofer, academics in the Heartland nations themselves are now rediscovering Heartland theory in the Eurasianist school of foreign policy, so that we have a situation where both East and West acknowledge the validity of Mackinder's theory, but find themselves diametrically opposed on the question of its realization. We have therefore seen how Mackinder identified the geographical realities that for centuries statesmen have had to heed, and how his reasoning continues to influence the policy makers and statesmen of the great powers. Of those policy makers it was George Kennan who was to provide the most substantive solution of recent times to the problem Mackinder had identified, one that has defined the geopolitical terrain for more than half a century.

CHAPTER 3

George Kennan and Containment

George F. Kennan has been variously described as the architect and father of the containment strategy that emerged in response to the Soviet threat after the Second World War. Such was Kennan's perceived influence in the formulation of American geostrategy that some went so far as to call him "America's Global Planner."[1] In *White House Years* former Secretary of State Henry Kissinger claimed that Kennan had come as close to authoring the diplomatic doctrine of his era as any diplomat in America's history.[2] Kennan is, therefore, popularly credited with having provided the intellectual framework from which initiatives such as the Marshall Plan and Truman Doctrine were begot, and which were to represent the Western attitude towards Russia for over 40 years. Yet Kennan's approach was fundamentally premised upon the geopolitical understanding rendered to us by Mackinder. Soviet policy, Kennan argued, could be attributed to a mixture of ideology and circumstances. The circumstances, Kennan said, were those power relations that had existed in Russia for the three decades of Soviet rule prior to the Allied victory in 1945. In fact, they were those of Russia's geography and chronic sense of insecurity, as traced by Mackinder. The ideology was that admixture of Marxism and Russian nationalism, in describing the effect of which Kennan was to make his most valuable contribution, drawing as he did on his years of service in Russia and Eastern Europe. The effect of Kennan's influence at the end of the Second World War was to reemphasize the paramountcy of Eurasia in the minds of American statesmen, at a time when their focus threatened to shift back to hemispheric concerns. In this way Kennan was instrumental in facilitating a continuation in the tradition of Mackinder-esque geopolitics, a timely example for today's Western statesmen, the vacillations of whom in their attitude to Eurasian affairs threaten losing that continent to domination by the autocratic organizers so implacably resistant to the progressive Western ideals of good governance and free trade.

DEFINING YEARS: RIGA AND MOSCOW

Kennan was raised for the most part in the midwest state of Wisconsin, but spent a part of his childhood in Cassel, Germany, picking up there something of the language as well as the culture of a world beyond America. George F. Kennan, his cousin twice removed and namesake, had been a well-respected nineteenth-century scholar of Imperial Russia and was acknowledged by Kennan as an inspiration to his interest in foreign, in particular Russian, affairs. After leaving Princeton and joining the Foreign Service Kennan's first posting was to Geneva, after which he took up another consular post in Hamburg. His first posting relevant to his later work was as vice consul in Tallinn, Estonia in July 1928. Tallinn at that time was a political backwater, and Kennan was employed on general consulate duties, which afforded him little if any exposure to the deliberations of policy making. However, in early 1929 he was transferred to the legation at Riga, Latvia, which, at a time when the United States entertained no diplomatic relations with the Soviet Union, was the closest Kennan could get to that country. That diplomatic relations had been frozen throughout the 1920s was chiefly a result of the Soviet Union's refusals to renounce its right to encourage revolutionary activity abroad, to honor the undertakings of the erstwhile Czarist government, or to compensate private American interests for losses incurred during the sweeping nationalizations of the years following the revolution. Already, then, the contempt in which the new Russian leaders held the established strictures of diplomacy was evident. The legation at Riga was occupied by men, many of whom had previously staffed their respective embassies in St. Petersburg before the revolution. From them Kennan was to get his first introduction to the realities of the Russian character and the seismic changes that had upset the mode of life in Russia.

There then followed a two-year interlude while Kennan returned to Germany to enroll in a Foreign Service-sponsored Russian language course at the University of Berlin's Oriental Seminary. The course encompassed not just Russian language, but also Russian history—especially constitutional and legal—and economic geography. It must be regarded as highly significant that Kennan gained the foundation of his knowledge about Russia from German teachers in a purely Eurasian setting. U.S. Foreign Service personnel had traditionally studied for Russian posts in Paris, which meant that Kennan was unique among his cadre for gaining his grounding from the German perspective. Only after he had built up a good repository of knowledge of Russian traditions was Kennan encouraged

to study the country in its Soviet manifestation. At the end of the course in
Berlin Kennan went back to the Riga legation, where he was to remain for
two years as third secretary before the reestablishment of U.S.-Soviet
relations in 1933 under Roosevelt's new administration. The reasons for
Roosevelt's decision to formalize relations are not fully known, but aside
from his characteristic desire to promote forums for straightforward talking,
the move may have represented a practical balancing response to German
and Japanese pugnacity. The upshot for Kennan was that his credentials as
a budding Russia expert were recognized, and he was posted to the new
embassy in Moscow with Ambassador William C. Bullitt.

By this time the fundamentals of Kennan's political outlook were established. He was a realist, albeit a moderate and idiosyncratic one. His
approach to foreign policy represented a departure from the Wilsonian
tradition that had preceded him. That tradition was wont to stress the
moral rationale of its arguments and to hold up ideals to which others
ought to aspire. Wilson's approach had itself been a self-conscious
departure from the derided Old World practices of secret diplomacy
and amoral political expediency, often directed towards maintaining the
European balance of power. Kennan, although deeply imbued with the
worth of his own liberal democratic political system, did not arrive in
Moscow carrying the same idealistic baggage as many of his contemporaries.
On the one hand he scorned what he claimed was an inveterate tendency
of Americans to judge others by the extent to which they contrived to be like
themselves.[3] On the other, he made an unfavorable contrast between the
callous and unyielding spectacle of the Russian diplomatic technique he
came to witness in Moscow and the strong Anglo-Saxon tradition of
compromise when trying to make common cause in difficult situations. Yet,
if this was Kennan's opinion of Russian behavior at the political level, it was
not representative of his experiences of ordinary Russians with whom he
came into contact.

During his time in Moscow, together with associates such as Charles
E. Bolen and Loy W. Henderson at the American embassy and Frank
Roberts, his opposite number at the British embassy, Kennan came to
appreciate the full extent of Soviet designs. Kennan's social life in
Moscow was restricted by the imposition of many and varied regulations
dictating travel and relationships. In the febrile climate of Stalin's great
purges, life for all was saturated with suspicion. As a foreign diplomat
Kennan faced not only the obvious obstacle of the People's Commissariat
for Internal Affairs (NKVD) discouragement of his attempts to interact
with ordinary Russians, but also the strain on his conscience of knowing
that, even were he to slip his guard from time to time and canvas the
opinion of his fellow Muscovites, the implications for them, if not him,
were potentially disastrous. Nevertheless, he did gather Russian friends
and acquaintances, ideas and impressions, and together these informed

a view of the Russian people as warm, intelligent, resourceful, and romantic, a view that was to stay with him for the rest of his life. Kennan was at pains throughout his writing to stress the need to oppose the Soviet government without demonizing the Russian people. This facet of his work was due in part to the complement it made to his prescriptions for bringing about a more agreeable Russia, but no less so to his evident compassion towards those people whom he met during his formative years in Moscow and to the admiration for the indomitable spirit that he believed had driven them through their misfortune. At the political level, however, the limits beyond which it was improper for a great nation such as America to bend in the pursuit of compromise and understanding were, Kennan thought, rapidly approaching.

FELLOW TRAVELERS AND REALISTS

Lenin had taught that unevenness of economic and political development was the inescapable law of capitalism. It was, as we have seen, a sentiment with which Mackinder himself was to empathize to some extent. But Marxism went much further than suggesting measures to ameliorate the existing system; rather, it described the pattern of capitalistic development in terms that highlighted its inevitable doom as the weaker of political systems when set against that of communism. A literal interpretation of Darwinist rationale had been in large part responsible for the scale of the recent calamity of the First World War. And it was the general inability of people across the developed world to comprehend exactly what had led to that conflagration that left them more than ever before receptive to novel and radical propositions about how they might better govern themselves in the future. Just why revolution had first occurred in comparatively undeveloped Russia, rather than in England or Germany, as Marx and Engels had predicted, was only to be guessed at. One peculiar feature that Kennan frequently made reference to was the habit of Russian factory owners to occupy living quarters on or next to their factory premises. While no doubt conducive to an effective regime of oversight, such arrangements allowed the workers a much more ready view of the signal disparity between their own living conditions and those of their masters, than did those of the country house-dwelling, capital-owning classes of Western Europe.

For Kennan the savage class distinctions of Marxist-Leninism seemed only a mirror image of the feudal institutions Russia had so recently rejected, by which he referred to the willingness to condemn whole classes of people on the basis of their being born bourgeois, serf, or Jew. In this sense Marxism was partisan, not universal, in its immediate aims, seeking as it did to reorder rather than abolish class-based society. Nevertheless, the message of utopian Marxism was making itself heard in the

universities and drawing rooms of the West as it had already in its coal
mines and dockyards years before. A considerable factor accounting for
the attraction of Marxism was probably the alternative it presented to
what was the more widespread political current of the day: fascism. It
was from among this sympathetic element of "Fellow Travelers" that the
Soviet Union had been able to recruit some of its most important agents,
most notably the Cambridge Five and Klaus Fuchs in Britain and the
Rosenbergs in the United States. All the people involved were destined
for high public office or important service and came into their maturities
as spies during the crucial war and immediate postwar years. Kennan
himself never had a "Marxist period" and at his most charitable was only
ever able to say that there were facets of Soviet life that he admired, but he
could find little patience for the ideology itself. It was for him a pseudosci-
ence, outdated in its terms of reference, plainly wrong in its most important assumptions, and overtaken everywhere by the real course of
events.[4] Nonetheless, he persisted to entertain a hope that it was possible
for communism and capitalism to coexist in the world in relative peace.

Yet while the foremost scions of capitalist development, the United
States and Great Britain, had allowed the waters of their opposition to
recede, the idea that the moneymaking culture that was an article of faith
in the former, and the tradition of inherited station and wealth, as
axiomatic in the latter, could contemplate with equanimity the tenets of
Marxism, was probably misplaced. Directing his remark at the Soviet
leaders, Kennan had said that no sane person had reason to doubt the
sincerity of moderate socialist leaders in Western countries. Yet the men
who held sway on both sides of the Atlantic viewed wealth creation as
their birthright, and the larger and more insatiable the markets in which
to practice it, the better. The great gentlemen of England had lived for
decades in perturbation about the lower classes finding the will to
descend on and confiscate their property in the name of the people. Often
nationalist wars had conveniently served the dual purpose of aggrandizing their own stake in the national wealth and at the same time diverting
attention from it by fixing peoples' minds on foreign bogeys. The emergence of a historically great state now purporting to represent the interests of these same people in their struggle against their political masters
was therefore one that those masters could not afford to tolerate if their
capitalist way of life was to survive.

The teaching of Marxist ideology of a hostile capitalist world was a
notion that resonated in Russia, where the people were in the habit of
looking back to regard the multitude of instances of invasion and intervention so captivatingly described by Mackinder. As Kennan said, the
powerful hands of Russian history and tradition were ever there to reach
up and support such ideas. Frank Roberts, at the British embassy in
Moscow, had pointed out how the constant striving for security of a state

with no natural frontiers and surrounded by enemies had been a fundamental of Russian foreign policy dating back to the small beginnings of
the Muscovite state.[5] Kennan, too, acknowledged the influence of climate,
the Asiatic Hordes, and Byzantium on the evolution of the Russian mind
as it perceived its relations with other peoples. In fact, Kennan saw many
parallels between American and Russian physical characteristics and historical development, both having experienced a race for the Pacific shore,
albeit in opposite directions—although a more resonant analogy might
have been that of the contemporaneous expansion of Tudor England over
the seas following Vasco da Gama and of Russia over the Heartland
following Yermak the Cossack. Another key difference was that the
United States had the great fortune of arriving at the Pacific to claim a
fertile land lapped by warm waters, whereas Yermak and the early
Russian pioneers had toiled through the wilderness of the Amurland only
to find a violent and often frozen sea that later came to be controlled by an
implacable enemy in the shape of the Japanese.

Nevertheless, in making that journey the Russian leaders had come to
sit astride half the resources of the world. In a passage that could have
been straight from Mackinder, Kennan described the five centers of
organization capable of producing military-industrial strength on a
serious scale. The five were the United States, Great Britain, Germany,
Japan, and the Soviet Union. Kennan drew the analogy between
Britain and Japan's respective positions flanking the great Eurasian
continent and highlighted the vast metallic and energy resources of
Germany and the USSR occupying its interior. So too did he adopt
Mackinder and Spykman's categorization of the United States, Britain,
and Japan as maritime insular powers. And echoing British policy
since Castlereagh at Vienna, Kennan acknowledged that the heart of
the problem was to prevent the gathering together of the military-
industrial potential of the entire Eurasian landmass under a single
power. For Kennan it was that crucial void between Narva and Bessarabia,
Mackinder's broad isthmus between the Black and Baltic seas, that had
historically separated the vast resources of the ast from the higher civilization of the west, thereby denying the consolidation of omnipotent power
in Eurasia.[6] But Kennan also acknowledged the limits placed on Russia's
political development by its geographic characteristics—characteristics so
little favorable to normal administrative control, to national unity, and to
self-confidence.[7]

Despite those difficulties, by the 1930s Russia was formidable. Trotsky
had been banished, and Stalin had consolidated his preeminence in the
lengthy internal power struggle that had ensued after Lenin's death.
The foreign intervention forces had long been smitten, as had the White
forces they supported. Yet still Stalin's message to the Russian people
remained one of caution about the foreign wolves everywhere padding

up around them. Soviet ideology and Russian nationalism had become indistinguishable. Russian nationalism, Kennan was to write from Moscow, was a centuries-old movement in which conceptions of offense and defense had become inextricably confused. The fiction was necessary to hold the people in awe to the patriarchal shield that the party had erected and to justify the rigor of Dzerzhinsky's police state that served it. The impressions Kennan accumulated as this era in history unfolded are worth quoting at length:

I came without false hopes or illusions, in the mid 1930s, to a more intimate acquaintance with the phenomenon of Stalinism at the apogee of its horror ... Here was a great nation helpless in the toils of an unbelievably cunning, in many ways great, but monstrously ruthless and cynical man. So insistently were the evidences of Russia's degradations borne in upon me during the years of my residence in Moscow—so prolonged and incessant were the hammer-blow impressions, each more outrageous and heart-rending than the other—that the effect was never to leave me. Its imprint on my political judgment was one that would place me at odds with official thinking in Washington for at least a decade thereafter.[8]

Kennan had been part of a coterie of American diplomatists based in Eastern Europe that considered themselves uniquely alive to the geopolitical threat posed by Russian power in its Soviet guise. American statesmen found it necessary to debate the emergence of the first Marxist state in a way the establishment in Great Britain did not. On an economic level the shibboleths of communism were clearly anathema to the American model. Yet politically, communism represented less of an obvious specter to republican America than it did to monarchical Britain. Roosevelt's reaction appears to have been quiet confidence that he could handle Stalin on a personal level, regardless of the real extent to which the ideologies of their respective countries were in opposition. However, once war had broken out the broader debate about what sort of relations the United States was to have with the Soviet Union, and how to go about pursuing them, quickly became academic when within the space of six months Nazi Germany invaded the latter and declared war on the former. Seapower was then matched with landpower in an uneasy alliance to oppose the similar seapower-landpower formation of the German-Japanese Axis.

AN UNFIT ALLY: THE ALLIED POWERS
AND THE SECOND WORLD WAR

For Kennan the alliance entailed a political intimacy not befitting of the traditions the United States was fighting to preserve. "Never—neither then nor at any later date—did I consider the Soviet Union a fit ally or associate, actual or potential, for this country."[9] That was Kennan's opinion in a nutshell. That is not to say that he did not recognize the sense in a formal alliance between two countries finding themselves on the same side in an unprovoked war, but nor did it mean he considered it acceptable, in the spirit of wartime camaraderie, to turn a blind eye to the plethora shortcomings of America's new partner. To demonstrate support for the Soviet Union was to be complicit in its crimes. Yet to have remained aloof to the extent Kennan might have wished would have been unrealistic, and the political capital afforded to Stalin by his association with the West was unavoidable. The same problem was shared by Britain as the other member of the Big Three. Churchill had famously declared that were Hitler to invade hell, he would at least have made a favorable reference to the devil in the House of Commons. This ungenerous compliment was the best he could manage, and by 1943 Churchill was making loud anti-Russian noises in cabinet meetings. Not for Churchill was Stalin's Russia a fit ally either, but it was tried and tested British policy to side with the second strongest power in serious European disputes in order to maintain the hallowed balance and prevent domination by any one power. In allying with Russia, Churchill was doing no more than following the logic of that tradition. Nevertheless, he saw clearly that the alliance only meant a situation of hostilities deferred, and as soon as the theoretical estimate of Allied victory began to be backed up by empirical results on the ground, Churchill began promoting strategies that would ensure to the Allies a head start in the new conflict to come.

The major strategic undertakings of the Western Allies depended not only on their own successes and failures but also on a close reading of the Eastern Front situation. Stalin was furious that a Western Front was not opened sooner and accurately ascribed the delay to more than mere prudence in ensuring the availability of sufficient men and machines. Although Operation Barbarossa launched in June of 1941 was devastating in its opening stages, and it looked as though the Russians might have been evicted from their political and industrial bases, as had they been already from many of their important agricultural areas, the failure to take Leningrad, Moscow, and Stalingrad before the coming of winter meant the Germans' momentum ground to a halt and inertia set in. British and American strategists looked to history for comfort. With the exception of the Russian story itself, of the great movements of peoples through the Heartland, the successful ones, whether military or migratory, had always been from east to west. Only Napoleon in modern times had attempted the countermovement, and the Germans looked to be stuck in direct imitation of him. For the Western Allies it therefore made eminent sense to sit back for a time while the two great Heartland powers broke themselves against one another. That is not to impute a false character to the spirit in which the majority of major strategic decisions were taken. There were, no doubt, many men, both military and civilian, who did not peer very far beyond the immediate objective of defeating Germany. However, we know from Churchill's memoirs, among others, that strategic moves designed to forestall Soviet consolidation were certainly countenanced by some, if not all, of the British leaders and were known to, even if rejected by, the Americans.

Once the Germans were in retreat and the prospect of a Nazi-dominated Heartland had been put paid to, the Western Allies felt confident enough to mount an offensive to retake Western Europe. How much that effort was designed to ensure against a Soviet-dominated version taking its place is a moot point. For the British, at least, the essential point was to push east to the maximum extent, subduing German units along the way, encouraging a German transfer of forces to the Eastern Front to continue the process of mutual destruction, and denying Russia as much central and southern European territory as possible. The best means of achieving these aims, suggested Churchill, was "an attack on the soft underbelly of Europe," in preference to the more direct route through France. The main advantage of this strategy was a drive into Germany that would incidentally leave Western Allied troops in control in the Balkans and Greece and possibly as far east as non-Slavic Romania. The disadvantage was its indirection and the necessity to land near and fight through mountainous terrain. In the end, American aversion to the necessarily lengthier and potentially much more costly strategy meant an attack on southern France in Operation Anvil to complement Overlord in the north was the preferred option.

Such was Allied confidence in the closing weeks of the war that Churchill was heard to have openly counseled against weakening Germany too much lest she was needed against Russia in the future. Nevertheless, Eisenhower rejected British overtures for a rapier strike to the heart of Germany in anticipation of Russian control there, insisting instead on a halt at the Elbe. At the Yalta conference in February 1945 the demarcation lines for Anglo-American and Soviet control were agreed upon, and at this time it appears Churchill felt he had made as good a bargain as British-American military prospects warranted. In the event, the Westerners advanced beyond the agreed line, and this gave impetus to Churchill's badgering for a more forward strategy. When the Americans were unforthcoming Britain's own self-help efforts in Italy and Greece soon ran into difficulties. And it was only at this point, at the war's end, and as the reality of Soviet gains began to crystallize, that Britain began supporting France in pushing for a defensive anti-Soviet bloc incorporating what had become West Germany.

The British effort to anticipate Soviet aggrandizement suffered from manifold weaknesses. It was principally a Churchillian enterprise, not fully supported by the rest of the British coalition government. It also smacked of warmongering at a time before the European conflict was all but won and while there remained the formidable proposition of an invasion of the Japanese mainland. Britain's evident bankruptcy, both financially and in terms of prestige, was also causing her voice to ring increasingly hollow. And most seriously, there was an escalating sense, sometimes rising to a pitch of hysteria, among some Americans engaged in Anglo-American strategy making that they were being systematically duped by the British into propping up the ailing British Empire. If anything could epitomize the negative aspect of Anglo-American ambivalence it was evidence of Perfidious Albion attempting to play fast and loose with American money and lives. An additional American idiosyncrasy, which acted to smother the eastern push, was the hope some seemed to entertain that the Soviet Union might voluntarily shrink back into its prewar borders. After all, the isolationist lobby in America was already being vocal in advocating a retrenchment once the job of beating Germany and Japan had been accomplished, and maybe others would follow suit.

In Kennan's own words, it was only after the war that there was suddenly brought home to people the truism that a combination of the physical resources of Russia and China with the technical skills and machine tools of Germany and the Eastern European countries might spell a military reality more powerful than anything that could be mobilized against it.[10] This prospect had, in large part, come to pass into reality. Soviet connivance at Nazi aggression in the opening years of the war and the iron grip in which she held the supposedly liberated peoples of Eastern Europe had borne out Kennan's prediction of 1933 that the Soviet Union was no fit ally. It had been clear by the time of the Potsdam conference that the Big Three was, in reality, the Big Two, and their interests were rapidly diverging. In March 1946 Churchill made his Iron Curtain speech at Fulton, Missouri, in which he described the reality of Soviet control of Eastern and Central Europe. The effect was to make an early case for continued American engagement in Eurasian affairs, one that was well received, delivered as it was just a month after Kennan had set out his own arguments to secure the same.

CONTAINMENT: FOUNDATION

The strategy that came to be known as containment, although not wholly original when popularized in 1946, did represent a departure for American foreign policy and a novel level of engagement in extrahemispheric affairs during peacetime. The first document detailing the strategy was written by Kennan while still at the embassy in Moscow. The Treasury Department was at a loss to explain the Soviet Union's refusal to support the newly created International Monetary Fund and World Bank. A request was sent to the Moscow embassy for insight, and Kennan took the opportunity to vent his anxiety regarding Soviet intentions and what he considered the confused American response to them. In 1946, prior to sending the five-part message that was to become known to history as the Long Telegram, Kennan enumerated a set of "rules" to underpin his arguments about how Soviet-American relations ought to be conducted from the American perspective. They were illustrative of all his subsequent thinking.

a. Do not be chummy with them.
b. Do not assume a community of aims which does not exist.
c. Do not make fatuous gestures of goodwill.
d. Make no requests of the Soviets for failure to grant which we are not prepared to make our displeasure felt.
e. Take up matters on a normal level and insist that the Russians take full responsibility for their actions on that level.
f. Do not encourage high-level exchanges unless coming at least 50 percent on Russian initiative.
g. Do not be afraid to use heavy weapons for what seems to us minor matters.
h. Do not be afraid of unpleasantness and public airing of differences.
i. Coordinate as far as possible American government and private activities involved with the Soviet Union.
j. Strengthen and support American representation in Russia.

These prescriptions constituted only the final part of the telegram. Kennan used the first four parts to describe what he thought were the real intentions and capabilities of the Soviet leaders, their modus operandi, and the background to these things. According to Soviet notions, there could be no permanent peaceful coexistence between the capitalist and Communist countries. There were internal conflicts in the capitalist system, insoluble by peaceful means, and at their greatest intensity between England and the United States. Non-Communist left-wing politicians in capitalist countries were the most dangerous and damaging elements for the Soviet agents to monitor. However, Kennan stressed that these extreme views did not represent the natural outlook of the Russian people. He argued that experience had shown that peaceful and mutually profitable coexistence of capitalist and socialist states was entirely possible—and that for the Soviets to speak of possible intervention by the West against the USSR in 1946, after the elimination of Germany and Japan and after the recent war, was sheerest nonsense. At the bottom of the Kremlin's neurotic view of world affairs, Kennan contended, was the traditional and instinctive Russian sense of insecurity. Originally, this was insecurity of a peaceful agricultural people trying to live on a vast, exposed plain in the neighborhood of fierce nomadic peoples. To this, he said, was added, as Russia came into contact with the economically more advanced West, the fear of more competent, more powerful, more highly organized societies monopolizing them too. They had thus learned to seek security only in a patient but deadly struggle for total destruction of rival powers, never in compacts and compromises with it.

In the name of Marxism, Kennan wrote, the Soviet leaders had sacrificed every single ethical value in their methods and tactics, so much so that they could not dispense with Marxism itself. It was the fig leaf of their moral and intellectual respectability. Wherever it was considered timely and promising, efforts would be made to advance the official limits of Soviet power. In 1946 those efforts were restricted to certain neighboring points conceived of as being of immediate strategic necessity, such as Northern Iran and Turkey. However, other points could at any time become significant as concealed Soviet political power was extended to new areas. Thus a friendly Persian government might be asked to grant Russia a port on the Persian Gulf. Should Spain have fallen under Communist control, the question of a Soviet base in the Gibraltar Strait might have been raised. There was, moreover, an underground operating directorate of world communism, a concealed Comintern tightly coordinated and directed by Moscow, intended to set the poor against the rich, black against white, young against old, newcomers against established residents, and so forth.

Kennan argued that resolution of the Soviet question had to be approached with the same thoroughness and care as would be the solution of a major strategic problem in war and, if necessary, with no smaller outlay in planning and effort. Kennan was clear when he said that he believed the problem was within America's power to solve without recourse to any general military conflict. Soviet power, he argued, was unlike that of Hitlerite Germany: it was neither schematic nor adventurist. It did not work by fixed plans. It did not take unnecessary risks. It was impervious to the logic of reason but highly sensitive to the logic of force. For this reason it could easily withdraw—and usually did when strong resistance was encountered. Thus, if an adversary had sufficient force and made clear his readiness to use it, he would rarely have to do so. If situations were properly handled there would need be no prestige-engaging showdowns. "I am convinced," he said, "that there would be far less hysterical anti-Sovietism in our country today if the realities of this situation were better understood by our people." However, from the response that was about to ensue, one might conclude that he had only succeeded in scaring his compatriots half to death.

The telegram fell on receptive ears, most notably those of James Forrestal, secretary of the navy. Forrestal had Kennan's telegram widely circulated among government departments, ensuring it became a cause célèbre. The effect was to raise Kennan from his obscurity and shake Washington officialdom out of its torpor at the same time. Forrestal was instrumental in bringing Kennan back to Washington to take up a post as deputy for foreign affairs at the Naval War College. At this time Kennan also held the post of State Department consultant to the National Security Council, and it was therefore at this time that he had the greatest ostensible impact upon policy making in Washington. Forrestal further requested that Kennan adapt the material from his Long Telegram into a report for Forrestal's own consumption. Kennan obliged but was soon approached by Hamilton Fish Armstrong, editor of *Foreign Affairs* magazine, and persuaded to seek permission to print the piece. Under the pseudonym "X" the article emerged in the July 1947 edition of *Foreign Affairs* and was almost immediately identified as being from Kennan's pen and therefore as representative of government opinion.

Kennan captured imaginations by describing the Soviets' chronic sense of insecurity and all that that entailed. He reiterated the notion of innate antagonism between capitalism and socialism. He described at length the infallibility of the Kremlin as sold to the people, as well as its flexibility in ensuring it filled every nook and cranny available to it in the basin of world power. The main element of any U.S. policy towards the Soviet Union, Kennan contested, had to be that of a long-term, patient but firm and vigilant containment of Russian expansive tendencies. Soviet pressure was something that could be contained by the adroit and vigilant application of counterforce at a series of constantly shifting geographical and political points. The aim was to promote sentiments in Russia that would eventually find their outlet in either the breakup or gradual mellowing of Soviet power and ultimately the emergence of a more agreeable Russia.

Once the Bolsheviks had consolidated power to the extent that their survival aligned fully with that of Russia itself, the historical precepts of Russian insecurity began to assert themselves in their thinking. And as Frank Roberts had concluded, the fundamental Soviet search for security was potentially limitless. With its frontier on the Curzon Line, the USSR would require a puppet Polish state with a Polish frontier on the Oder, which, although this had not been possible with Poland under the direction of the staunchly Russophobe Pilsudski, had become a reality after the war. This in turn would necessitate control of the Eastern Zone of Germany, and encouragement of Communist influence in the rest of Germany and even in France. "In fact," Roberts asserted in his own long telegram to the British Foreign Office, "Soviet security has become hard to distinguish from Soviet imperialism and it is becoming uncertain whether there is, in fact, any limit to Soviet expansion."[11]

In the X Article Kennan sought to modify some of the views expressed in the Long Telegram. However, the differences were subtle, and already in March 1947 President Truman had announced in Congress the set of principles that came to be known as the Truman Doctrine, which relied heavily on the reading of the Soviet threat as furnished by Kennan in the Long Telegram. Containment became the watchword. In April 1947 George C. Marshall, former U.S. Army chief of staff during the Second World War and the "Organiser of Victory," in the words of Winston Churchill, became secretary of state. Marshall immediately acted to institute a centralized planning staff to coordinate medium- to long-term strategy, such as he had been accustomed to in the War Department. The product was the Policy Planning Staff, with which Marshall acknowledged his admiration of Kennan's recent thesis by appointing him director. Elevation to the post meant that for the first time Kennan was assured a direct avenue of influence to the top echelons of foreign policy making. Upon admission to the heart of the State Department apparatus, the first thing that struck Kennan was the lack of general agreement about basic concepts underlying the conduct of the United States in its external relations, especially vis-à-vis the Soviet Union.

The policies that grew out of the new arrangements at the State Department represented a synthesis of the ideas of a number of influential men at the center of that apparatus, not least those of Kennan as they came to be refined by contact with the inner realities of the foreign policy establishment. However, because the effect of the Long Telegram and, even more so, the X Article was to elevate the Soviet question to the broader governmental and national level, it was no longer merely an inner core of professionally trained and experienced old hands suggesting policies to the top echelon of the executive branch. In the vibrant democracy of America the varied influences on policy making were dispersed across the executive and legislature. And it was the language of Kennan's seminal documents that stuck and afforded a broad spectrum of influential men the confidence that they had an insight into the Soviet mind. The spirit of American foreign policy towards the Soviet Union from then on rested on the intellectual foundation provided by Kennan, but extrapolated by some much more belligerent characters.

ENDS

The starting point for Kennan was that America, and by extension the West, should know in the first place what it wanted and in the second how to properly conduct itself in order to facilitate and not impede achieving that goal. Policy had to be anticipated in terms of what American action could realistically achieve. And Kennan's nuanced but innate sense

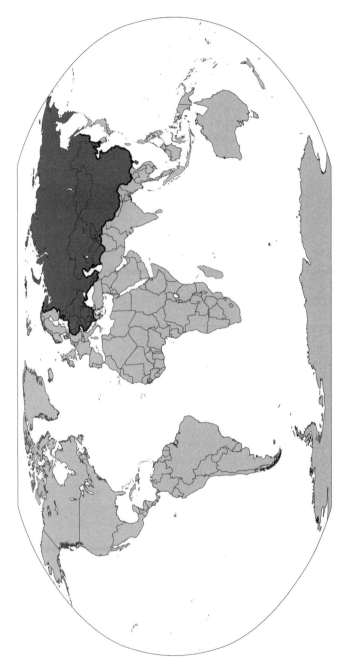

Containment of the Communist Eurasian Powers during the Cold War

of realism taught him that to hope for a Soviet Union that converged with the Western model of liberal-democratic capitalism was a chimera and transmogrification that would never happen. This was not least because the Russian people themselves had scant, if any, experience of living in a society organized according to either principle, neither government by the majority nor complex industry and artisanship. And to think that the USSR once industrialized would be anything other than an economic rival to America was romantic. "No members of future Russian governments," Kennan wrote, "will be aided by doctrinaire and impatient well-wishers who look to them ... to produce in short order a replica of the Western democratic dream."[12] This was "the evil in misplaced enthusiasms,"[13] especially pronounced when peddled in isolation from considerations of realpolitik, the effect of which was often to divert attention from matters of real significance.

However, to despair utterly of the Russian peoples' capacity to dispute their sorry condition was to ignore the fine, if delicate, liberal tradition that had once existed in the country. Therefore, a realistic aim was to induce by America's behavior the emergence of a more agreeable Soviet Russia, a Russia that was more "tolerant, communicative and forthright in its relations with other states."[14] That goal, Kennan argued, should be the reference point against which all proposed policy initiatives were weighed. It was common for discussion of the Soviet question to hold up "liberation" of the Soviet Union's subject peoples as an ideal. And in the sense that he hoped for a reduction in Soviet influence, Kennan was supportive of such an aim. However, he knew that liberation in the popular sense often implied a plan to actively raise the Russian people from their servitude, by force if necessary. This Kennan thought was impractical and dangerous. A more sober objective was therefore to prevent Soviet influence flowing into areas it had not yet already reached. And it was this idea that gave to Kennan's strategic vision the character of containment. The problem of containment was, therefore, chiefly a question of the reaction of the peoples of the non-Communist world to American and Western initiatives. If Western Europe could be regenerated in imitation of its prewar capitalist system, then its prosperous functioning would first balance then expose the weaknesses of Soviet imperialism.

In the struggle to counter Soviet imperialism Kennan derived little comfort from the rampant establishment of multilateral institutions, the most conspicuous of which was the new United Nations organization. While he acknowledged the worth of international law as one of the cherished pillars of the diplomatic world and especially the role it could play in mediating nonvital interests, he saw that its utility in moderating the insecurities of great nations was limited. "The mark of genuine concern," Kennan wrote, "for the observation of the legal principle in the affairs of nations is the recognition of the realistic limits beyond which it cannot be expressed."[15] The task of bringing about a more agreeable Soviet Russia was therefore one "best achieved by devices of political expedience, not rigid legal norms."[16] And the fostering of institutions and initiatives to include the minority peoples of the Russian orbit risked leaving those people in irredeemable dispute with Russia, because, while such nations might achieve a certain degree of political independence from Russia, the question of their economic independence by no means comported to it.[17] The means for containing the Soviet threat had to be robust and subtle at the same time. However, this caution stands in contrast to the way the West should be engaging the smaller Eurasian states today when East-West tensions are pronounced but not at a comparable hostile level to those of Kennan's day. It is the fluidity of today's Eurasian geopolitics that means it is precisely the empowerment the West is able to provide through economic independence that will allow for the growth of Western institutions without the sorts of risks that would have entailed at the beginning of the Cold War.

MEANS

Kennan advocated a policy of strength and patience, because, while the Soviets believed that time was on their side, Kennan rather thought the converse. He suggested that perhaps the Soviet system already had sown within it the seeds of its own decay. Not only that, but their growth was well advanced and, as with the lives of many great organisms—empires especially—that decay was evident even when their light shone most brightly, as did that of the Soviet Union directly at the war's conclusion. Soviet power was, Kennan thought, overextended, and this was primarily due to its suzerainty over the peoples of Eastern Europe. However, that was not to say that the Soviets would not attempt to extend their clammy embrace yet further into Central and Western Europe whenever the opportunity presented. Western European economic revitalization was therefore essential, and in June 1947 Marshall announced in his Harvard address the European Recovery Program. Kennan believed that the Soviet Union was impotent in many ways, not least because of its historically poor economic development. Industrially, it lacked the general culture of production and technical self-respect that characterized the skilled workers of the West. By the end of the war it was "only able to export its enthusiasms and the strange charms of its primitive political vitality."[18] For this reason it was essential to revive productive capacity in decimated Western Europe, as it would be that very economic vitality that would constitute those countries' greatest weapon in the struggle to come. The Marhsall Plan was therefore an obvious concomitant of the political campaign that Kennan lobbied to be waged.

Fundamentally, Kennan saw the struggle as political and economic rather than military: political containment of a political threat, aided by economic superiority. There had never been any evidence, he declared, of a desire on the part of the Soviet leaders for general war with the capitalistic powers. In fact, it was not the Soviet style to militarily invade other countries; they had tried it in Finland and had their fingers burned, so preferred political infiltration. Soviet ideology taught that the capitalists themselves would seek war as a release from the political frustrations engendered by the inherent conflicts within the capitalist system. And because mutual retaliatory capabilities meant that nuclear weapons were unlikely to ever be used, the struggle from the Soviet perspective would take the form of expediting the inner decay present in the capitalistic societies. Capitalism's failings and assumed inevitable decline, perhaps coupled to the perceived lethargy of the Russian character in general, afforded Soviet policy a leisurely timetable for completion. Their chief strategy would be the cultivation of Communist parties in other countries where domestic weakness had allowed them a foothold. Routing of these insidious factions was thus essential, although they were not, Kennan believed, sources of mortal danger. Ultimately Kennan was confident, for if the Western system really was the more finely attuned to the nature of man, then it could afford to be patient, placing its confidence in the longer and deeper workings of history. But others disagreed, pointing to other developments as evidence of a broader design for Soviet world domination.

Those who disagreed held up the Berlin Blockade of 1948, the development of the Soviet atomic bomb in 1949, and contemporaneous development of the long-distance bomber and guided missile technology as the most conspicuous examples indicating that such a plan was in the offing. Kennan acknowledged that these events had indeed shaken America's geographical sense of security. However, he opposed the establishment of NATO—instead promoting an Atlanticist United States-United Kingdom-Canada pact—seeing it as a step across some sort of Rubicon, the other side of which lay militarization and possible war. He attributed the drive for NATO to European rather than American security fears, especially those of the British and French who, he argued, at the end of the war feared even more than the newly resplendent USSR a unified Germany cobbled together from the ruins. Kennan argued that the political concomitant to German economic revitalization should have been reunification at the earliest opportunity. Instead, with the support of Dean Acheson as secretary of state, the division of Germany was entrenched by the incorporation of West Germany into NATO and its contemporaneous rearming, the latter also something that Kennan objected to. Even in 1989 many west European leaders, most notably Margaret Thatcher and Francois Mitterrand, were initially opposed to the idea of German unification and secretly entreated Mikhail Gorbachev to reign in the events that began to unfold then.

With respect to the newly bipolar nuclear world, Kennan's position was in concord with what he saw as the Soviet view. He thought the retention of a certain amount of retaliatory capability a prudent measure, but saw that it rendered atomic weapons practically useless in the instant struggle and foresaw only limited uses of force from there on. In the putative war, Russia could not be wholly occupied or blockaded after all, so a policy of unconditional surrender would not have been feasible. Yet the chief point of being strong and looking strong was the confidence it imparted to the peoples of the non-Communist world about the prospect of their future should they not acquiesce to Soviet encroachment. In this way the people of the non-Communist nations would be attracted and come to the side of the democracies of their own volition rather than by subterfuge. Kennan argued for the maintenance of a special reserve and dignity, seriousness of purpose, and fundamental reasonableness of approach.[19] He distinguished between direct and indirect American action, preferring the indirect variety with an emphasis on oppressed peoples determining for themselves their conditions of life. This he hoped they would do by drawing on the shining example of American democracy: demonstrably strong and prepared, and surrounded by friends from the "free world." Ultimately, the darkness would be banished simply by shining a brighter light.[20] The small nations would be encouraged with institutions such as Radio Liberty and Radio Free Europe, in the formation of which Kennan was a central figure.

CRITICISM

The most immediate and forthright criticism of Kennan's containment policy came from the journalist Walter Lippmann. Lippmann did not object to Kennan's conclusion that force was going to have to be met with counterforce, but instead argued that containment would be a misuse of American power. Lippmann's central complaint was that containment missed the point with its focus on responding to Soviet encroachment at a series of constantly shifting geographical points, making it therefore an essentially reactive policy. This was despite Kennan asserting that it did not amount to a policy of simply holding the line and hoping for the best, rather that U.S. action could achieve positive results. Nonetheless, Lippmann thought it allowed the Soviet Union the initiative to probe and prod until it achieved its objectives, while containment had no real objective of its own beyond trying to react in time to Soviet moves and hoping that at some point the Soviet attitude would mellow or the empire break up. Moreover, it required the United States to make allies of historically unproven nations at the expense of alienating traditional allies in the Atlantic community. Lippmann criticized Kennan's analysis of the interaction of Soviet ideology and Russian nationalism as incomplete and amorphous, citing it as the reason for the corresponding lack of shape to the strategy of containment. It was the mighty power of the Red Army,

Lippmann contended, not the ideology of Karl Marx, which had enabled the Russian government to expand its frontiers.

The real debate for American foreign policy, Lippmann contested, was therefore whether, when, and on what conditions the Red Army could be prevailed upon to evacuate Europe. The necessary accompaniment of Soviet evacuation was the contemporaneous evacuation of the American, Canadian, and British armies, which also remained in Europe. To evacuate the victorious armies and leave Europe to the Europeans would be to honor the agreements reached at Yalta that intended the division of Europe between the Allies to be temporary while the details of the armistice were worked out. After the withdrawal of the Soviet Army, any attempt to return would be an invasion—an open, unmistakable act of military aggression, against which the legitimate power of the United States to respond militarily would stand as the opposing and deterrent force. All other pressures at the "constantly shifting geographical and political points," were to Lippmann secondary and subsidiary to the fact that the Red Army was in the heart of Europe. It was to the Red Army in Europe, therefore, and not to ideologies, elections, forms of government; to socialism; to communism; to free enterprise that a correctly conceived and soundly planned policy should have been directed.

Lippmann's criticism was in large part a response to Truman's evident adoption of Kennan's evaluation and prescriptions in the announcement of what quickly became known as the Truman Doctrine. However, the American obsession with doctrines, something the Marshall Plan had only encouraged, was a phenomenon Kennan himself later spoke out against. "I think of foreign policy in terms of principles, not doctrines," he wrote in 1954.[21] The Truman Doctrine had declared it "the policy of the United States to support free peoples who are resisting attempted subjugation by armed minorities or by outside pressures." Kennan took objection to the sweeping commitments it implied. The statement was, he said, too general and implied a departure from a case-by-case pragmatic approach based on clear national interest. In theory it invited applications for American assistance from all manner of governments simply on the basis of their having some Communist element within their societies, which effectively meant all societies. However, others in the administration held the flexible approach to foreign policy in equal contempt. Secretary of State Dean Acheson in particular carped at what he called "the sin of ad hocery."[22]

The National Security Council strategy document of 1950—popularly known as NSC-68—was a product of this yearning for a strictly defined and referable rubric for strategy. Despite his obvious, if inadvertent, contribution to the establishment of the Truman Doctrine, Kennan was at pains to stress the need for a pragmatic, nondoctrinaire approach to foreign policy making, which, if not so loose as Roosevelt's version, would still only be guided by preconditioned concepts, not enthralled to them. Doctrine as the determinant of foreign policy was, he argued, facile, but "trust," he said, had only a relative meaning in foreign affairs. Kennan recognized that his ideas were "a far cry from the outlook of FDR himself, and particularly from those whom he was soon to choose as advisers on policy towards the Soviet Union."[23] Another casualty of differing views was William C. Bullitt, who Kennan contends was sidelined after espousing a tougher stance in contrast to Roosevelt's conciliatory tone before the war. Yet after the war the policy that evolved took a much tougher stance still.

MILITARIZATION

Ultimately Kennan's view of the struggle as chiefly political rather than military in character was shared by few in Washington. The Berlin Blockade, Soviet development of the atomic bomb, the Communist take-over in China, and the subsequent Korean War all reinforced the contrary view. Kennan's ability to shape policy was rapidly overtaken by events. The arrival of Dean Acheson as secretary of state, who eschewed much of the prescriptions in Kennan's thinking for a submilitary strategy, prompted Kennan to resign his post as director of the Policy Planning Staff and move permanently into academia. The use or threat of force in Greece, Iran, and Turkey was aimed at preventing Russia from gaining access to ice-free ports on the great seas and oceans and threatening Suez. Such efforts were laudable, and it was for this same reason that Vietnam after the Sino-Russian split did not command the strategic importance that was afforded it. Ultimately, the Long Telegram and X Article had been intended to advocate a middle road between the doves and hawks. Such was the determination to prevail over the Soviet menace that containment policy in Europe was briefly superseded by the much harder-edged policy of "Rollback," introduced by the Eisenhower administration but soon abandoned as unproductive and dangerous in anywhere other than parts of the developing world. In this way Kennan argued that it was not containment that failed but the intended follow-up.

Kennan claimed in the first volume of his memoirs that his views diverged from the policies that actually emerged in much the same ways that Lippmann's had from his own. Those divergences ranged from the absolute misreading of containment as a military rather than a political strategy to the differing geographical scope attributed to his ideas on opposing Soviet expansion. However, Kennan's qualifications, in public if not in private to his superiors, came after the events. And on a reading of the headline statements it is easy to see why his audience took from them the impression that America had to be prepared to use large-scale force. While Kennan had yearned to find an audience willing to heed the dangers he had witnessed multiplying, he had not anticipated the whirlwind that followed. Kennan had let the proverbial cat out of the bag. Of course it was the bold statements rather than the many nuances of Kennan's Long Telegram and X Article that were seized upon by the Washington policy-making machine. In that sense those early statements certainly did have profound and far-reaching implications for American foreign policy, but they were, in fact, not representative of the totality of his views. Once influential persons had digested and, they thought, grasped the import of those statements, they were little interested to heed the many qualifications its author immediately began appending to them. Kennan stressed that the material for the X Article had been intended for consumption by Forrestal only, and he was at pains to point out that there were some important omissions on his part with respect to the piece as a comprehensive policy document. First was his failure to discuss what he considered to be the overextension of Soviet power in Eastern Europe. Second was the failure to delineate a clear geographic distinction between areas of vital interest. After all, when looking at the world from a distance it was the diversity rather than the uniformity which had impressed Kennan.

Of the five areas he had described as capable of producing serious military-industrial power, only one of them, the Soviet Union, was in the hands of the Soviets. Therefore a primary policy objective should have been to prevent Soviet influence spreading to the remaining four, rather than challenging the Soviet Union head on in an existential contest. But as Wilson Miscamble writes, "The ease with which [Paul] Nitze assumed control of the Planning Staff and used its members in the drafting of NSC-68 suggests that, while Kennan enjoyed his colleagues personal loyalty, he had not managed to convert them fully to his basic ideas on how the US should deal with the Soviet Union."[24] The appellation of "America's Global Planner" was clearly, then, in truth, well wide of the mark. During that critical period between the end of the Second World War and formation of NATO the paranoia about foreign intentions demonstrable in the Soviet mentality had come to act as a self-fulfilling prophecy, as Soviet actions induced the very countermoves they had early on feared but had little real evidence to expect. On the Western side too, the proclivity to court aggression became more pronounced, and Kennan cautioned against the tendency to permit the image of a different, more acceptable Russia to be eclipsed by or identified with the question of victory or defeat in a future war. The Russo-Chinese schism is probably explained to a considerable extent by nationalistic geographic factors. Kennan came to believe that containment had become redundant as soon as the Sino-Russian split emerged, for that was itself the greatest measure of containment that could have been conceived.[25] Stalin's death further altered the validity of the basic assumptions upon which Kennan had first proposed containment, but by then the attitude was entrenched, as was the faith in a "doctrine." To escape the schizophrenia of conceiving of the world as divided between "two planes of reality," the one surfeited by Soviet mendacity, the other the "free world" of the capitalist nations, was something Kennan had advised in 1954.

ENDURING GEOPOLITICS: BEYOND CONTAINMENT, THE CASE FOR INVOLVEMENT

Only in the late 1980s did U.S. officials begin speaking of a new era of transition and moving beyond containment. Terry Anderson remarked how it fell to Reagan to complete the task of containment, and how he did so in a way that Kennan himself had anticipated—by enlisting a Soviet leader in the task of altering his own regime.[26] Fast-forwarding to our own day, the reality is that the incumbent Russian leaders continue to employ the tactic of demonizing the West, usually with the suggestion that all overtures are simply ruses by which to "steal" their energy, and in doing so they seek to justify the oppressive conditions that still prevail. Russia remains more receptive to authoritarianism than almost any other European nation as, indeed, it has known little else. At an early stage in his career Kennan had a conversation with a Russian acquaintance who gave him this insight into the Russian character: "The better things go for a Russian the more arrogant he is ... It is only when we are having hard sledding that we are meek and mild and conciliatory. When we are successful, keep out of our way."[27] It was clearly the basis of Kennan's assertion that the Russians were impervious to the logic of reason but highly sensitive to that of force, the corollary being that to wrest a concession from them required first making them uncomfortable. Before the buoyant commodity markets collapsed in the autumn of 2008, Russia had had good sledding and displayed much arrogance in acts such as planting the Russian flag on the seabed at the North Pole, flying provocative missions of its "Bear Bombers" over EU countries, and, finally, invading Georgia. It can, therefore, be convincingly argued that Kennan had overemphasized Soviet ideology at the expense of highlighting the driving force of Russian nationalism.

A further result of Kennan's influence while director of the Planning Staff had been the concentration of American political and economic efforts on Japan in preference to China. This was despite the entreaties of many congressmen and senators for a policy focusing on China, which had since the nineteenth century been seen as a fruitful prospect for American expansion; the logical next step in America's great drive west. In this way Kennan advocated an approach more in tune with Spykman's Rimland thesis than Mackinder's Heartland. In response to requests for a "Marshall Plan for China" Kennan had protested that the country was not economically or politically receptive to such aid in the way that developed-but-depressed Europe was. Despite Kennan's entreaties to oppose Soviet imperialism, his policy advised that beyond essential economic aid and political support to areas outside the Soviet sphere, the United States ought to remain aloof from much of what was done within it. However, with the many examples of Russian concessions when faced with staunch opposition, it must be asked, what if nuanced involvement rather than militaristic containment had been the preferred strategy as the lines were drawn at the end of the Second World War? Might the long struggle that Kennan accurately foresaw and, in fact, relished, have been foreshortened? So it is at a time when Western governments, especially those with forces committed in Iraq and Afghanistan, are asking themselves frank questions about what is an appropriate level of involvement for them in Eurasian affairs, and how far it is prudent to press particular issues such as the expansion of NATO, that it pays to recall the ideas of a Polish leader who bequeathed policies which might sensibly form the basis for Western involvement in Eurasia today.

CHAPTER 4

Josef Pilsudski and Prometheism-Intermarum

The alternative to Kennan's policy of containment would have been involvement: in other words, engagement of the myriad captive Eurasian peoples within the Russian orbit. This was the strategy espoused half a century earlier by Josef Pilsudski, the first leader of the modern Polish state as it emerged from the Partitions after Versailles. Pilsudski argued that any great Eurasian power would crumble if its many minorities were empowered from without. This assumption drew on Mackinder in highlighting the debilitated state of Russia when confined to its historic northern wastes. Pilsudski named his policy "Prometheism," an allusion to the actions of the Greek Titan Prometheus, who stole fire from the gods to give to mankind, thereby raising him from ignorance and representing the triumph of light over dark as mankind emerged from the shadow of the overbearing gods. Alongside his policy of Prometheism Pilsudski advocated and pursued a second complementary concept called, in Polish, "Międzymorze," or in Latin, "Intermarum." In the place of Mackinder's "broad isthmus" between the Black and Baltic seas, Pilsudski had envisaged a federation of the small states united in their desire to be independent from both Russia in the east and Germany in the west—the two great Eurasian powers of their day.

Pilsudski's Prometheist vision has been partly realized with the fall of communism in Eastern Europe in 1989 and the breakup of the Soviet Union in 1991, when Russia's former satellites regained their independence. However, the great Eurasian powers of today—Russia and China—still encompass hundreds of minorities, and the small states of Eurasia have not always made linear progress in consolidating their nascent sovereignty and emerging from the political and economic tutelage of Russia. The specter of regression is mainly relevant when looking at the bilateral relations of the smaller Eurasian states with Russia. Yet the problem of nurturing their emergence into the free-trading democratic world is compounded by the trend which has seen China simply filling the vacuum created by any Russian retreat. More worrying still is the evidence that the Eurasian great powers are acting in concord to ensure the subservience of these peoples. Similarly, Pilsudski's Intermarum has been partly realized in the post-2004 form of the European Union, which firmly binds Germany and the East European states into its Western institutions at the expense of Russia's alternative model. But again, the process has not been wholly successful in achieving its strategic potential. Vagueness and incoherence in the European program undermine its attraction to the as yet unincorporated fault line states on Russia's border, as well as the ability of the established ones to deal with Russia as their numbers and economic might ought properly to dictate. It therefore pays to revisit Pilsudski's concepts and reassess them as part of our troika of ideas from Mackinder, Kennan, and Pilsudski to be used as a basis for informing today's Western strategy in Eurasia.

FORMATIVE YEARS DOMINATED
BY THE HEARTLAND POWER

Born in 1867 Josef Pilsudski was a contemporary of Mackinder's; yet, growing up the fortunes of the two men's respective countries could not have stood in starker contrast. While Great Britain was approaching the apogee of her imperial grandeur, Poland was wallowing in the humiliation of partition. Pilsudski's family of disestablished nobility held lands in what is now Lithuania, previously a part of the Grand Duchy of Lithuania and the Polish-Lithuanian Commonwealth, but following partition, under the Russian yoke. The Pilsudski family was staunchly Polonized in its habits but powerless to shelter the young Pilsudski from the Russification policies that pervaded life in that part of the partition. His family owed its position to the Polish-Lithuanian Commonwealth, which had represented the alliance of the Polish and Lithuanian monarchs under the Jagiellon dynasty, brought about when Poland's Queen Jadwiga married Lithuania's Grand Duke Jogaila, the latter becoming King Wladyslaw II Jagiello of Poland. After its momentous defeat of the Teutonic Knights at the Battle of Grunwald in 1410, the Polish-Lithuanian alliance emerged as one of the indisputable great powers of Europe, dominating its central portion. Schooled in the history of Poland's greatness as the dominant partner in that enterprise, Pilsudski matured in an attitude of resentment at the interlopers from both east and west who had fallen upon and devoured what historians generally hold to have been a quite progressive and enlightened commonwealth-empire. So it must be borne in mind that Pilsudski came to theorizing about Eurasian security not as one of Churchill's pygmy nationalities[1] but as the descendant of one of Europe's past giants.

The Commonwealth had been formed largely in response to Germanic aggression, as the Monastic Order of the Teutonic Knights continued to prosecute their wars against the Latvians of the Baltic coast, despite the latter's conversion to Christianity and invalidation of the Knights' raison d'être. At the time of the Treaty of Lublin at which the Commonwealth was formed, Russia was ever avaricious under Ivan IV (the Terrible), but was directing the greater weight of its energies against the non-Slavic tribes between Muscovy and the Pacific. The Commonwealth enjoyed almost two centuries gathering new territories, mostly in the Baltics, Ukraine, and Belarus, and swelling in wealth and culture. The Commonwealth had as its foundation a constitutional apparatus that severely curtailed the power of the monarch, maintaining him in a position as head of state, but playing second fiddle to the parliamentarians, who were composed mainly of Szlachta noble families, such as the one from which Pilsudski himself was descended. During this time the Commonwealth traded profitably in grain and other agricultural products and was a hive of artistic and scientific advancement, even at the time other European nations were being wrought apart by the Thirty Years War.

The Commonwealth's woes began with revolts among some of its subject peoples, most significantly the Cossacks. However, other underlying factors had been further and more significantly eroding the structural integrity of the union. As the western European countries increased their reach upon the ocean, the new markets they exploited and developed, and the new trade routes they pioneered, meant a reduction in demand for the Commonwealth's products, as well as the importance of its position on the historic east-west trade routes. Another factor was Russia. In the early seventeenth century the Commonwealth had actually succeeded in occupying Moscow, albeit for a brief period of only two years. Thereafter, however, the tide of influence and then outright occupation flowed wholly in the opposite direction. Russia had become the menace Poland was to endure for another three centuries and more. Compounding these problems was the Commonwealth's inability to take timely executive action to avoid disaster. In the spirit of democracy a unanimous voting system, the *liberum veto*, had been introduced into parliamentary procedure, which, owing to the disharmony in the vested interests of the parliamentarians, meant resolution of nearly all major reform and other issues became deadlocked. This constitutional disease soon manifested itself in visible outward signs of decay—so often the invitation for dismemberment of an empire. The warlike Prussians and expansive Russians were ready to take what they could, but so too was comparatively liberal Austria, a traditional Commonwealth ally but one not prepared to let Russia and Prussia fill the void left by the vacuum. Ironically, Europe's first codified constitution came just four years before the Commonwealth was totally dismembered in 1795.

The partition came in three parts—1772, 1790, and 1795. After the last, the Prussians and Russians finally met on a line running to the northeast of Warsaw, with the Prussians taking Warsaw itself. The Austrian segment, including Lublin, Krakow, and Lwow, retained a modicum of autonomy with inhabitants enfranchised to a limited extent and allowed to maintain and establish their own universities. The other segments, however, were subjected to intense Pruss- and Russification policies. It was in this way that the Jagiellonian University in Krakow survived while the University of Vilnius did not. For Pilsudski this meant that he was compelled to attend school lessons in Russian and was indoctrinated into the strictures of the Orthodox Church. All in all, Pilsudski grew up in an atmosphere of hatred for the Russians and desperate to fight for Poland's independence.[2] It was these formative years which forever colored his attitude towards Poland's eastern neighbor and, once he had gained power, informed his policy in respect of securing its safety from that menace. Although popularized as the "Marshal of Poland," Pilsudski was not, in fact, a professional or career soldier. He began by studying medicine at Kharkov University in modern-day Ukraine, but had that course interrupted when he was arrested for revolutionary activity and transported to Siberia. Inevitably, the rigor of the frozen wilderness only served to intensify Pilsudski's Russophobia and facilitate his capacity to plot against the country by introducing him to other radicals he would probably not otherwise have met. On returning from exile, Pilsudski joined the Polish Socialist Party and set up an underground revolutionary newspaper. For the latter he was briefly detained, but escaped to Austrian-controlled Krakow.

It seems Pilsudski's attraction to Marxist-socialism owed much less to ideology than the fact most of its Russian and Eastern European protagonists defined their belief in defiance of the Czar. For Pilsudski, radical leftist politics represented no more than the best vehicle by which to arrive at a restored Polish state. In the words of his famous remark made after Poland's independence in 1918 and familiar to Polish school children today, "Comrades, I took the red tram of socialism to the stop of independence and that is where I get off" However, despite his lack of ideological commitment to socialism, Pilsudski's anti-czarism was genuine. In 1904, on the eve of the Russo-Japanese War, Pilsudski set out for Tokyo where he propositioned the Japanese government about a bilateral arrangement to upset Russian efforts in the coming war. Pilsudski saw the opportunity to offer the Japanese a hand in diverting Russia's attention in return for armaments and financial support for an uprising in Poland. In a memorandum preceding his visit to the Japanese government, Pilsudski emphasized "the importance of taking advantage of the many nationalities within the Russian Empire, with the Polish people in the forefront."[3] Pilsudski's military experience began with his initiative to establish a paramilitary wing for the more bellicose faction of the Socialist Party that he led. Later, these paramilitary units were trained at a military academy in Krakow tolerated by the Austrian authorities. The paramilitary units' activities were more terroristic, criminal, and saboteurial than military, being involved in assassination and theft of Russian assets. The paramilitary units were later augmented by recruits to the Riflemen's Association, a front, tacitly sanctioned by the Austrian authorities, for the establishment of a Polish army in waiting. Pilsudski's position at the head of these organizations ensured that with the outbreak of the First World War and transformation of his fighting men into the Polish Legions, the military pretender become an actual commander-in-chief.

Pilsudski placed his Legions at the disposal of the Triple Alliance, with the stipulation that they be used exclusively for fighting the Russians. The Legions proved to be capable units and scored many successes against the disintegrating Russian army. Towards the end of the war Pilsudski felt confident enough to demand from the Austrians a promise of independence once the Alliance was victorious, but knew that the only sure way of achieving that goal was for it to be beaten by the Triple Entente, to which end he gave secret assurances to the British and French that the Legions would not fight them. Despite the Legions' successes against the Russians, they were later deemed by both the Austrians and Germans to be a seditious element. Pilsudski's tenacity in the First World War, where he came to blows with all three of the erstwhile partitioning powers, cemented his domestic image as Poland's protector. However, the corollary was a residual sense of distrust amongst the victorious powers that was to prove an obstacle to Pilsudski's postwar schemes for ensuring Poland's security in a geopolitically hostile Europe.

POLISH IMPERATIVES

Poland, from the river Odra in the west to the Bug in the east, the "land of the plains," consists of that predominantly flat land occupying the basin of the larger Vistula River, between the Baltic Sea in the north and the Tatra Carpathian Mountains in the south. It straddles the historical fracture line where the Slavic and Germanic peoples have met. In it constitutes the western approach to Eastern Europe proper. With no natural defensive boundaries save for the mountains in the south, throughout its history Poland has been hemmed in by the virile German principalities in the west and the Russians to the east. For that reason the country has inevitably been contested over in a centuries-long running battle between the

Germans—who, with a powerful France to their west, tended to divest themselves of their expansive urges in the weaker lands to their east—and the Russians, who were continuously pushing east to achieve defense-in-depth and who, in any case, and as Mackinder said, had considered Russia the rightful preserve of all Slavdom. The imperative for Poland, therefore, was a march land between the two peoples. It was in this way that Poland and Lithuania had overcome their differences to make common cause against the Germans. From a mixture of avarice and insecurity the Commonwealth had then absorbed many of the Ruthenian peoples of modern Belarus and the struggling Ukrainians in the south. In doing so it ensured for the first time a viable security situation in which the buffer between the Russians and Germans was sufficiently large for a time to keep those peoples from clashing at Poland's expense. When they finally did come together once more, the result was 123 years during which Poland ceased to exist on the map of Europe.

Yet even after both Russia and Germany were in turn defeated and Poland's independence restored at the culmination of the First World War, it took little time for the double threat to reemerge and once more press in on the country. In the wake of Russia's humiliation at the Treaty of Brest-Litovsk a new, more ruthless Russia emerged behind the guise of the USSR, ostensibly more principled in its aims but much less so in its means. Pilsudski's false devotion to the socialist cause was underscored when the Polish-Soviet War broke out in February 1919. Poland's stand against Lenin and Trotsky's drive to support Communist movements vying for power in the ruins of other European states put paid to those ambitions and aligned Poland in principle with the Western powers that were limply trying to rout the Bolshevik movement in Russia. Not only did Pilsudski aim to emasculate the Soviet reconquest and ensure Poland's newly regained independence, but his plans envisaged orientating the whole of Eastern Europe and the Caucasus in direct opposition to Moscow. Apart from seeing the opportunity to recover lands in western Ukraine that had slipped from Polish control, Pilsudski saw that an alliance with Kyiv was essential to his broader plans for opposing Russia. Pilsudski made similar overtures to the Lithuanians and Latvians, both of whom, but especially the Lithuanians, proved recalcitrant, fearing Polish dominance almost as much as Russian. The key to Polish security was thus cooperation between Poland, the Baltic states, Ukraine, and possibly Belarus. This was also, by extension, the key to broader European security, as Russia could be pinned back to her natural frontier in the east and the Germans prevented from overspilling into Slavic lands from the west.

However, the fate of Eastern Europe was not hers to decide. The great powers at Versailles had determined not to let Europe degenerate again into general conflagration and were alive to the need to micromanage the Germano-Slavic struggle in Eastern Europe and its proxy clashes in the Balkans. That said, the general approach of those powers, as Mackinder cautioned, was remiss and apt to shy away from making any dramatic changes to the European status quo. In fact, the overwhelming concern in the years after the Armistice was to punish and emasculate Germany rather than forestall the spread of Bolshevism. The Allied foray into Russia soon ran out of steam when it became apparent that the feared domino effect of Communist revolution had not materialized and that prosecuting the struggle into the deeper reaches of the Russian interior was an ideological crusade for which none had the stomach. So like Mackinder, Pilsudski similarly sought to establish the importance of Eastern European and Caucasian politics in the minds of Western statesmen. Pilsudski argued that alignment and reorientation of the states of Eastern Europe and the Caucasus was the key to influencing politics further east and denuding Russia of its proclivity for westward expansion. That proclivity arose from the traditional and inevitable Russian sense of insecurity and was premised on the idea that occupation of the country's peripheral regions would fundamentally provide defense-in-depth, in addition to the economic benefits to be derived from controlling the populaces and resources there. The corollary, thought Pilsudski, was that if Russia were to have wrested from it the nations it had absorbed, that it would become insecure and more accommodating to the states on its western flank, specifically to their aspirations of independence. In other words, Pilsudski would have understood the sentiment of Kennan's Russian acquaintance, that to make Russia meek and conciliatory was first to see to it that she had hard sledding. His policy therefore came to consist of a double-pronged approach of supporting secessionist movements in the Russian imperial lands, on the one hand, and consolidating those lands into a reoriented defensive federation, on the other.

PROMETHEISM

The scope of the Promethean concept was set out by one of Pilsudski's most trusted intelligence officers and organizers of the Promethean program, Edmund Charaszkiewicz, in an extract from his memoirs that is worth quoting at length:

The author of the Prometheism concept was Jozef Pilsudski who, as early as 1904, wrote in a document to the Japanese government of the need to utilize the potential of the non-Russian nations in the fight against Russia, which included, in the Marshal's view, the nations surrounding the Baltic and Caspian Seas. He noted that Poland, with its history and most assertive stance under the partitions, and love of freedom, would act as the leader in this process of emancipating the other nations from Russian rule. Special attention should be paid to the following excerpt from the Marshal's memoirs: "the strength of Poland and its importance amongst the nations under Russia, allows us to set ambitious political goals—disintegration of the Russian Empire and the granting of independence to the countries placed under Russian rule by force. We do not only believe this to be the fruition of the cultural aims of our nation for independence, but also a guarantee of its existence, as Russia without its conquests, will be so weak to cease to be a dangerous neighbour."[4]

Pilsudski's Prometheist concept had its roots in his childhood and was something he was busy promoting long before the First World War and his rise to power. In the months leading up to the Russo-Japanese War of 1904–1905, Pilsudski sent a memorandum to the Japanese government explaining his idea. Then following up the memorandum he traveled to Tokyo to lobby the government there for support in an insurrection in Poland. This move, however, was scuppered by the opposition of Pilsudski's domestic rival Roman Dmowski, leader of the Polish National Democrats, who was on the spot to pour water over what he thought was a counterproductive and ultimately doomed initiative to further the cause of Polish independence. Nonetheless, Pilsudski returned to Poland determined to continue his uncompromising and virulently anti-Russian means of bringing about his goal. The essential idea was to counter Soviet imperialism by fomenting and supporting irredentist movements among the non-Russian peoples of Eastern Europe and the Russian Empire. In the 20 years following Pilsudski's return from Tokyo, his position in Poland changed from outlaw revolutionary to acknowledged father of the modern nation. After a coup in May 1926 power in Poland became concentrated in Pilsudski's hands, and the newly established Pilsudski regime supported the Promethean ideology.[5] Richard Woytak writes that the Promethean concept had been "based on the assumption that the changes caused by the post-World War One national revolutions were still in progress; according to this view, the emergence of Russia was an unfinished business."[6] For Pilsudski it followed that mechanisms had to be put in place to ensure the business was finished in a manner satisfactory for Polish and, by extension, East European, security.

Woytak divided the history of the Promethean movement into four periods: 1918–1921, 1922–1926, 1926–1932, and 1932–1939. During the first the movement was at its most active, signing a formal pact with the Ukrainian nationalist leader Symon Petlura, recognizing the governments of Georgia and Azerbaijan, founding research and educational establishments, admitting officers from Soviet bloc countries to the Polish army, and subsidizing over a hundred irregular periodicals and more than twenty regularly published journals dealing with Promethean topics.[7] At one point the Russian State Political Directorate (OGPU) security services discovered that the Pilsudski government had been subsidizing the

Prometheist movements of both the Azerbaijani Tartars and the Armenian Dashnaks at the rate of at least $1,000 a month "in anticipation of a Western crusade against Russia which was to liberate these national minorities of the Caucasus."[8] Charaszkiewicz's own work in the Polish General Staff's intelligence section involved planning, organizing, and conducting clandestine operations outside of Poland, primarily in neighboring countries, as well as establishing cells within Poland to lead resistance in the event Poland was occupied. Office B of Charaszkiewicz's department was responsible for clandestine actions against the USSR, targeting its ethnic minorities, such the Ukrainians, Belarusians, Cossacks, Caucasians, and Tartars. Office A, however, was responsible for running similar operations in the west, with a view to monitoring German and Austrian development and gauging support for the Promethean program among the Entente powers.

However, the virility of the movement subsided as Pilsudski became disillusioned about the prospect of securing support from the West and grew more cautious, seeming to prioritize other, less provocative foreign policy initiatives. Woytak contends that the Polish state was "too weak to challenge openly the prevalent Western concepts of Russia, [and that] Poland's main goal was to retain her newly gained independence."[9] This is accurate; however, Pilsudski never lost sight of his cherished Promethean goal of denuding Russia of her non-Russian gains and reversing her expansion in the west beyond the Russian core of old Muscovy. Mackinder and Pilsudski had both idealized an Eastern Europe divided into allied but self-contained nations, just like the Western portion. The scarcity of documentary evidence relating to Pilsudski's conception of the Promethean program means that exactly from whence his grand plans originated is to be guessed at. However, it does not take much consideration to show that Mackinder and his ideas could have figured in his strategy. Essentially Pilsudski's initiatives, although most likely formed independently, constituted a solution to the problem outlined by Mackinder. The approach of both men was to facilitate the estrangement of the non-Russian nations from within Russia's orbit. Both fully appreciated East Europe's fraught position straddling the Germano-Slavic fault line and the need for a viable march land between the two. And both received little wider acknowledgment during their lifetimes for the sense in their plans.

The ultimate failure of the Promethean concept during Pilsudski's lifetime is attributable to a number of factors. Pilsudski's domestic rivals were quick to criticize anything they saw as a diversion from the task of building Poland proper. Additionally, relations with other important East European nations sometimes soured over the incidental, which in turn held back the fundamental. Pilsudski's use of severe methods to crush the Ukrainian uprising of 1930 is one example. Because the Promethean program was a Polish initiative, Poland's neighboring states were ever wary of Poland's own imperialistic ambitions in emulation of the Commonwealth. This was especially the case when the manifestation of Polish influence in neighboring lands was so often intensive policies of Polonization, and that even with the irony of Poland having spent over a century nonextant under the partitions. Lithuania, especially, was averse to substituting one form of tutelage for another and had firsthand knowledge of Poland as the dominant partner in the sort of alliance Pilsudski was proposing. Moreover, aside from the question of bilateral relations between Poland and the putative members of the Intermarum federation, relations between those members themselves were often strained, something which compounded the problem of securing commitment, even if the common anti-Russian, anti-German ground on which they all stood was readily apparent. It was for those reasons that only a Polish-Romanian alliance was managed in 1921.

The definitive factor, though, must be the reluctance and aversion of the great powers—"the cartel of great powers," as Pilsudski called it[10]—to support the project beyond tacit identification with it. Initially, the Western powers had been averse to seeing Russia lose territory while the Entente was still fighting the Germans in 1917–1918. Their aim was to support the recovery of former Russian imperial lands ceded to the Germans at the Treaty of Brest-Litovsk. One manifestation of that policy was the pressure put on Skoropadsky, the Ukrainian leader, immediately after the Armistice to propose a federation with Russia in preference to Pilsudski's overtures. As Woytak writes, "The movement never experienced moderate or even lukewarm support from the Western countries. Generally they 'intended [simply] to build a unified and indivisible pro-Entente Russia.' "[11] Miron Rezun contends that "the British continued to manifest their traditional interest in the Caucasus and in the Baku oil fields, which led them to support Prometheism in Soviet Russia."[12] This, however, was very much in principle. When Maurice Hankey, cabinet secretary to British Prime Minister Lloyd George, returned from a postwar fact-finding mission to the Eastern European states, he communicated his feelings to the prime minister thus: "My hopes do not rest on the Poles," he said, "for in them as yet I can see not the smallest sign of capacity or efficiency."[13] Regarding Pilsudski himself, Hankey was dismissive of his ideas for European security, saying that "his interests are entirely military."[14] Norman Davies concludes that "the emotional tone and bitter criticisms of Poland which pervade [Hankey's] letters to Lloyd George and his personal report, cannot but have confirmed the prime minister in his determination to avoid involvement in Poland at all costs."[15]

With his plans to reorganize Eastern Europe snubbed from all sides and Poland's closest Western ally, France, looking less and less as a guarantor of her security, Pilsudski, ever the realist, was left to make what he could from Poland's situation. The results were the dual nonaggression treaties with Poland's great neighbors. The Polish-Soviet Non-aggression Pact of July 25, 1932 was followed on January 26, 1934 by the signing of the Polish-German Non-aggression Pact. Yet Pilsudski was contemptuous of their capacity to do anything other than buy time before the seemingly inevitable clash portended by the unfinished character of the great process of change that was begun in 1914. "Having these pacts," mused Pilsudski, "we are straddling two stools. This cannot last long. We have to know from which stool we will tumble first, and when it will be."[16] Pilsudski was criticized for the treaties and accused of underestimating Hitler's preparedness to renege on Germany's Versailles agreements and flaunt her aggression towards and contempt of East European states. He was criticized for giving Germany time to rearm and simultaneously allowing Stalin a free hand to consolidate the Soviet position in Ukraine, Belarus, and the Caucasus. Realistically, however, the choices open to Pilsudski were limited by the reluctance of the Western powers to take a tough stance with Russia and later Germany. In Pilsudski Eastern Europe and the West had a man who understood Eurasian geopolitics and how they hinged on Eastern Europe. They had a man with vision but one who was largely left to whistle in the dark. For the Promethean program in Eastern Europe, his death in 1935 left a vacuum of initiative that was never to be filled.

The following years saw Hitler's consolidation of power in Germany and the reshaping of the political landscape so that once more Eastern Europe's fortunes were weighed in the balance. The attitudes of Great Britain and France, which were essentially those of appeasement, meant, as Zygmunt Gasiorowski notes, that "in the West the ranks of those who were willing to pay nearly any price for the conciliation of Germany were swelling—especially if that price was to be paid with Eastern European territories."[17] Ultimately, Pilsudski's Promethean and Intermarum ideas were abandoned as works in progress and, as Woytak points out, "it is noteworthy that the Promethean harvest was reaped by none other than Hitler in his invasion of Soviet Russia in 1941 when the peoples of that country, not understanding the real intentions of the Nazi Germans, greeted the aggressors as liberators."[18] The second great war of the century that was the result concluded with a Russian stranglehold over half of Europe. Russia's quest for security knew no bounds as world power shifted west from Europe to America, drawing with it the fulcrum on which the East-West balance lay and giving a truly global character to the Cold War situation that was developing. As already documented in chapter 2, Mackinder's star was in the ascendant immediately as the dust was settling, and Western policy makers were clawing about in it for an explanation of the process that was unfolding and what should be their course in it. Kennan's policy of containment was the one adopted, and it was in opposition to a more direct program of trying to "liberate," as Kennan chastised it, the peoples of Eastern Europe already firmly within Russia's orbit. Thus it was, that with little Western support it took another four decades for those people to liberate themselves and Pilsudski's vision be partly realized.

THE FALL OF THE SOVIET UNION: PROMETHEISM REALIZED?

Since the Prague Spring of 1968 and the crushing of the reforms that were introduced into Czechoslovakia at that time, the so-called Brezhnev Doctrine had prevailed in the Warsaw Pact countries. Any attempt to destabilize the "legitimate" socialist governments of Eastern Europe, in other words, those sanctioned by Moscow, would become a casus belli for Warsaw Pact troops to act in defense of them. But come 1985 and the elevation of Mikhail Gorbachev to the Soviet leadership, that policy had long been relaxed as the USSR's economy was in tatters and the country had failed to subdue even backwards Afghanistan. At a time when people were beginning to talk of moving beyond containment there was a palpable sense of impending change in the winds of East-West relations. Between 1986 and 1988, it was Gorbachev who had set the pace in the recalibration of those relations by his announcement of the new official Soviet attitude, as represented by the policies of Glasnost and Perestroika. This had the desired effect of calming Ronald Reagan's language and inducing the Americans into arms limitation and trade talks. However, with the process of change that had been started it was really a case of floodgates, and once opened, the Soviet leader was borne along by the current. By the late 1980s the Soviet presence in Eastern Europe was not serving its intended defense-in-depth purpose, but rather it required enormous injections of capital and micromanagement of numerous internal crises, an unaffordable commitment of military resources and the continued risk of a major dislocation with the West. Ultimately, what Gorbachev called openness and restructuring was perceived in Eastern Europe as weakness, and stood in stark contrast to the confidence of the incumbent Western leaders, chief among whom were pugnacious characters such as Reagan and Britain's Margaret Thatcher.

It has often been said that the USSR's policy towards Eastern Europe by 1989 was simply not to have a policy.[19] Gorbachev's cautious approach seemed at first to succeed in extracting maximum political advantage out of a situation in which Russia was destined to lose a great deal of prestige and influence. With the exception of the brief Soviet intervention in Lithuania, Eastern Europe was essentially abandoned without a tantrum to the irresistible forces that were at work there. When the fighting erupted in Bucharest, it was the United States that urged Gorbachev to intervene, but Gorbachev declined. Local Communist leaders who had spent years and, with their predecessors, decades trying to legitimize themselves as independent of Moscow quickly entreated their patrons for help, but Moscow was unresponsive. Indeed, Gorbachev was the recipient of the Nobel Peace Prize in 1990, principally on the basis of what he had *not* done and his capacity to constrain the more hard-line elements within the Soviet leadership who were for reaction. The peoples of Eastern Europe essentially liberated themselves. But it was the manifest redundancy of the Brezhnev approach helped by the tough talk from the West that allowed them to do so. That said, Moscow viewed the question of independence as wholly separate from that of Western integration.[20] Even key reformers, such as Foreign Minister Eduard Shevardnadze, opposed Eastern European states switching their allegiance to the West and warned the West not to try to make immediate political capital from the upheaval,[21] something the Western European countries themselves, although encouraged by the United States, actually had very little desire to do.

The collapse of communism in Eastern Europe gave Russia cause for concern about the future of the USSR itself. But in some quarters that concern went even further, extending to actual fears over German revitalization and renewed power should that country reunify. As a result, certain institutions, foremost the Warsaw Pact organization, were to be retrenched and reorganized rather than abandoned. In 1990, in negotiations with the Czechoslovak government over the number and status of Soviet troops in Czechoslovakia, the Russians seemed to show no intention of giving up what was a crucial part of their European war-fighting capability. The Warsaw Pact was thus to be reformed, albeit outside the context of ideological confrontation.[22] Yet in the West itself, especially Britain and France, the dislocation of Eastern Europe from the USSR was not wholly welcome, as the stability provided by the old East-West divide had, in fact, suited them—once the possibility of major nuclear war had become practically unthinkable, following both blocs having peered into the abyss at Cuba. In particular, both Britain and France feared German reunification and preferred a divided Germany, something that suited all the major European powers, not least the Russians themselves.

It has been widely reported from Kremlin archival sources that shortly before the Berlin Wall came down, Britain's Margaret Thatcher informed Gorbachev that Britain and Western Europe did not want German reunification. France's President Mitterand similarly implored Gorbachev to intervene should the process of reunification begin. A yet worse outcome envisaged by the Western European allies was German reunification aided by the Russians and the possibility of Russo-German partnership that could have been entailed. The Russians carped about how German reunification would dangerously alter the NATO-Warsaw Pact balance of power, but ultimately Gorbachev was unprepared to use force to prevent the process. But that process, if inevitable, was to have its limits. The Soviets supported Poland's position on the retention of its post-Second World War borders with Germany, aiming to ensure that Moscow had a say in the shape of the new Germany and at the same time trying to justify the lingering presence of Soviet troops in Poland. However, Poland ultimately rejected the Soviet overture in the knowledge that playing the Soviet card was the last thing that would be conducive to dealing profitably with a reunified Germany in the future. [23]

As far as Moscow was concerned, German reunification would mean the total withdrawal of Soviet forces from Germany, which would in turn amount to the dismantling of the Warsaw Pact. Soviet troop withdrawal depended to some extent on the preparedness of NATO to make like concessions (just as Walter Lippmann had predicted nearly 50 years earlier), and as the East European states' agitation for Soviet withdrawal became more pronounced, the Soviets actually attempted to short circuit the arguments by proposing to the Americans the total withdrawal of Soviet forces from Europe and the German Democratic Republic, contingent on the United States doing the same. In the knowledge that such a proposal would never be accepted, the Russians were able to credibly buy some time in their dealings with the East European governments. Moscow's position appeared to be that it wanted the Warsaw Pact organization transformed from a defensive into a political alliance, although how sincere was its belief in such a possibility is open to question. In reality, the best the Russians could hope for was East European neutrality once those states became independent of the Warsaw Pact. But at the same time, they knew how attractive the Western model was to these peoples and that it would not be long before applications for EU and probably NATO membership would be made.

Again it was the East Europeans themselves who made the moves over the question of their membership in the Warsaw Pact, by condemning the legacy of the 1945 Yalta agreement and the premise that it was the way of things for Eastern Europe to be cleaved between East and West. But far from a falling out over the development of independent Eastern Europe, the period was marked by unprecedented levels of East-West cooperation at the international level, with the Persian Gulf War being the most trenchant example, sanctioned as it was by the sort of agreement in the UN Security Council that would have been impossible in previous years. Moscow generally made increased use of the United Nations; however, this was also viewed as evidence of decrepitude by most. Moscow sought to establish new security structures and develop more subtle methods for influencing the Central and East European nations. It was then time for a proper but necessarily lengthy accommodation with the USSR's former colonies. One response to the rejection of Soviet power in the region was an insistence on hard-nosed economic relations and the withdrawal of preferential trade agreements, especially concerning Russian energy exports. This was to establish a modus operandi to be seen in Eastern European-Russian disagreements up to today, the last significant example being the Ukrainian gas dispute of January 2009.

Once the inevitability of military withdrawal had been accepted, it was intended to be a phased affair, but in the event it was rapid, so much so that the Warsaw Pact was effectively nonexistent by the end of 1990. Moscow was concerned that its withdrawal from Eastern Europe should not entail its isolation from the continent altogether. Indeed it was concerned not to be left essentially an Asian power, and it is for that reason that it cleaves so strongly to Ukraine now. After reunification, Gorbachev was against German membership in NATO, but eventually relented in return for beneficial economic agreements. Interestingly, it was the Germans who were "by far the most positive in their readiness to extend material help [after 1989]."[24] A process of ironing out of strategic arms limitation issues soon followed, and relations with the West improved. But for the East Europeans, proper economic backing from the West was not immediately forthcoming, and the conversion to payment in hard currency to Russia meant the Kremlin was able to make sure "the East Europeans finally understood how tough it actually was to be free."[25]

The Moscow line today holds that Ukrainian membership of NATO would dangerously upset the East-West balance. The question of to what extent Russia would be prepared to intervene to stop that process, if Ukrainian public opinion appeared to support it, is moot. The 2010 election of Victor Yanukovich has necessarily meant Moscow's confidence has grown as the specter of Ukrainian Western incorporation and the concomitant compromising of Russian power in the Black Sea region seems to have been averted for the time being. Moscow has similarly opposed Georgian NATO integration by making threats about how it might be forced to act should Georgia go ahead. In 1991 it had been the Baltic countries that were first to leave the union. The Central Asian states, however, had been much more in favor of the revised union treaty, as they feared more keenly the removal of preferential trade links with Russia while having few historical links with the West. Thus, Pilsudski's vision had been partly realized with the breakup of the Soviet Union and the independence of its former satellites, but there had been only limited emergence from Russia's shadow. The great powers of Eurasia today still encompass hundreds of minorities, and the small states of Eurasia are still fighting for their sovereignty. There is therefore a current policy shortfall in the West, when one considers that the Promethean program was a very genuine inspiration for Georgian, Armenian, and Azerbaijani patriots (there is a Prometheism statue in the Georgian capital Tbilisi) but is not now being pursued in those states or the rest of Eurasia.

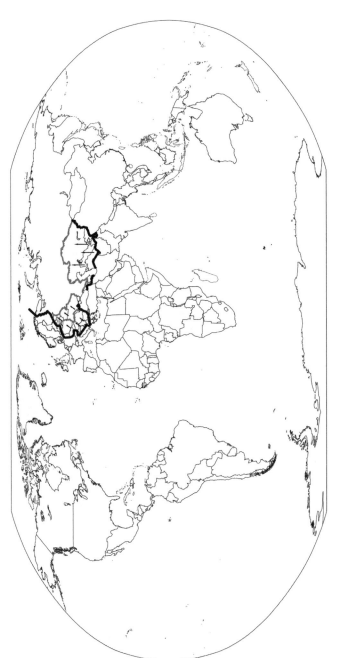

The Fall of the Soviet Union: Prometheism Realized?

INTERMARUM

To his Promethean idea of downsizing Russia, Pilsudski added a second, complementary initiative. This was his Międzymorze or "between the seas" program, also variously known in Latin as Intermarum or Intermarium. The concept focused on the countries of the broad isthmus between the Black and Baltic seas that Mackinder had described. Just as Mackinder had looked forward to the emergence of a constellation of minor nationalities in South East Europe, suggesting that Hungary, Romania, Bulgaria, and Serbia be federated to provide strength,[26] so Pilsudski conceived of a federation of White Russians, Ukrainians, Lithuanians, and Poles occupying the eastern European approaches. Although Pilsudski's vision was for a federation, it was to be the Poles of the reborn Polish state who would be first among equals. Mackinder had sought a further compartmentalization of Eastern Europe and the Caucasus where a group of buffer states including White Russia, Ukraine, South Russia, Georgia, Armenia, and Azerbaijan would help reverse the historical process of Russian expansion. Similarly, Pilsudski's Międzymorze concept contemplated an Eastern European and Caucasian security pact as the only realistic and effective way of consolidating the independence of those states achieved through the Prometheist program. This would then deter Russian westward expansion in the future.

Pilsudski's Intermarum recalled the work of Adam Czartoryski, Polish prince and one-time foreign minister to the Russian Czars Paul and Alexander I. Czartoryski's own analysis of the threat Russia posed anticipated that of Mackinder. "Having extended her sway south and west," Czartoryski said, "and being by the nature of things unreachable from the north and east, Russia becomes a source of constant threat to Europe."[27] Czartoryski had advocated the revival of the Polish-Lithuanian Commonwealth to counter this process, and Pilsudski's plan was to federate the East European and Caucasian nations in a similar geographic grouping to be reoriented as a defensive security pact against Russian expansion south and west. Pilsudski believed it was possible for Poland to regain her natural weight within Europe, and the idea of reestablishing the sixteenth-century Jagiellon Polish-Lithuanian Commonwealth in a more modern form must have been the basis of his Intermarum concept. Central to this concept was the maintenance of the Baltic countries as independent states.[28] However, what Pilsudski really needed to see his vision realized was backing from the Western great powers, specifically Britain and France. In order to promote the federation of independent nation states, drawn from within the Russian orbit and guided by Poland, Pilsudski pointed to Poland's bridgehead position between east and west Europe and hoped to impress upon those powers the sort of understanding Mackinder had striven to provide. Poland's historical alliance with France was key to this maneuvering.

Indeed, Norman Davies has said that the French would "move heaven and earth to get Galicia for Poland, which they consider[ed] a French preserve."[29] Yet as much as French protection was cause for confidence on the face of it, Pilsudski worried about Poland being considered a vassal of France and the Baltic states unimportant transitory phenomena inevitably to be reabsorbed by either Russia or Germany.[30] So long as French power remained predominant in Europe Poland's security could be hoped for, but by the 1930s this was in doubt. A politically like-minded and robust Eastern Europe, therefore, seemed to serve as an alternative security structure, performing the role of buffering German and Russian animosity and, in addition, deterring Germany herself from a move against Poland. This meant, as Litauer summed it up, providing "active opposition to Russian pan-Slavism and the Prussian raison d'état."[31] This double Eurasian threat was precisely what had worried Mackinder, and the conclusions of Mackinder and Pilsudski about how best to ensure Eastern European security could not have been in greater concord. At a cabinet meeting upon his return from the abortive ambassadorship to South Russia, Mackinder's policy recommendation was to "assemble all the anti-Bolshevik states from Finland to the Caucasus; giving them a certain amount of support." "Once an alliance such as contemplated has been created," he went on, "and the morale of the anti-Bolshevik forces has been re-established, we should be in a much better position to obtain a peace with a Soviet Russia which was not triumphant."[32] Mackinder further advocated the material support of all anti-Bolshevik forces from Finland to the Caucasus, the reequipping of the White Russian General Denikin's forces for reasonable defense, British control of the Baku-Batum railroad, and British control of Denikin's fleet on the Caspian.

As Brian Blouet noted, Mackinder's policy "amounted to . . . an alliance between Poland and the South Russians."[33] From *Democratic Ideals and Reality* one can see that Mackinder thought it vitally necessary that the tier of independent states between Russia and Germany should be properly linked with infrastructure and with secure access to the Baltic, Black, and Adriatic seas. Ultimately, however, Mackinder's assertive solution to the problem he identified found little support beyond other assertive figures such as Foreign Secretary George Curzon in war-weary London, and, crucially, the policy proposals he put to the cabinet met with little enthusiasm and even less support.[34]

Both Mackinder and Pilsudski effectively had their respective Intermarum concepts vetoed by the Western governments. For those governments both concepts represented too radical a reordering of the East European map and the balance of power that hinged upon it. In Pilsudski's case the Western powers—principally Britain and France— were reluctant to lend their political capital to a figure with such a checkered history, if not one of perceived general failure, both political and military, before his success in the Polish-Soviet War. In some ways Pilsudski was seen as a treacherous character, to be trusted by neither the West nor Russia. Mackinder had said that it was worse than useless to set alien teachers to work to inculcate the theory of freedom—that freedom could not be taught, only given to those who could use it. With Pilsudski's death in 1935 the Międzymorze concept inevitably lost its driving force, and all the countries he had viewed as possible candidates for membership had been absorbed by either Soviet Russia or Nazi Germany. The opportunity to give freedom to nations who did know how to use it was lost for generations.

THE EU-NATO INTERMARUM: MORE TO BE DONE?

In many ways the expansion of the European Union into Central and Eastern Europe in 2004, beginning with the Visegrad process of 1991, and the concomitant extension to those countries of NATO membership has meant that Pilsudski's Intermarum federation has been realized in outline. It is the first time any sort of Intermarum federation has been extant since the Polish-Lithuanian Commonwealth, in fact. The reunification and incorporation of Germany into the EU was a Western success story, given that Germany, before that time, must be considered an anti-Western authoritarian state. In this sense the EU went a step better than that which Pilsudski had hoped for. The Slavic lands that Russia had drawn into its orbit under the czars and shackled to it under the Soviets quickly moved to distance themselves from Russia and adopt the Western model as represented by the EU. The Warsaw Pact fell to pieces, and many of its members rallied to their former adversary, NATO. Perhaps the most important result of this process, as Walter Lippmann would surely have thought, was the withdrawal of Russian forces back within Russia's borders. However, at the time of writing that process remains incomplete as, in the Black Sea, Russia's lease of Ukraine's Crimean base has been renewed once more. This schizophrenia in postdissolution relations between Moscow and the former Soviet states that remain outside the EU has come about largely as a result of Western hesitancy in extending meaningful support for the stronger inclinations within most of these states to pull free from their old masters. Nevertheless, that is the situation as it exists today and, as such, Pilsudski's vision cannot be said to be wholly complete. There is, therefore, more to be done.

The effect of European Union membership on the East European countries has meant market orientated, democratic governments have come to the fore in each. Such a colossal reversal is ample testament to the fundamental preference for the capitalist system, with all its shortcomings, over that of the centrally controlled economy and polity. At the most basic level the likelihood of war as a means to resolve disputes between EU members has now been reduced to an absolute minimum. Of course there is no guarantee that will remain the case, but the stability that prevails is quite astonishing given the historical extent of the turmoil that preceded it. The position of Germany in the new European model is something to be celebrated. Germany might be said to be the European nation with the greatest natural weight. She has the largest population, and that popula- tion is creative and productive. As such, German orientation can make or break the continent. Prior to her defeat and division in the First and Second World Wars Germany was vain and dissatisfied with her incongruous lot of great power without great possessions. The result was authoritarianism and calamitous war. Decolonization since the end of the Second World War has meant that reunified Germany has been able to assume her lead role in the European project without the hindrance of jealousy. Germany has come into her maturity as a (for the moment) benign giant critically driving the European economy and generally satisfied with her borders, as well as with those of her consolidated East European neighbors.

Abolishment of tariffs, normalization of trade standards, infrastructural improvements, marked reduction in corruption so that new infrastructure can be put in place in a timely manner, and the certainty ensured by the rule of law are all factors that have allowed trade to flourish across Eastern Europe. Although problems of social security remain and have, in some instances, become more pronounced in these countries, the general trend has seen huge rises in living standards and disposable income. As such, the Eastern European model is a good example to follow with respect to the other former Soviet states still languishing in the shadow of Russia's influence and too unreformed to have access to EU benefits. With the exception of Belarus—which, despite the efforts of groups such as the Union of Poles in Belarus (Zwiazek Polakow na Bialorusi), it has to be accepted has little inclination, even with a new administration, to emerge from the Russian sphere—the countries belonging to the Common- wealth of Independent States (CIS), both current and former, are in need of a geopolitical incentive for good governance—in other words, staunch Western support and the possibility of the benefits that integration brings. A robust EU-NATO presence in Eastern Europe and the Caucasus could do much to ensure, for example, that Azerbaijan—"the cork in the bottle containing the riches of the Caspian Sea basin and Central Asia"[35]—is safeguarded from a repeat of the Georgian experience of summer 2008 and, moreover, to safeguard energy supplies in the region.

The European Union's relationship with Russia is a prism through which to understand why Pilsudski's vision requires completing. The EU numbers over 500 million citizens and is Russia's most obvious and necessary market in which to sell its vast energy resources. Russia needs

EU custom as much as the EU needs Russian energy. The newly independent Caucasian states similarly control huge deposits, the efficient sale of which to European countries would go far in allowing them to modernize and draw clear of Russia's lingering influence. However, the incoherence and provincial character of the EU approach to its dealings with all these countries has meant that Moscow has been able to extract maximum political advantage from what ought to be recognized as the weaker of the two positions. EU commitment to the sovereign integrity of the Caucasian states, assistance in reforming their economic and institutional settings, and delivery of benefits should those goals be met would deepen and better diversify the EU's energy sources; at the same time force Russia to be more competitive and dissuade Moscow from so freely using energy as a political tool. Although the EU has no territorial ties with China, a stronger, more coherent voice would better position the union to dictate to China terms of good practice in trade matters, and similarly discourage Beijing from attempting to fill any political space vacated by Russia. It is in these ways that the EU can finish the process Pilsudski envisaged and be a determinative force in Eurasia.

One could seek to cast aspersions on the importance of Pilsudski's concepts by highlighting his and his country's historical paranoia about Russia and therefore their lack of utility in addressing the greater problems of the region today. While Mackinder and Pilsudski were inspired to focus on Eastern Europe for different reasons and to present its significance within different contexts, the parallels between their work are marked. Essentially Mackinder identified and conceptualized a danger from the Western perspective. In his turn Pilsudski devised solutions to the problem which, although borne of a Central and Eastern European perspective, are equally pertinent to that of the West. It may just be, then, that Mackinder's conceptual analysis and Pilsudski's operational policies can provide timely aid to those European and American statesmen currently seeking to understand and further their shared interests in the Eurasian theater. The appropriate prism for looking at the problems already exists in Mackinder's analysis, and so too does the appropriate blueprint for a solution going beyond Kennan's Cold War containment, in the form of Pilsudski's twin concepts.

CHAPTER 5

The World Island in the Twenty-First Century

THE UNSTABLE WORLD ISLAND

The geofinancial system established at Bretton Woods in 1944 paved the way for American dominance through the remainder of the twentieth century. The U.S. strategy of permitting European nations free access to its markets while not demanding the same of theirs, in return for a hand in determining the direction of their foreign policies, proved so successful with the Western Europeans that it was subsequently extended to the Axis powers of Germany and Japan. In the aftermath of the Korean War the scheme was similarly extended to key Western allies in the Asia-Pacific region: Korea, Taiwan, and Singapore. Militarily and economically the Bretton Woods system facilitated Kennan's containment strategy. Yet the system that so effectively underpinned Western dominance for 60 years is now threatening to unravel, and the economic linchpin of that system, the United States, is countenancing protectionist measures to insulate it from increasing global competition compounded by the effects of the global financial crisis of 2008. The capricious global financial system is hugely important in the way it overlays more immutable geopolitical realities. The risk now is that these major financial crises may be followed by major fiscal crises, a trend strongly supported by history. Indeed, the history of all the great European empires and their imperial decline is replete with such episodes. The point is that such crises matter more for preeminent great powers, as financial struggling means that something has to give, and that something is usually the defense budget. Long-term curtailment of the defense budget means a reduced extraterritorial presence for major powers. In this climate there is a danger that China may emerge as an alternative source of economic sustenance for much of the developing world.

The twenty-first-century geopolitics of the World Island are thus in flux, making Mackinder's warning all the more relevant. A revanchist Russia, once again asserting itself in the post-Soviet space, is met by the tide of Western integration that is NATO and EU expansion in the west and the American presence in Central Asia. Many of the major Western states are deeply invested in Iraq, Afghanistan, and Pakistan, where effective governance and the establishment of stable civil society are proving difficult to achieve. Meanwhile, China spreads its economic and, increasingly, military influence from the Pacific to the Black Sea. In this context Beijing and Moscow have made quiet but concerted common cause to muscle Western actors out of Eurasia, while Iran's nuclear ambitions threaten to spark the security vacuum that could provide the two great Eurasian powers with the opportunity to finally do so. These broader geopolitical trends have been evidenced by a multitude of disagreements between Moscow and Beijing in Eurasia and the West at the peripheries. In the wake of 9/11 Islamic extremism seemed to provide a common focal point that allowed the major East-West powers for a time to ignore their traditional antagonisms. However, that climate of cooperation soon gave way to a hardening of relations as Russia, China, and the West began to repose in attitudes of mutual disappointment.

For Russia, the clear refusal of the United States to recognize it as an equal partner in global affairs jarred with the agenda of nationalist pride being pushed by President Vladimir Putin. This was compounded by the series of "color" revolutions, starting in Georgia in 2003 and spreading to the Ukraine in 2004 and Kyrgyzstan in 2005. The Orange Revolution in Ukraine was the pivotal event that convinced Russia the West was attempting to deliver a geopolitical knockout in the post-Soviet space. For China, U.S. insistence on criticizing its approach to human rights, currency valuation, and unbending stance over Taiwanese and Tibetan autonomy all emphasized the way the West was unwilling to accept the larger process of economic and societal development being undertaken by the Communist Party as a quid pro quo for authoritarian governance. Together these things left the Chinese dismayed and irritable. For the West, Russia's rollback of the democratic reforms introduced under Yeltsin and retreat into authoritarianism, along with China's similar refusal to accompany its economic liberalization with political, has meant similar disappointment at what some thought could have been a genuinely different and new world order at the beginning of the twenty-first century.

Since the election of Barack Obama in 2008, the United States' quarrel with Russia over the planned U.S. missile defense shield in Eastern Europe has come full circle. The Obama administration first made noises about the cancellation of the system, to the delight of the Kremlin, but then announced a revised system to be based principally in Romania. Over the same period the United States and China have been in open dispute over the United States' sale of advanced weaponry to Taiwan, engagement with the Dalai Lama, criticism of Beijing's monetary policy, and support for the internet company Google in its decision to pull out of China rather than remain subject to Beijing's draconian censorship laws. To compound the situation, China has adopted the Russian position over sanctions against Iran, with whom it is already close economically, thereby palpably undermining the preeminent medium-term strategic challenge for the Obama administration. Together these quarrels have been instances in the broader pattern of East-West divergence in recent years. However, such differences might be characterized as only the public face of the East-West struggle, which, in reality, is focused on Eurasia and the jockeying for influence there. That struggle has assumed a heightened level of intensity since the end of the stabilization period after 9/11. We might now number among the major concerns for Western civilization a China Question, a Russia Question, an Energy Question, and an Islamic Question, all of which have their ultimate solution in Eurasia.

The Islamic Question is a prime example of the way the greater East-West geopolitical struggle prevents resolution of very genuine but inflated problems, the conclusion of which ought to benefit Russia, China, and the West in outline—but the ramifications of which are far reaching for their respective future positions in Eurasia. The specific problem of Islamic extremism, and the terroristic tactics employed in pursuit of its political goals, is potentially equally detrimental to both the Western and Eurasian great powers. However, whereas political stability within the Middle East is desirable for the West and most probably for China too, for Russia there exists a perverse attraction in the destabilization of the region. It is only in this way that Russia is able to augment its influence in weapons and technology trade with the political presence of an honest broker in the region's disputes. The Iranian Republic was founded in direct opposition to Western culture, and, while currently lacking the delivery capabilities to threaten the West directly, a nuclear Iran could exert significant pressure on Turkey, Azerbaijan, and Turkmenistan, in particular on their energy policy and strategic alignment. The augmentation of Iran's power, whether with nuclear weaponry or not, would mean further menacing of Israel and other Western allies in the Middle East and the very real possibility of a nuclear armament domino effect throughout the volatile region. For these reasons the rise of Iran, nuclear or not, must be viewed as inimical to Western interests, and no fundamental rapprochement between the Iranian regime and the West led by the United States can be reasonably expected. Syria is not far removed from Iran in its authoritarian anti-Western outlook and shares with Tehran not just its desire but its determination to rid the region of its most conspicuous Western presence, Israel. Israel, for all its faults, represents a beacon of functional representative government and a liberal market economy for other states in the region to aspire to. The emasculation of Iran under its current leadership and concomitant survival of Israel is therefore a key Western strategic priorityand not one that should be lost sight of in the face of Russian and Chinese obstructionism.

Of course a clear consequence of growing Western institutions and norms in the Middle East has been the stimulation of anti-Western organizations utilizing terroristic methods to achieve religiously-tinged totalitarian ends. Al Qaeda remains the foremost example of such an organization. In Niall Ferguson's words, "Its members seek to undermine the market-state by turning its own technological achievements against it in a protracted worldwide war, the ultimate goal of which is to create a Sharia-based 'terror-state' in the form of a new caliphate."[1] In furtherance of these objectives the organization certainly aspires to acquire nuclear, chemical, or biological weapons of mass destruction. More disturbingly still, as the influential U.S. lawyer and former National Security Council member Philip Bobbitt has argued, "precisely because of the nature of the market-state, as well as the actions of rogue nation-states, the key components and knowledge are very close to being available to them—witness the nuclear Wal-Mart run in Pakistan by A. Q. Khan."[2] With such weapons, argues Bobbitt, the terrorists will be able to unleash a "super-9/11," with scarcely imaginable human and psychological costs. So much then for the most immediate and conspicuous dangers emerging from the World Island; what of the underlying structural trends that are less dramatically but more seriously eroding the foundation of the Western model in Eurasia?

In 2001 the Shanghai Cooperation Organization (SCO) was formed out of the erstwhile Shanghai Five group, which itself had been formed in 1996 largely to demilitarize the border between China, Russia, and Russia's former satellites. The SCO has since dispatched the task of border normalization with aplomb and evolved into a multilateral partnership of some substance and increasingly far-reaching geopolitical objectives. China appears to be the linchpin and driving force of the organization, whereas Russia displays a more cautious approach. Nonetheless, the two major Eurasian powers appear to be in genuine concord in appreciating the facility of presenting a common front on a broad range of issues, some of which have historically divided them and some of which constitute an effort to eclipse Western influence in Eurasia. In the Goldman-Sachs-designated "BRIC" grouping of developing economies, which is comprised of Brazil, Russia, India, and China, the influence of Russia and China has similarly been to emphasize the intent of the group to "work towards a more multi-polar world," which is, of course, tanta-mount to saying a less American- and, by extension, Western-dominated military, economic, and cultural space. Independently, Russia and China have also increased their respective presences outside their borders on the Eurasian continent. In particular, China has begun to construct a blue-water navy and expand its naval presence from North Korea clock-wise down the coast as far as the Red Sea, where it is part of the international patrol squadron intended to deter Somali piracy around the Horn of Africa. This "string of pearls" of naval bases and attendant matériel to stock them represents a fundamental extraterritorial expan-sion for China beyond its traditional "Middle Kingdom" territory. In Central Asia, China and Russia have been active in strengthening their presences, both economically and politically. Central Eurasia had become something of a vacuum since the dissolution of the Soviet Union in 1991, but has reemerged since 9/11 as the critical geopolitical arena it always was and always will be.

The broader pattern of geopolitical flux engendered by the recalibration in relations between East and West is perhaps nowhere better encapsulated than by the schizophrenia of the Ukrainian situation. Ukraine appeared for a while to be well on the road towards Western integration. Its Orange Revolution of 2004 was part of a process of similar "color" revolutions that spread east through the former Soviet satellites. Roadmaps for EU and NATO membership were loudly discussed, and rejection of Moscow's tutelage appeared tantalizingly close. Yet, just one parliamentary term later, the Ukrainian people have, in what has been deemed a free and fair election by international monitors, chosen the very candidate who in the 2004 election stood, and continues to stand, for the maintenance of the status quo ante, or in other words, Russian supervision. Clearly part of the reason for the volte-face is that a large proportion of the Ukrainian population, if not identifying themselves as ethnically Russian, nevertheless identify more closely with what they perceive to be Russian culture, particularly the Russian language. Clearly another part of the reason points to public dissatisfaction with the performances of Viktor Yushchenko and Yulia Timoshenko while in office. However, further explanation for the change of heart can also be found in the failure of the West, in this case chiefly the EU, to sufficiently promote their agenda for integration and the benefits to be derived from it. The EU's approach has stood in stark contrast to that of Russian President Dmitry Medvedev who, echoing Boris Yeltsin, encour-aged Russian government ministers every morning to think of Ukraine. In this context of the West's failure to grasp the importance of Eurasia, of its hesitant approach to furthering its interests there, and of the simultaneous invitation of competition from the great Eurasian powers, Russia and China, it pays to analyze in detail the key developments threatening to preclude Western actors from the Eurasian space altogether.

THE REVANCHIST BEAR

At the beginning of April 2010 U.S. President Barack Obama was in Prague to sign a new treaty to replace the Strategic Arms Reduction Treaty of 1991. Both the United States and Russia took the opportunity to highlight the improvement in relations since the Georgian War of 2008. However, Russian Foreign Minister Sergey Lavrov also pointed out Moscow's continuing concerns over the missile defense shield, which, although in its present guise of a Romania-based interceptor system is more agreeable than its erstwhile Polish/Czech variant, nevertheless presents a potential threat to Russia's deterrent capability and, by extension, the regional balance of power. But is this really the Russian position? In reality, Russia does not feel so much threatened by the proposed missile shield as supremely insulted by it. Aside from the acknowledged unlikelihood of nuclear brinkmanship becoming a feature of Russian-Western relations in the foreseeable future, Moscow knows that its deterrent capability as it stands is not seriously impaired, because Russia simply has far more missiles than could ever be shot down. Much more important is the symbolism of the United States blithely going about installing a weapons system superior to anything the Russians can produce, and in what was not long ago their undisputed backyard. The Russian nuclear apparatus is one of the only properly maintained parts of its armed forces. Any perceived slight to that apparatus that cannot be countered in the traditional arms race fashion is feared by the Kremlin as an embarrassment to its revanchist agenda, which enjoys so much support domestically. It is just this kind of national insult that reminds the Russian people of the situation they found their country in shortly after the last strategic arms treaty in 1991 and during the generally lamented years of Yeltsin's leadership.

Yet the years following the dissolution of the union properly deserve to be regarded with at least some ambivalence. For a time there even existed the question of whether Russia could have become a part of the EU program. As the forces of democracy brought about regime change in Moscow there was a window when Yeltsin, through a mixture of international weakness and a genuine desire to embrace market and democratic reforms at home, could conceivably have moved towards partnership with the Euro-Atlantic community. However, the West, especially the European nations, remained deeply suspicious of Russia and were for the most part still enthralled to Lord Ismay's prescription for NATO—keep the Americans in, the Russians out, and the Germans down. The assumption was that Russia would never swallow its pride and move for genuine EU partnership and would anyway be obliged to adopt Western values and institutions, therefore not requiring them to be forced on it. Thus it was that little constructive advantage was made of Russia's debilitated state in the immediate postdissolution years. It was never likely that Russia could have been put on course for EU and NATO membership at that time, as opposition would have been too strong from too many quarters—not least the East European states who were desperately trying to get away from Russia and not wanting to find it already proposed for membership in the club they sought to join. However, massive investment (as was actually expected in Russia) on Western terms, not unlike the manner of that made as part of the Marshall Plan, might have bequeathed to today's policymakers a much more pliant Russia.

So it was that Russia was left to stew in its murky political and economic juices, and by the time the Central and East European states had acceded to the EU it was clear that the window for partnership on strictly Western terms had closed. Moreover, it was clear that with the exponential rise in world commodity prices and the partnership with China, Russia was acquiring a pretension to great power status once more. Vladimir Putin's strategy for justifying his anointment and consolidating domestic support after 2000 soon came to focus on criticizing the Western-centric policies of his erstwhile patron, Yeltsin. Putin pointed out the disparity between Russia as a superpower and Russia as it had become when it tried to accept Western political, social, and economic strictures. His pitch struck a chord with the disillusioned Russian people, and now Moscow no longer strives for Western integration but wants to see itself as an independent power center. However, the reality is that Russia does not have the necessary institutionalized business and industrial structures necessary to compete with the EU or the West in general. But despite this the EU is in disarray over the question of the proper attitude to take towards Russia, and while no consensus is reached on presenting a common front to deal with Russia's energy imperialism, the EU contents itself with spiteful and pointless anti-Russian restrictions such as the anachronistic visa requirements. If Europeans are looking for reasons to be confident and to reduce the unwarranted latitude Moscow enjoys in their relations, then the figures speak for themselves. More than 90 percent of Russian gas is exported to the EU, whose states constitute its highest and best paying customers. There is no alternative market for Russian energy on that scale. The EU accounts for 50 percent of Russian trade turnover, yet Russia accounts for just 8 to 9 percent of the EU's. Similarly, EU foreign direct investment accounts for 90 percent of Russia's, while that of Russia in the EU is nowhere near comparable.[3]

All this points, as Bobo Lo has noted, to Russian power vis-à-vis Europe being more psychological than material. Nevertheless, Russia has scored some considerable foreign policy achievements in the past decade. These include the establishment of the Collective Security Treaty Organization (CSTO) in 2002, which includes Armenia, Belarus, Kazakhstan, Kyrgyzstan,

Tajikistan, and Uzbekistan, therefore incorporating many of the important post-Soviet states of the Heartland. The CSTO is clearly intended as a replacement for the ineffective Commonwealth of Independent States, which has fallen by the wayside as a serious international organization. Of the CIS states the black sheep had always been Georgia, withdrawing from the Council of Defense Ministers in 2006 after declaring its intention to join NATO, drawing further away from Moscow with the "Rose" revolution of 2003, and finally leaving in 2008. However, Georgia's bumptiousness, abetted by Western pronouncements on its roadmap for EU and NATO integration, led it to misjudge its position in 2008 when it responded to Russian provocation and fired the first shots in that brief but bloody conflict, which was pregnant with meaning for the future of other Western-inclined Eurasian nations. The true cause of the Georgian conflict was less the future status of Abkhazia and South Ossetia, and more Georgia's desire to go West and Russia's determination to stop it. And for all intents and purposes Russia *has* stopped it, at least for the time being. Since the conclusion of hostilities Georgia has realized that not the United States' and certainly not Europe's security umbrella extends to include it, consequently leaving it at the mercy of Russia's superior forces. Many NATO members who were once countenancing the inclusion of Georgia have also begun questioning the extent of the liability that might be entailed by doing so, as well as whether they would really be prepared to honor Article V of the constitution, which states that an attack on one is an attack on all and requires a collective response.

The ramifications for other former Soviet satellites seeking to draw away from Moscow's orbit have been profound. Russia's action and the policy by which it was operating represented a kind of neo-Brezhnev doctrine, intended to deter secession in the post-Soviet space. Such is the confidence the successful invasion has inspired in Moscow that Russian Foreign Minister Sergey Lavrov has concluded that "the centuries-old bonds that unite the people of Russia and Georgia are stronger than any political 'butterflies' that foreign winds bring to this part of the world."[4] In Lavrov's view this feeling of kinship is equally strong throughout the post-Soviet space: "In recent years," he said, "and particularly in the wake of the world financial crisis, we see the CIS countries increasingly come to the understanding that it's better to keep together."[5] In these words is contained a clear signal that Russia will continue to disrupt Central Asia and the Caucasus' integration with the West, especially where that integration represents diversification that threatens to undermine Russia's leverage through energy imperialism.

It is indicative of Russian confidence deriving from these foreign policy coups that since his promotion in 2008 Medvedev has consistently pushed his vision of a new European security initiative. Moscow's initiative is little more than the expression of the hope that the West will promise not to encroach any further upon Russia's traditional sphere of influence. While of course Western leaders have commented positively on some of the detail of the initiative and expressed a punctilious interest in furthering a mutual sense of security, most, including the United States, have wisely rejected the essential thrust of the plan, which calls for mutual acknowledgment of demarcated security interests and is clearly aimed at undermining NATO. What Moscow considers its sphere of influence clearly extends as far into modern Europe as the Balkans, where it has done all it can to stall the process of Serbian EU integration, not to mention meddling in the challenge of Bosnian consolidation. Moreover, Russia has taken advantage of the West's mistake in recognizing Kosovan independence in the region by citing the precedent in its recognition of Abkhazia and South Ossetia. Of Medvedev's new security initiative Lavrov has said that the sincerity test is still underway. By this he means that the proposal is a test of the preparedness of and degree to which Western actors will honor the collective political statements the Russians claim were made in the late 1990s, when OSCE and NATO-Russia Council documents were signed, including the Charter for European Security approved in 1999. Those statements, Lavrov claims, said that security was indivisible and that no country would strengthen its security at the expense of the other Euro-Atlantic states. He pointed out that the statements also guarantee the equality of organizations—NATO, the CSTO, and the OSCE.

Indeed, in early 2010 UN Secretary-General Ban Ki-moon signed a cooperation agreement with the Collective Security Treaty Organization's secretary general, Nikolay Bordyuzha, specifying cooperation between the two secretariats. Inevitably Moscow presents the development as representing UN recognition of the CSTO as a legitimate and equal partner to NATO and the OSCE. The CSTO is Moscow's preferred vehicle for safeguarding its sphere of influence in Eurasia. Under the auspices of the organization Russia plans to coordinate peacekeeping, military, and "antiterrorism" operations throughout the Heartland region. Moscow is prepared to act unilaterally if necessary, but it knows the products of its actions will derive greater international legitimacy if realized through multilateral action encompassing regional actors. A great hypocrisy exists in the preparedness of Moscow to contribute troops to a range of UN-mandated peacekeeping deployments around the world, while insisting on a "peacekeeping" monopoly within the CSTO territory and even in the post-Soviet space beyond, in countries such as Moldova. It is just one example giving the lie to Russia's sincerity in its engagement with the norms of respectable international conduct. So, it must be asked, as far as the new European security initiative goes, what can Russia bring to the table? While Medvedev's proposals sound, to all the world, egalitarian and inclusive in their precepts for European security, in reality they threaten to seriously undermine the true pillars of European security: the 1975 Helsinki Final Act, the 1990 Charter of Paris, and the pivotal roles of the OSCE and NATO. All this comes at a time when Russia has insisted it will go ahead with building Iran's first nuclear power station at Bushehr, despite widely held concern within the United Nations that before developing civilian nuclear power Tehran must first allay suspicions over its suspected weapons program.

Russia's interest in the West's difficulties with the Islamic world extends to other areas too. Moscow is currently divided about what position to take on Afghanistan. There is general recognition that the Western presence in Afghanistan is in Russia's interests. There is genuine concern about a corridor of Islamic militancy from Afghanistan to the Caucasus through Central Asia, a worry heightened by the 2010 Moscow metro bombings. NATO's role in stabilizing Afghanistan is essentially achieving an outcome Russia might otherwise have had to attempt for itself, with all the historical baggage that would burden the effort. Nevertheless, Moscow wants as great a say as possible in Afghanistan's development, both politically and economically, and is seeking to revitalize Russophile lobbies in Kabul. Dmitry Rogozhin, Russian representative to NATO, and General Boris Gromov, a Russian general who fought in Afghanistan, recently published an open letter to the *New York Times* to the effect that Russia in no way objects to NATO, and especially the United States, fighting in Afghanistan and that Russia could even increase its already important logistical help to the coalition, although it would never again send troops to Afghanistan.[6] In this way Russia is content to allow the West to do its job for it, although in return for simply countenancing the presence it expects a significant geopolitical quid pro quo.

Nor should the West place much faith in the capacity or even will of Medvedev to set Russia on a new course. Medvedev claims that Russia is a functioning democracy that protects the liberties of individual Russians. Russians may be content to some extent because the government appears to protect the egregious international liberties of Russia, but the same cannot be said of Russian citizens. Since graduating to the presidency in May 2008, Medvedev has failed to signal any departure from Putin's revanchist agenda. Georgia has been invaded, Abkhazia and South Ossetia annexed, and Russia continues to threaten its neighbors in the post-Soviet space and advocate the new European security initiative to undermine NATO in Europe. Ultimately, Russia remains, as others have already put it, the last European empire in Asia, with a territorial extent that would have delighted Peter the Great. It therefore behooves Russia's leaders to consolidate and if possible reanimate its power in that space. However, the Kremlin's embrace of the Soviet past entails a considerable degree of risk. There appears to be a limit to how far both the leadership and the people are willing to go. The tentative rehabilitation of Stalin in some quarters of the legislature and press has led Medvedev to publically state that any revision of the now generally accepted history of Stalin as a tyrant is unacceptable. This is one of the few issues that apparently puts him at odds with Prime Minster Putin. Moreover, the practice of reminding Russians of the Soviet Union's past glory has the drawback of drawing attention to the disparity between yesterday's world position and today's, which is a political risk unless success in recovering lost ground is seen to be made. It is a contradiction that may ultimately play to the West's favor and encourage more deep-rooted democratic and market reform in Russia, for the reason that Russia fundamentally lacks the organization and means to achieve the Kremlin's ends. The reality is that Russia cuts a poor economic and demographic picture, with the upshot that perhaps the biggest danger for the United States and, by extension, the West, is that they overrate Moscow, whether as a potential partner or an antagonist.

THE RISING DRAGON

Kennan had said in the 1950s that China was a distinctly resource-poor country.[7] Indeed, most assessments of China at that time were wont to emphasize a negative outlook for the country. China's reluctance to modernize in the nineteenth century had allowed European interlopers to come close to partitioning the country. By the end of the century the country was effectively partitioned into economic spheres controlled by the European great powers and the United States. Even then, however, taking a longer view, it should have been clear that to condemn China's prospects was to ignore history. Chris Patten, the last British governor of Hong Kong, makes the startling point that for 18 of the past 20 centuries China has ranked as the world's preeminent global economic power. The economic disarray that prevailed until the 1980s has seemingly done little to harm China's potential in the longer run. For three decades since Deng Xiaoping opened China up to market reform, the country has averaged annual growth rates of close to 10 percent. China is now the world's second-largest economy in terms of GDP. Although a key factor of this dramatic rise has been China's reticence in international affairs, economic might is nevertheless increasingly being converted into military. Through a combination of real increase in strength and modesty in advertising the fact (in contrast to Russia's specious revival and insouciance), China has come to command respect, even if tending more often towards fear, in the international community. But for China itself this state of affairs represents no more that the restoration of the historical status quo.

The lingering presence of an attitude of Chinese cultural superiority, deriving from Middle Kingdom assumptions that China, the Celestial

Empire, is at the center of the earth, surrounded on all sides by barbarian people to be subdued and made tributary, has not gone unnoticed by careful outside observers. Sensible of the disconcerting effect this certainly has on Western powers, especially the United States, the Chinese government has spent many years espousing a policy of "Peaceful Rise." Peaceful Rise was the brainchild of Zheng Bijan and goes hand in hand with "Harmonious World," in which China emphasizes its positive-sum view of international relations. The incoming "fifth generation" Chinese leadership—expected to take the helm at the 2012 18th Party Congress—is likely to continue the supreme caution demonstrated by the fourth generation in most spheres of policy, not least foreign. The Chinese leadership recognizes that confrontation with the West is highly undesirable and that it pays to assuage the anxieties of China as the proverbial ant nest and peril in those they consider geopolitical hotheads. For that reason, the unspoken but undoubted rivalry between China and the West has taken on nothing of the dramatic hue that characterized East-West relations during the Cold War. But is the contrast with Russia's typically extrovert style of geostrategy something to be welcomed or feared?

Despite the global financial crisis that unfolded in the summer of 2008, China's economy maintained enviable growth in 2010. China's capacity to produce and the United States' capacity to buy is therefore what will drive the economic recovery worldwide. Yet many economists have argued that China exists in a mercantilist bubble. Policies such as maintaining the yuan (renminbi) at an artificially low level in order to increase the appeal of Chinese exports is a strategy that riles not just the United States, its most vocal detractor, but also most other major economies. China currently owns in the region of $1.4 trillion in U.S. Treasuries, agency bonds, and U.S. instruments. In this way China can exert considerable leverage over the United States. However, the economic corollary is that Washington has the ability to decimate China's export economy instantly by shutting its markets with massive tariff barriers. And the path to global economic recovery is strewn with a number of other significant stumbling blocks. The year 2010 saw a number of United States-China disputes, from the relatively trivial egress of Google from the Chinese internet market and acrimony over U.S. arms sales to Taiwan, to some progress on China's yuan revaluation. Chinese media has accused the United States of "information imperialism" acting through its major transnational, Google, over Google's decision to withdraw after China refused to amend its internet censorship laws. In unusually irritable language the Chinese State Council responded by launching a tirade accusing the United States of "serial villainy." "In the US," it said, "the civil and political rights of citizens are severely restricted and violated by the government [and] workers' rights are seriously violated."[8] It also claimed that "the US, with its strong military power, has pursued hegemony in the world, trampling upon the sovereignty of other countries and trespassing their human rights."[9] Furthermore, laying the blame for the financial crises clearly at the feet of the United States, it said: "At a time when the world is suffering a serious human rights disaster caused by the US subprime crisis-induced global financial crisis, the US government revels in accusing other countries."[10] In response to the $6.4 billion-worth of weapons sold to Taiwan, China has promised sanctions against any U.S. firm that took part in the deal. It has further threatened to ban Boeing from selling and operating in China.

Of the more strategic developments that underlie these quarrels, the Chinese military is currently constructing nuclear submarines and aircraft carriers, as well as planning a space launch to put a Chinese astronaut on the moon by 2015. The most significant development in terms of power projection is China's construction of a blue-water navy. China is in the process of securing long-term access to North Korea's Rajin Port, allowing it access to the Sea of Japan—a long-term strategic objective. The agreement is indicative of Pyongyang's growing dependence on Beijing and Beijing's concomitant long-term commitment to Pyongyang. Negotiation for the agreement comes at a time when North Korea has recently agreed to lease another pier at the port to China's SCO partner, Russia, for a 50-year term. For China the agreement enables it to bypass the so-called First Island Chain, including the Yellow Sea, the East China Sea, and the South China Sea, which Chinese analysts see as a U.S. containment strategy. China is also making strategic capital out of the financial crisis and the blame dealt out to the Anglo-Saxon laissez-faire financial model by pushing for a novel international financial architecture, by which it hopes for one not dominated by the United States and the Bretton Woods institutions. Overall, China seeks a much-enhanced level of power projection in both the hard and soft variants and is determined to meet the challenge of the West in Central Asia that has so worried it in the years following 9/11.

But what sort of power will China be projecting? It must be remembered that China is an autocratic, antidemocratic state with a huge population that has historically demonstrated little desire to depart from the Confucian prescription to suppress individualism for the purposes of the greater whole. Of course such a mentality was a key facilitator of the Communist takeover. And although the 1980s saw significant liberalization relative to the Mao era, the clampdown marked by the Tiananmen Square massacre was comprehensive, and no comparable democratic expression has since been seen in the country. However, despite the years of communism the Chinese have displayed very strong consumerist tendencies in the last two decades. To visit a Chinese east coast city is to be reminded of Japan and to feel as though in a developed country, not a developing one. Although the status of developing nation may only apply to the Chinese countryside, the Chinese government will continue to eschew vanity and employ the appellation when it suits it internationally, even as it becomes increasingly inaccurate. Domestically, however, the situation is different, and the trend is for the government to showcase the country's development as justification for its control. Although the marked increase in levels of Chinese education in recent years seems in no way to have begotten a comparable rise in democratic sentiment, the Chinese government is highly sensitive to the spirit of giving the people what they want, in contrast to the spirit of the Mao years when everything was taken away. Although high levels of austerity appear to be naturally occurring in Chinese society, the modern Chinese government is not in the austerity business, and it is for this reason that China's growth in the coming years and expansion of its capabilities is likely to be accompanied by increasing instances of China asserting itself to get what it wants from the rest of the world.

However, China is ringed by states that have an interest in its containment. Japan, Korea, Taiwan, the Philippines, and India are all American allies and, despite any notions of racial allegiance (in the non-European sense), know that preservation of the liberal, democratic market economies they have come to embrace with such success lies in supporting the United States, in contrast to the many questions raised by the prospect of a Chinese alternative. On its northern flank China faces Russia along a 4,000-kilometer border, over which Chinese migrants are seeking work in increasing numbers. In Russia, Lieutenant General Vladimir Chirkin, commander of the Siberian Military District, has announced the deployment of two brigades to the Chinese border near Chita. Although they do not represent any new animosities, Chirkin stated that the brigades were deployed there to counter the presence of five People's Liberation Army combined-arms groups across the border. Chirkin stated, "We are obligated to keep troops there, because on the other side of the border are five Chinese armies and we cannot ignore that operational direction." More tellingly still, Chirkin characterized them as part of a deterrent force aimed as a friendly reminder to Beijing: "Despite friendly relations with China, our army command understands that friendship is possible only with strong countries, which can quiet a friend down with a conventional or nuclear club." This hard realpolitik stance belies the fact that the Kremlin has spent the Putin years avoiding confrontation with China (indeed, China probably represents some sort of model for the post-Yeltsin Kremlin—Perestroika without Glasnost), knowing that its position vis-à-vis the United States and Europe is better enhanced by cooperation with it. Nevertheless, it takes little consideration to show why many Russian strategists consider China a serious, perhaps the ultimate, long-term threat to Russia. So what of the deeper Sino-Russian strategic relationship?

BEIJING-MOSCOW COLLUSION

SCO member states include China, Russia, Kazakhstan, Uzbekistan, Kyrgyzstan, and Tajikistan. Together they occupy a territory of over 30 million square kilometers, which makes up three-fifths of the Eurasian continent, and have a population of 1.5 billion, making up a quarter of the world's population. Incomparable oil, gas, and mineral wealth is also contained in the area, prompting the appellation "OPEC with bombs." China appears to form the linchpin and driving force of the organization. This is in contrast to Russia's more cautious approach, which is understandable given that in Central Asia China has everything to gain and Russia everything to lose. Bobo Lo, in his book on the Beijing-Moscow relationship, has termed this an "anti-relationship," ultimately describing it as constituting an "Axis of Convenience." In the grand strategic sense, however, a change in the particular combinations of power brought into balance in the World Island may not alter the fundamental dynamics of the region. As Mackinder said, "The substitution of some new control of the inland area for that of Russia would not tend to reduce the geographical significance of the pivot (Heartland) position." "Were the Chinese," Mackinder went on, "organised by the Japanese, to overthrow the Russian Empire and conquer its territory, they might constitute the Yellow Peril to the world's freedom."[11] For many, however, the notion of a united Eurasia seems fanciful. Indeed, most are likely to incline towards to Zbigniew Brzezinski's view that Eurasia is too big to be politically one.[12]

Nonetheless, the formation and, more importantly, development of the SCO has piqued the interest of a number of major Eurasian states. India, Pakistan, Mongolia, and Iran have been granted observer status. Even the United States applied but was, perhaps inevitably, rejected. In March 2008, Iran applied for full membership. However, the SCO responded by saying that "as of now, there is no clear mechanism in place to expand the SCO and offer Iran—or any other potential member—formal membership."[13] The possible inclusion of Iran must be seen as a provocative act. It would be confirmation of the organization's hostile disposition towards the West, which has already been made fairly clear in numerous SCO joint statements about the intention to evict the United States from the Central Asian bases it currently enjoys the use of. Practically, however, although the inclusion of Iran would certainly cause concern in the West, any would-be Chinese-Russian-Iranian coalition is not likely to materialize in the immediate future. For China Iran's pugnacious anti-Americanism is counterproductive to its purpose of avoiding confrontation over nonvital interests, and for Russia the inclusion of another major energy supplier in the organization would only dilute the limited leverage Russia already enjoys. Many questions therefore remain over the eventual direction of the SCO. However, what is not in question is the potential for it to be a major and perhaps even determinative force on the Eurasian continent, depending on the evolution of its internal relationships and the attitude of the Western powers.

Peace Mission 2007 saw the SCO hold historic military exercises in China and Russia in August of that year, building on the precedent of Peace Mission 2005. In 2005 Russia spent approximately $5 million on the exercises. In 2007 this figure increased dramatically to around $78 million. The ostensible purpose of the exercises was to train multilateral forces in combating the much maligned evils of terrorism, separatism, and extremism (Russia supports China over Taiwan, Tibet, and Xinjiang, and China supports Russia over Chechnya and the rest of the North Caucasus). The exercises involved military forces provided primarily by China and Russia, although the other members did send token units. The maneuvers begot speculation that the exercises would be used as a foundation for transforming the partnership into a military bloc to compete with NATO and to counter the Western presence and influence in Central Asia. One purpose of the exercise was clearly sending a message to the Central Asian states that they need rely less on security assistance and influence from the United States and NATO in the future. But of course the Central Asian states may equally see the potential for future SCO operations to be used for quashing rebellion or dealing with political instability—broad brush terms that may include reversing their own sovereign and democratic political developments that Russia and China take issue with. There has been further speculation that a joint SCO-CSTO program may be developed. Indeed, joint military exercises are a priority for China's military planners. However, in many ways these organizations are in competition with one another, the one essentially a Chinese enterprise and the other a Russian. Of the two, however, it is the SCO that has the greater potential as Chinese leverage increases and Moscow prefers Beijing to the West.

The SCO has been described as the most dangerous organization Americans have never heard of. The senior partners, China and Russia, know that their respective quests for energy, China to fuel its continued growth and Moscow to export, mean that cooperation is necessary. This is despite the fact that plethora historical misgivings lurk within the relationship. These span the centuries, from the Mongol invasions of Muscovy in the thirteenth century (the fact it was not actually the Chinese Han seems to have little bearing) to Russian encroachment and racial condescension in the nineteenth, the latter most trenchantly represented by the unequal treaties (Aigun, 1858; Tientsin, 1858; and Peking, 1860) where collectively Russia took 1.5 million square kilometers of Chinese territory. Although Russia's political and cultural history is so intertwined with the major European nations, Germany, France, and England, in that order, the question of whether Russia fundamentally identifies itself as

European or Asian power for the future is not straightforward to guess at. The Eurasianist school of thought within Russian foreign policy, which argues that Russia's future lies in its eastern relations, has gained more adherents and greater influence in recent years. That said, if hostility towards the West and a focus on quintessentially "Russian" values of autocracy (*samoderzhavie*), orthodoxy (*pravoslavie*), and nationhood (*narodnost*) persists, the Russian view of Asia is no more practical than sentimental. At best, Russia sees itself as a bridge between East and West. Although the economy of the declining Russian Far East is propped up by Chinese migrant labor, the dislike of their presence is palpable in the streets of many towns in the region. Yeltsin's willingness to disregard Chinese "friendship" when other opportunities seemed to present themselves in closer integration with the West in the immediate dissolution years has not been forgotten in China. Nor has China overlooked Russia's willingness to allow Western transnational companies property-buying rights in energy concerns, while denying access to China's state-owned rivals. Therefore the West must beware of regarding the Moscow-Beijing relationship as a monolith. However, the interest China and Russia have in eclipsing Western influence in Eurasia is paramount, and just as people in glass houses should not begin throwing stones, Moscow and Beijing will not allow their differences to come in the way of achieving their end.

The SCO Moscow-Beijing relationship represents in outline the specter Mackinder had so ominously warned of. Although the Japanese have really played no part as Mackinder thought they would have to, nevertheless, China has partnered if not overrun Russia, and now practically the entire Heartland and a majority of the World Island are under the control of the strong influence, if not direct control, of two powers. Recalling the strategic implications of Germany's Berlin-Baghdad railway in the early twentieth century are China's recent proposals for a transcontinental rail network in the early twenty-first. In April 2010 China announced plans for a high-speed rail network linking the country with Germany in the north, Turkey in the west, and Pakistan, India, and Singapore in the south. In Eurasia India is the only major functioning capitalist democracy. India's rise is often spoken of in the same breath as that of China, but in reality China is leaps ahead. Moreover, Chinese foreign policy is, in many ways, vectored against India's ascent, especially in the naval sphere, where the Chinese refuse to accept India's primacy in the Indian Ocean where that would leave their Middle East oil imports as so many hostages to fortune. Chapter 4 described how Pilsudski's Promethean concept had been in part realized with the dissolution of the Soviet Union in 1991. However, even that incomplete process threatens to be reversed if Russia is allowed to reoccupy the post-Soviet space or, perhaps more likely, China is able to usurp that position. The maintenance of the United States as the only state with a truly global capability for power projection means that containment of Eurasia is still possible, and if one looks at the distribution of major U.S. forces around the world—Europe, Turkey, Iraq, Afghanistan, Taiwan, South Korea, and Japan—it becomes clear that containment of Eurasia remains the default position for U.S. grand strategy. However, although important, containment is not a sufficient strategy for the twenty-first century. In that way the part realization of Pilsudski's Intermarum concept, in the guise of the EU, remains as one of the few constructive answers the West has to the problem of authoritarianism in the Heartland and all that entails for the resources of those lands. More, therefore, needs to be done.

EURASIAN GEOECONOMICS

In 1954 George Kennan aired Malthusian concerns when he said of the post-Second World War population explosion that "I am sure future historians are going to point to it as one of the determinant factors of our time."[14] Such concern remains apposite when the historical record shows that the rate of resource development has often failed to keep pace with that of population. Competition for resources and the impact their pursuit and possession can have on a state's foreign policy strategy is nowhere more pronounced than in the World Island. With the exception of Russia, the populations of most of the major international powers are steadily increasing and have been doing so since the end of the Second World War.[15] China's population is predicted to plateau and slowly decrease steadily in the coming years, but will nonetheless remain massive. Accompanying this rise in population has been a concomitant increase in the energy demands of the various states, not just in absolute terms, but proportionally per unit of those populations. Modern lifestyles in developed countries are dependent on artificial energy. Despite climate concern and the drive for green fuels, production of that energy remains overwhelmingly derived from fossil fuels: coal, oil, and gas. Deposits of the first are widespread, and its supply is not currently an issue of global significance. Deposits of oil and gas, however, although still significant, are becoming increasingly costly to extract, thereby pushing up prices and the degree of leverage that possession can confer. It is not just the specter of the wells and reservoirs drying up that is cause for concern. Indeed, this is unlikely to happen for a long time. Rather, even a minor destabilization to the global system of supply precludes business from planning and therefore from investing. The consequential effect is disruption of trade and the international flow of money. The story of Eurasian geoeconomics is thus one of a struggle to control and protect the consistent production of energy in the World Island and its distribution beyond.

The dynamics of that struggle focus on China's insatiable thirst for energy to power gargantuan economic development and Russia's determination to hold on to its monopoly as the most comprehensive energy supplier. China possesses large deposits of coal, but lacks oil and conventional natural gas. The Chinese leadership recognizes that diversification of its oil and gas supply is the best way to both secure their flow free from interruption and to discourage and minimize the effect of any one supplier from exercising geopolitical leverage against it. Despite the SCO partnership, China's chief concern with respect to energy blackmail is Russia. For that reason it has been dramatically ramifying and deepening its energy supply network. in the established energy-producing states of the Middle East but also in the emerging ones of Africa and South America, the latter affording China particularly rich opportunities for manipulating local governance with pervasive infrastructural and other investment. Russia also recognizes that its ability to influence China in Eurasia depends upon the degree to which it can ensure China's demand for its energy products. Energy policy has become such a central and consuming plank of Russian foreign policy that the two are practically one and the same.

Nowhere is this conflation more fully represented than in Russia's state-controlled energy giant Gazprom. In Europe Gazprom controls a raft of non-transparent gas trading operations that together exercise considerable influence upon a number of states through their links with politicians, legitimate business interests, and organized crime. The uncertainty the mysterious workings of these companies introduces into European energy security is significant. Ukraine has been at the epicenter of revelations about these trends. Although there existed a genuine commercial dispute, albeit between various oligarchs and compromised officials, about revaluing Kyiv's artificially low gas payments inherited from the subsidized Soviet era, Russian gas trading companies have nevertheless been highly active undermining Ukraine's energy independence and consequently maximizing its political dependence on Moscow. However, the dramatic decisions to switch off the gas in 2006 and 2009 may have actually backfired from Moscow's point of view. The moves were intended to put Viktor Yushchenko and Yulia Timoshenko's administrations under immense domestic pressure, but because that sense of discomfort was so pervasive it had the effect of generating in Western European minds at least a sense that they needed to take a firmer stance with Russia and at the same time diversify. Unfortunately, little has been done since then. In the meantime Ukrainian and Russian energy cooperation continues apace as the coup of maintaining the Russian Black Sea Fleet at Crimea is consolidated.

The development of liquefied natural gas (LNG) markets is another avenue by which Moscow hopes to project its power beyond its existing pipeline networks in Eurasia. Currently other countries, especially

Australia, enjoy better established positions in the global LNG supply market than Russia. However Russia, as the world's largest producer of gas, in 2009 inaugurated a new LNG terminal on Sakhalin Island, south of the Kamchatka Peninsula, ideally placing itself to supply Asia-Pacific markets, including China, should LNG demand recover. Moscow clearly intends that LNG will augment Gazprom's global reach as well as short-circuit attempts at diversification by existing Russian-dependent Eurasian states. However, Russia may have overestimated its production potential and capacity to supply disparate new pipeline projects from an antiquated core transport network that relies too heavily on its non-Yamal fields in Western Siberia, ones that are mostly at or past their projected peak production levels. In Europe both the Nord Stream pipeline under the Baltic Sea to Germany and the fantastical South Stream to rival the EU's Nabucco pipeline in southern Europe must compete for gas from these fields. Added to this is the priority of supplying domestic demand in Russia, which is steadily recovering from the global financial crisis. The fact that the Blue Stream pipeline running under the Black Sea to Turkey has often operated at half capacity is indicative of this problem.

The problem derives from a strategic miscalculation whereby Moscow assumed a continuing Russian monopoly over Central Asian gas. However, in 2009 Turkmenistan, the largest repository of Central Asian energy reserves, made a clear statement on its desire to diversify its exporting options beyond the existing Russian contracts and infrastructure. Unfortunately a major aspect of that diversification involves the China-Central Asia pipeline from Turkmenistan transiting Uzbekistan and Kazakhstan to Xinjiang Province. The result is that China is now the most influential energy player in Turkmenistan. Kazakhstan and Azerbaijan are also seeking enhanced export capacity and must make choices between a number of offers from both Eurasian and Western states and companies to develop their deposits and infrastructure. In November 2008 Kazakhstan and Azerbaijan finalized an agreement to develop a trans-Caspian oil transportation network to include "an onshore oil pipeline in Kazakhstan and a tanker fleet in the Caspian Sea to ship Kazakh oil to the Baku-Tbilisi-Ceyhan ()pipeline and on to the world markets."[16] At the Budapest summit of January 2010 on the Nabucco pipeline project, it was noted that "significant progress had been made on the development of a natural gas link between the Caspian and Europe, within which Georgia had an important role to play." However, diversification of export options for the Caucasian and Central Asian states requires substantial and unwavering support from the West. Through NATO and Turkish security guarantees the West can secure Caspian energy resources, of which those actors are the major consumers and beneficiaries. The Turkish factor is essential and for that very reason potentially problematical. Turkey is a key country to Europe in its own right, but it is also an important interlocutor with regard to the "New Eastern Europe" comprising Belarus, Ukraine, and the Caucasian states. Turkey is eminently aware that it straddles a key geostrategic location with respect to European energy security, as well as a number of other matters. It uses its position as political leverage to further its aspirations for EU membership. As such it must be handled with care, lest it become either too confident of its EU prospects and cause an unwanted schism in that bloc before the reluctant states are brought round to the idea, or too disenchanted by broken promises, causing it to withdraw from key initiatives to protect Caucasian and Central Asian energy trade and to move closer to Russia, which has been courting it.

Since the revitalization of the energy corridor through Georgia and Azerbaijan in the late 1990s, the security and infrastructural situation has improved dramatically because of support from the United States, Europe, and Turkey. Astana has also expressed interest in alternative pipeline routes and in March 2010 suggested creating a new route through Azerbaijan and Georgia to the Black Sea, to take Kazakh oil from the Kashagan field to Constanta, Romania by tanker and from there to Trieste in Italy. The new route could form part of the EU-supported Interstate Oil and Gas Transportation to Europe (INOGATE) network, which includes most of the Black Sea, Caucasian and Central Asian states (Russia has observer status). The project is, however, politically dormant at the moment, but has great potential should it be revivified in the future. The Turkish deal also suggests that Kazakhstan is seeking to limit its dependence on Russian pipelines. However, despite moderating supply routes, in 2008 trade between Russia and Kazakhstan, not confined exclusively to energy, rose to $20 billion—meaning that Kazakhstan remains Russia's third-largest post-Soviet trade partner. Putin has promoted an agenda of continuing to enhance that bilateral trade, creating a joint company to implement civilian nuclear power projects and possibly the integration of power supply systems of both countries.

The Northern Distribution Network (NDN), which constitutes a land route from Riga through Russia to Central Asia and Afghanistan, as well as another route from Turkey, is being successfully used to supply coalition troops in Afghanistan. The project is fundamentally aimed at diversifying supplies away from dependence on the inherently unstable Pakistan road from Karachi (although that will continue to take the bulk of supplies). However, the project is expected to create substantial long-term economic opportunities for the numerous Eurasian states it passes through, prompting some to term it the "Modern Silk Road." Indeed, the ability to trade and transport goods across Eurasia with the same ease as by sea, something that would be possible were it not for the draconian authoritarian customs regimes in Eurasia, would mean a lot less time to drive a container from Beijing to London than to ship it around the Cape

or through Suez. Uzbekistan has held talks with the United States about
military-technical cooperation.

Elsewhere in Eurasia Russia has similarly been trying to bolster its trading relations, notably in South Asia with its BRIC partner, India. Trade
between Russia and India has historically been confined to military hard-
ware, energy, and space technology. Indeed, Russia is India's chief arms
supplier, providing $4 billion-worth of matériel and know-how—mostly
in relation to a new generation of fighter jets and a refitted Soviet-era aircraft carrier—to the Indian Navy over the coming years. However, Russia
is looking to diversify its exports to India beyond the government-to-
government level and to tap into the $1 billion-strong commercial market,
where huge potentialities exist in areas such as telecommunications. The
$10 billion trade balance for 2010 is a figure with which there is much
room for improvement when one considers the size of the respective
economies. However, there is little evidence that Russia is able to offer
India much in the private commercial sector that it cannot already get better elsewhere. In this scenario, Russia will have to fall back on its traditional geoeconomic strategy of guns, space, and nuclear. Russia was
responsible for transferring nuclear weapons technology to India in the
1970s and continues to be a major partner helping to build and maintain
the country's civilian nuclear power apparatus today. Russia's state-
owned nuclear company, Rosatom, is set to build up to 16 nuclear reactors
at three sites in India. Moreover, during Putin's 2010 visit to the country it
is widely suspected that Indian Prime Minister Manmohan Singh used
the opportunity to request the transfer of nuclear reprocessing technology,
something the West is reluctant to do, but which Russia will cater to if it
means filling a niche left vacant by Western high-mindedness and by
which it might extend its leverage with a major Eurasian actor. Further
east Russia has also been trying to expand its trading presence. Russian
Foreign Minister Sergey Lavrov remarked that it was commonplace to
say that the Asia-Pacific region had become the locomotive of world economic growth and that Russia would structure business strategy accord-
ingly. But at the geopolitical level, here Russia must acknowledge a
security debt to the United States for the stability brought by the long-
term United States-Japan and United States-South Korea alliances and
its essential conservatism there, where for Russia the worst case scenario
would be China slipping into the United States' shoes.

Fyodor Lukyanov of the *Russia in Global Affairs* journal has said of the
last decade of Russian trade that it was "marked by all-out mercantilism."[17] He went on to note that theirs is not a value system best suited
to the fostering of new ideas and explains the invention of "Russian conservatism" or "conservative modernization," which are, in fact, just bluff
for the country's lack of economic strategy and innovation. And it is for
this reason, contends Lukyanov, that Medvedev's various modernization

initiatives lack constructive substance. Those initiatives have professed a desire for Russia to graduate beyond the status of a producer of raw materials and military technology to create a knowledge-based economy, diversify, and add value to products before export. To complement these goals, two key aspirations of the Kremlin had been to join the World Trade Organization and the Organization for Economic Co-operation and Development. Doing so, the Kremlin had hoped, would encourage Russian companies to go overseas and attract foreign investment into the country. However, Russia resents the obligations of the very strictures that will enable it to secure such membership and is wont, when acceptance into certain international social circles is not as readily forthcoming as it would like, to withdraw in attitude of resentment.

ISLANDS ADRIFT

In strict Mackinder-esque, the Islanders as concerned in our Eurasian saga are the United States, Canada, Britain, Japan, and Australasia, and it was the set of "special relationships" between them that facilitated containment in Kennan's era. But for more practical purposes we must include Europe, now that Germany is fully and constructively incorporated as a Western state. Leaving Japan and Australia out of the equation, the one geographically too remote and the other still constrained in its ability to project power, the core of the West as discussed in these pages means the Atlantic community as represented by NATO. If Eurasia is to be preserved from domination by authoritarian, mercantilist powers, and its resources made competitively available for the benefit of both its people and the West, as prescribed by the Smith-Ricardo free trade model, then the West must be grown into Eurasia and its values and institutions transplanted there. NATO's role in this process is crucial, as is that of the EU, which in its eastern reaches constitutes the West's bridgehead into the crucial Heartland region of the Caucasus. The EU's Eastern Partnership program, which includes Armenia, Azerbaijan, Belarus, Georgia, Moldova, and the Ukraine, has meant those countries adopting the moniker "the New Eastern Europe." However, the schizophrenia of progressive democratic forces and conservative Russian allegiance pulling at once in different directions, as described with especial respect to Ukraine, is endemic throughout the bloc. In this climate it is vital that the people of these small Eurasian nations are treated as sovereign subjects and not objects in dialogues between the Eastern and Western great powers. The West should not repeat Yalta and negotiate the fate of these countries with other powers over their heads. What is needed is an expanded European security presence on the ground in the most vulnerable areas, such as Georgia in particular, and a Western strategy that engages the small states themselves.

In March 2010, recalling some of the proposals emanating during the euphoria of 1991, but deriving from pragmatism rather than sentiment, a group of influential German politicians and military officers, including the former German Defense Minister Volker Ruehe, published an open letter recommending that NATO offer membership to Russia. In this way such an offer would constitute the proverbial "Europe from Vancouver to Vladivostok." The démarche was representative of broader German moves to assert itself both within and independently of the EU. Chancellor Angela Merkel has striven to reestablish Germany's histori-cally strong trade relations with Russia, represented nowhere better than the Nord Stream pipeline project, in which the rest of the Islanders had little or no say whatsoever. However, Germany is aware of the sensible boundaries it ought to respect when acting independently of the EU and NATO and is anyway still suspicious of Russia, just as Russia is of it. An alliance between Moscow and the West even if indirectly through Germany thus seems unlikely. Even if the door to Russian Western integration were genuinely open, and there are many in the east of Europe that would wish to see it kept firmly closed, there has been little indication that Russia would warm to the move. Russian media peddles the twin myths that the EU seeks no more in a potential alliance than to steal energy and dump waste. Russia must also tread a careful path with China, which wields increasing leverage over the Russian economy. Western integration, as attempted in the early 1990s, would alienate China, leaving it as the sole "enemy" for NATO to be vectored against. In the Kremlin's view the West has no interest in adopting it as a partner equal to the United States, therefore "these contradictory perspectives, suggest that in the long term, Moscow has a vested interest in the emergence of Beijing as a global player."[18] The Russian view is that the United States is scared of confrontation with China, and this allows scope for Moscow to indulge in its pastime of international mendacity.

"The space between an enlarging Europe and a regionally rising China will remain a geopolitical black hole at least until Russia resolves its inner struggle over its post-imperial self-definition."[19] That was how Zbigniew Brzezinski saw the situation a decade ago. During Putin's tenure Russia appeared to have resolved its struggle in preference of a reemergence upon the world stage and particularly into the post-Soviet space. This process has been continued by Dmitry Medvedev and has chiefly taken the form of gauging the West's mettle in a series of provocative but calculated acts, beginning with a simple turning off of the gas tap in 2006 and culminating in the invasion of Georgia's northern and central provinces in 2008. Although Russia was necessarily cowed in Central Asia by the wrath of the American response to 9/11, further west in the Caucasian pivot zone, it has been able to make consistent, incremental gains in the area that matters to it—and that in Mackinder's theory should matter most to us all.

Retired Russian General of the Army Makhmut Gareev, now president of the Russian Academy of Military Sciences and regarded as one of the country's leading strategists, has argued that Russia must give greater priority to the development of the Urals, Siberia, and the Russian Far East. "The increasing importance of the Asia-Pacific region to the global economy, the flow of capital to the region, and its emergence as a geopolitical center of gravity," says Gareev, is evidence of that need.[20] In this theater the "Key Resolve/Foal Eagle" joint exercises between the United States and South Korea have attracted attention in Russia, as well as predictable protests from Pyongyang. "If the entire world is turning its face towards the Asia-Pacific region," said Gareev, "the Eurasian area needs to be a priority for us too."[21] This Eurasianist school prescription recognizes the importance of the Urals and Siberia as a northern transit route to complement the ancient Silk Road routes between Europe and Asia, "while in parallel exploiting northern sea routes across the Arctic Ocean."[22] The importance of the Central Asian lands, as described in strategic outline by Mackinder, is put into contemporary context in an essay by S. Frederick Starr, part of which is worth quoting at length:

This vast region of irrigated deserts, mountains, and steppes between China, Pakistan, Iran, Russia, and the Caspian Sea is easily dismissed as a peripheral zone, the "backyard" of one or another great power. In impoverished Afghanistan, traditionally considered the heart of Central Asia, U.S. forces are fighting a backward-looking and ignorant Taliban. The main news in America from the rest of Central Asia is that the Pentagon is looking for bases there from which to provision the Afghan campaign. In China, the region is seen chiefly as a semi-colonial source of oil, natural gas, gold, aluminum, copper, and uranium. The Russian narrative, meanwhile, dwells on Moscow's geopolitical competition there with the West and, increasingly, China. It is not enough to view them simply as a "zone of [our] special interest," as Vladimir Putin's government does; as a source of raw materials, as the Chinese do; or as a fuelling stop en route to Kabul, as the United States does. The better alternative is to acknowledge that somewhere in the DNA of these peoples is the capacity to manage great empires and even greater trading zones, to interact as equals with the other centers of world culture, and to use their unique geographical position to become a link and bridge between civilizations.[23]

Gareev sees NATO's military presence in Central Asia as an emerging threat to China, as it affects a region where Russia is itself weaker than at any time in the last 200 years. He has also warned of other threats by nonmilitary means to undermine Russia's position through subversion and information warfare, such as with the color revolutions. In an interview with *Russia in Global Affairs*, Mikhail Gorbachev has conceded that NATO expansion was inevitable after the collapse of the Soviet Union, yet that has not precluded him from complaining that promises of nonenlargement have been broken. The solution to the problem of NATO

expansion now might have been a pan-European security apparatus insti-
tuted in the aftermath of the Soviet dissolution. In many ways this
appears to be what Dmitry Medvedev is trying to achieve with his
proposals for a New European Security Initiative, though on much more
Western-preferential terms. Gorbachev lamented the resilience of the
sentiment expressed by Lord Ismay, NATO's first secretary general, of
NATO "to keep the Russians out, the Americans in, and the Germans
down." However, the view from the West, excluding Germany, is that
little has changed to undermine the logic of that statement. Russia clings
to its NATO-phobia and worries that the organization will evolve into a
more proactive global force prepared to act well beyond its original remit.
Those were certainly ambitions entertained by some members of the
alliance before 9/11. However, once those events had provided the stimulus
and appetite for realizing the expansion, it soon became clear that through
internecine disagreements over policy and contribution levels, NATO was
unable to become a "global gendarme." Many see the war in Afghanistan—
the first full-fledged NATO military campaign outside the alliance's
traditional zone of operations—as its last. Yet the difficulties of Afghanistan
notwithstanding, the Western presence there remains a key geopolitical
foothold in a place in Eurasia where Russia perforce enjoys little if any
leverage. If the violence can be contained, the situation provides unique
opportunities to engage with the rest of Central Asia while not having to
suffer Russia's influence as a medium.

However, in recent years discussion of NATO ambitions has become
more modest. NATO Secretary General Anders Fogh Rasmussen underscored his reassurance that "NATO will never attack Russia" by airing the
idea of NATO playing the role of an international security think tank, coordi-
nating its activities with other international organizations and regional alliances, including the CSTO and SCO. This seems like a response to
Zbigniew Brzezinski, who acknowledged that the United States cannot rely
on its European allies alone to address problems in distant locations around
the globe. However, given the refusal of many NATO member states, not
least the United States, to even acknowledge the CSTO as a comparable
organization, it seems unlikely that cooperation will be easy in the near
future. More likely is that NATO will retrench and reinforce its status as a
regional organization with the primary goal of guaranteeing the security
of its member states in the European-Atlantic region. Thus the current
choice appears to be between expansion by way of cooperation that would
adulterate its values, versus outright retrenchment. However, a third way
for NATO and the Islanders might yet be found, provided member states
can reaffirm their principles and show solidarity in exporting them anew.

The consequences of outright NATO retrenchment are nowhere more
manifest than in the Ukraine. Ukraine has had a torrid time redefining
its stance toward Russia and its European neighbors. The country remains

a geopolitical pivot because, as Brzezinski notes, "its very existence as an independent country helps to transform Russia. Russia without Ukraine can still strive for imperial status, but it would then become a predominantly Asian imperial state."[24] "Therefore," Brzezinski continues, "if Moscow regains control over Ukraine, with its 52 million people and major resources as well as its access to the Black Sea, Russia automatically again regains the wherewithal to become a powerful imperial state, spanning Europe and Asia."[25] On that basis it has generally been assumed that much therefore depends on the contested expansion of NATO and the EU to Ukraine. However, it is precisely because the Ukraine means so much more to Russia than to the West that it can only be a very long investment with the prospect of little yield in the short term. This will remain the case so long as Ukraine's population is genuinely split between Russophiles and Russophobes. Medvedev had shunned Yanukovich's predecessor, Viktor Yushchenko, since August 2008 when Yushchenko had backed Georgia in that war. However, with the election of Yanukovich in January 2010, Putin and Medvedev have buoyantly reengaged with Kyiv and set in motion a process that will see much that we must consider progress over the last parliament disappear. In 2010, Ukraine announced its "non-bloc" status, in other words, its policy of not joining either NATO or the CSTO. In this way Yanukovich hopes to steer a course over the coming years between his grassroots support in the Russian segment of the population and the majority Ukrainian segment, which numbers among it a high proportion of Ukrainian nationalists. Yet the decision to withdraw from the NATO integration processis far more significant than any pledge not to join the CSTO, and NATO's dithering stance leading up to the election did nothing to encourage that slow progress before the withdrawal could be made.

Immediately upon taking office Yanukovich dismissed Ukraine's head of naval forces, Igor Tenukh, who Moscow claims initiated the information war against Russia's Black Sea Fleet in Crimea during the Georgian conflict. During the conflict "Admiral Tenukh ordered Ukrainian ships to block the entrance for the Russian navy to Sevastopol's bay."[26] Post-election discussions over the future of the Russian Black Sea Fleet base in Sevastopol ended with Moscow achieving its priority of extending the lease beyond the 2017 deadline (25 years beyond, in fact), even though the decision is at odds with the Ukrainian constitution. As if to avoid the charge of being wholly in Moscow's hands, Yanukovich has refused to recognize Abkhazian and South Ossetian independence. However, the Orange Revolution suddenly seems a long time ago and, for the many Ukrainians who see a better future in closer Western integration, the day may be long off when that comes to look as assured as it did in 2004. Ukraine's location, large mass, and population make it an indisputably important piece on the Eurasian chessboard, but that it is geopolitically lost for the near future must be accepted. That, however, even coupled with other setbacks, should not be a fact detrimental to the greater program of growing the West into the Heartland. The West has suffered a drop in its prestige as a result of various misguided strategic and nonstrategic choices in the previous seven years. Iraq represented the opening of a geopolitical Pandora's box, as knocking out the country and failing to quickly reconstitute it as a strong Western ally has meant that the Iranian question has occluded the horizon more menacingly than it did before. Recognition of Kosovan independence has given Russia license to meddle much more pervasively in Central Asia and the Caucasus. The decision to explain the significance of Afghanistan to Western electorates not in terms of hard geopolitical clarity but in the opaque terms of human rights and prevention of terrorism has fatigued those electorates, reducing their capacity to support the military and reconstruction effort. In this way "the West is having obvious trouble convincing the world [and itself] that it is still the predominant global leader, particularly against the backdrop of the rise of China and other Asian states and the multiplying number of regional conflicts."[27] Yet it is not too late to turn the tide and redouble the effort in Eurasia, provided there is a coherent program for action.

THE NEED FOR A 21CGSE

Russia's invasion of Georgia in 2008 and, more specifically, the lack of response beyond "strong condemnation" from the West has altered the strategic landscape in the Caucasus and beyond. The episode marked Russia's reemergence as a determinative force in Caucasian affairs. The main causes were a weak U.S. strategic position, a divided European and uncertainty as to Turkey's strategy. Furthermore, "the war made clear that Russia is willing to use force to deepen and promote its interests, while Western powers are not."[28] Of course the move was condemned wholesale in the international community and Russia was in the pariah sin bin for some months afterwards. However, because Moscow is impervious to most types of criticism, much less sensitive than Beijing, such rarely translates into remedial action, especially if it stands in contrast to popular sentiment in Russia itself, which Georgia did. The situation around Georgia remains fraught. Russian forces are still in a position to break out of the enclaves they occupy and dominate the entire former Soviet South Caucasus. Now that there is a pro-Russian government in Ukraine and Russia is gaining confidence from rising oil prices, Georgian president Mikheil Saakashvili appears to be isolated and the West impotent. It may just be then, that "when everything is ready, including propaganda ploys to explain to the world why Russia was compelled to use force, a series of provocations may ignite a war that could allow Russian forces to break out of the seclusion of the South Ossetian and

Abkhazian enclaves,"[29] finally displacing the anti-Russian military and political forces in the South Caucasus.

Although still focused on consolidating control in the restive northwestern provinces and on the recovery of Taiwan, China has similarly made progress in enhancing its position in the heart of Eurasia and weaning itself from dependence on Russian resources in the Russian Far East. In a quieter but surer way than Russia, China has filled power niches as they have become available through either local, Russian, or Western stumbling. China has completed the enormous gas pipeline from Turkmenistan through Kazakhstan and Uzbekistan, along the way supporting Turkmenistan in the face of Russian pressure and depositing political credit to be drawn upon later. And "while this strengthened China vis-à-vis Russia and the U.S. in Central Asia, it also deflected gas from Europe to China, making it harder for the U.S. to compete in gas-rich Turkmenistan."[30] Chinese global power remains rather more sophisticated than that of Russia. Western policy should therefore focus on promoting the Eurasian balance of power between Russia and China, rather than allowing them to paper over their differences and make common cause against the West through the SCO or in other formats.

In December 2009, Deputy Assistant Secretary of State George Krol told the U.S. Senate that "the [Central Asian] region is at the fulcrum of key U.S. security, economic and political interests. It demands attention and respect and our most diligent efforts."[31]The costs of not being diligent enough were more than exemplified by Moscow's almost successful attempt to have the Kyrgyz government expel the United States from the Manas airbase. In April 2010 the Kyrgyz opposition, led by Roza Otunbayeva, overthrew President Kurmanbek Bakiyev, who had come to power in the Tulip Revolution of 2005, in a series of bloody street riots that later led to widespread ethnic violence throughout the country. Otunbayeva is known to have been in Moscow, together with a number of other opposition leaders, just prior to the revolution. The opposition had previously been campaigning on a platform of ejecting the United States from the Manas airbase. The future of the Manas base and the Western presence in the region beyond is key to facilitating a strong geopolitical position for Western actors in Eurasia, one not just confined to the rebuilding in Afghanistan.

The Pivot-Heartland theory, containment, and Prometheism have clearly been the three dominant concepts governing Western policy in Eurasia through the twentieth century. However, there has been support from some quarters for a return to reliance on the naval doctrine of Mahan, of complacent satisfaction with control of the sea lanes and protection of international shipping (though one need look no further than the Horn of Africa to see that even that is something far from achieved). This is to be avoided. Philip Bobbitt has argued that old doctrines such as deterrence and containment are obsolete and must now give way to new strategies of "preclusion." Bobbitt contends that the United States and its allies must recognize their common fate as the natural defenders of the "society of states of consent." One way to promote these values, he says, is for the United States and the European Union to form a new G2, committed to a post-Westphalian notion of sovereignty, yet assuring that their overseas interventions are governed by a new instrument of international law. Though for preclusion "the electoral rewards for success are slight because the public finds it hard to be grateful for a nonevent. [Retaliation, by contrast, is a surefire vote-winner," [32] Bobbitt's organizational G2 concept is representative of the way the West should think proactively about the values that need promoting on the world stage. However, as Mackinder said, democracy refuses to think strategically unless and until compelled to do so for the purposes of defense.[33]

Former British ambassador to Moscow Sir Roderic Lyne has answered the question "what should the West do" by advising not to fall back on the strategies of containment and isolation. Russia, says Lyne, is as free as anyone else to try to exercise influence peacefully and legitimately through the power of attraction. But if the West is ever to wean Russian policy makers from their zero-sum mentality, it must avoid practicing zero-sum itself. However, there is always a palpable fatality in even the warmest Western prescriptions for progressive relations with Russia, and the continuation of NATO in its essentially negative, anti-Russian orientation seems inevitable. The EU is an organization that may well have much greater scope for interacting constructively with Russia. However, it lacks a strategy for doing so and is, in Fyodor Lukyanov's words, "now a hostage to the idea of success and influence and entangled in the insoluble contradiction between expansion and closer integration."[34] It is important to remember that for NATO and the EU to resolve their crises of identity and purpose they must focus on their core values. Unlike Russian or Chinese nationalism, NATO and the EU stand for a set of values and have prevailed once member states have been anchored in interrelated institutional ties. Often the reason Russia blocks sanctions and pushes for further negotiations and resolution by nonmilitary means over stalemated regional issues in the United Nations is because it fears these normative threats and resolute insistence on these values that come with the West's military presence. In contrast, Russia is fundamentally opportunistic and a wrecker in international affairs. China's approach is more nuanced, and it is much more attractive than Russia to a range of actors, large and small. However, China remains antithetical to many of these Western values in theory and very negative in the detail. And it is through promotion of these values that there is no need for the West to resign itself to the increasingly widespread prediction that China will become the next global superpower sometime in the first half of this century.

It is not necessary to identify as a neoconservative to advocate for good governance around the world. Invading Iraq in the name of spreading democracy was certainly a crusading agenda going beyond the realm of cold geopolitical calculation. However, Bush's outspoken public support for democracy promotion in the Middle East and beyond had a profound effect on politics in the region. Steven A. Cook in *Foreign Policy* has argued that it did nothing less than change the terms of the debate "in a way that Arab leaders could no longer control and allowed democracy activists to pursue their agendas in new ways."[35] Of course, there is a flip side to the democracy promotion coin. What happens when political undesirables are elected freely and fairly? Well, as in the case of the Ukraine, all disappointed observers can do is to support the legitimacy of the process and remain diligent for the next elections, by which time, if the incumbents really are that bad, they will probably have steered from the electoral straight and narrow. Ultimately, a utilitarian approach must be taken. So-called Democratic Peace theory is not a water-tight hypothesis. Nevertheless, democracy is clearly the best system on offer and in the overwhelming majority of cases its triumph favors the full spectrum of Western values, from rule of law to free trade and beyond. The goal is therefore independent, democratic, market-orientated Eurasian states that respect civil and humanitarian norms and the rule of law. However, to ensure this goal it is time for the West to pursue a strategy that is coherent and forthright. At the moment, the overwhelming Eurasian trends are those of Russian rollback of Western influence and the steady increase of Chinese; all the while the West is pinned down in Iraq and Afghanistan. In Mackinder's words, best let us be rid of cant: democracy must reckon with reality.[36]

CHAPTER 6

A Twenty-First-Century Geopolitical Strategy for Eurasia

THE NEED FOR A 21CGSE

For many the numbers are sufficient. Statistical figures for China, such as those indicating that its population will soon approach the 1.5 billion mark and the value of its economy balloon to $123 *trillion* by 2040,[1] appear to many in the West and elsewhere as empirical proof of the peril they had always feared. Yet it is in the relationship between these figures and corresponding predictions for the West that the cause for alarm becomes acutely apparent. The trends paint a picture of a future marked by Western decline relative to the Asian ascendency. Numbers, productivity, and wealth equal power and the ability to project power. Of course the other great Eurasian power, Russia, falls foul of this equation. Yet what Russia lacks in numbers and productivity it compensates for to some degree with ruthlessness and aggression. So it can only be that a China and a Russia that continue to operate somewhere outside the strictures of economic normalcy and untrammeled by Western limits on their expansion will, at some point, tip the geopolitical balance against Western primacy. One could argue, as Mackinder suggested in "The Round World," that the pivot on which that balance now rests is to be found in the Atlantic. However, to do so would to be to concede Europe to the Eurasian powers. In reality, the Atlantic must be considered a Western preserve. The pivot is therefore to be found somewhere between the edge of Western encroachment in Eastern Europe and the eastern reaches of Central Asia. In other words, the pivot of world politics remains more or less where Mackinder first identified it to be—in the Heartland. It is for this reason above all others that Mackinder remains important for us today. The geopolitical balance will continue to be determined in the Heartland, and Mackinder's warning about who dominates there still resonates in the specter of a Russo-Chinese condominium or simply collusion—an outcome that would mean the loss of the World Island to authoritarianism and mercantilism, whether through the SCO or otherwise. If the West is to avoid strategic eclipse and remain preeminent globally, championing the values of good governance that provide for stability and prosperity at home and abroad, then it is imperative that it maintain a dynamic foothold in the World Island and its Heartland.

This is no zero-sum cant. If cooperation can bring about new realities where the values held dear in the West are promoted to the benefit of all concerned, then it should be pursued in every instance. Yet we must be clear that there is no better political or economic paradigm on offer in the Russo-Chinese vision of a more "multi-polar" world. Both powers have shown themselves averse to democracy, suspicious of free markets on anything but the most controlled terms, and wholly indifferent to civil and human rights. If the West is criticized for ignoring international norms it is usually with reference to the use of force. Yet we know that the exercise of power by the powerful is the thing least amenable to constraint by consensus. Examples of the use of force as a form of international interaction by the West, principally the United States, are rare and, more importantly, quite predictable. It is at the subconflict level that the observance of international norms has so much practical day-to-day value as it collectively facilitates economic and cultural interaction. And here, as well as with use of force, the great Eurasian powers have consistently shown themselves contemptuous. The question for Western policy makers is therefore an objective one of what sort of world they would like to see develop in the twenty-first century. The best assessment is by values. There is ample scope for discussion of the relative merits of various cultural norms and aspirations across the world. Yet when it comes to the basic political, economic, and legal frameworks by which we might be governed, as promoted in the West and alternatively in Eurasia, any agonized debate becomes redundant. "West is Best."

The centrality of the World Island to the wider global balance and the potentialities of that yet largely unexploited region mean that the blanket establishment of Russia and China's antithetical value systems there would have disastrous consequences for the safety of countervailing Western ones. A world in which the World Island is dominated by authoritarian, mercantilist, and potentially hostile powers is one where marginalized Western powers will find themselves not only on the back foot but potentially split and dominated, strategically and economically, around the globe. Although Mackinder's analysis is often represented as being in conflict with Mahan's seapower-centric predecessor, in fact,

Mackinder readily acknowledged the importance of seapower—yet went beyond Mahan's static assumption of the West on the sea and the Eurasians on land and posited the idea that, by dint of the territory they controlled, the Eurasians had the potential to become the ultimate seapower. In 1898, on the eve of the Spanish-American War, the United States was, by most indices, already a wealthier nation than Great Britain. Yet in terms of real power, at the time best expressed by naval power, it lagged some way behind—the United States had just two first-rate battle-ships next to Britain's forty-four, not to mention a comparable deficit in smaller vessels. By the time of the 1921–1922 Washington Naval Treaty, however, the United States was successfully negotiating with Britain for parity in battleships and aircraft carriers. The point is that it took compa-rably little time, albeit expedited by a world war, for the United States to convert massive wealth into massive power. The development of China's blue-water navy over the coming years may be expedited by any number of events and, together with expansion into the Eurasian hinterland, will similarly represent the conversion of wealth into power. In this climate, Western policy makers need desperately to rally behind a twenty-first-century strategy to further their interests in Eurasia and secure their values in the world.

The West needs to be involved in Eurasia, in particular in the "New Eastern European" states of Ukraine, Belarus, and the Caucasian states, as well as in the Central Asian states: together, the "small Eurasian states." In this way the West will be able to create a bulwark against the major Eurasian powers—between Russia's soft underbelly and China's back door. If good governance—meaning stability, trade, the rule of law, and democracy—is promoted in these regions, Russian and Chinese power will necessarily be blunted. The Chinese see power in the region princi-pally in terms of economic penetration leading to soft political influence. For the Russians it is security links leading to hard political influence. The Russia-China nexus is represented less by the prospect of a genuine alliance than by some sort of agreement to partition Central and Inner Asia—whether actively or in terms of spheres of influence—and thus to effectively control the trade and strategic potential of the World Island. This would have the intended effect of freezing out Western influence, marginalizing Europe, isolating the United States in the Western Hemisphere, and relegating India, which is an important democratic bulwark in the monsoon coastlands, to the status of a purely economic, not strategic power. While Russo-Chinese condominium is a potential (and possibly overwhelming) threat, the prospect of Western expulsion from Eurasia is almost just as daunting, and this remains the case even if Russia and China compete rather than cooperate. The purpose of the Twenty-First-Century Geopolitical Strategy for Eurasia (21CGSE) is therefore to section off Central, Inner, and South Asia for Western cooperation and involvement, while splitting the Middle East and Iran from Russia and China. Western involvement in Eurasia can allow for the flourishing of trade routes across the World Island under the informal aegis of Western security and trade practice, just as with maritime trade today. Part of the strategy's strength as a practicable policy is that it would not cut off connections, just the potential for geopolitical dominance. Therefore, while enhanced Western geopolitical involvement in Eurasia limits the geopolitical ambitions of the great autocratic powers, it is relatively benign in that it does not directly threaten them in the way they threaten the smaller states—because the West is peripheral and outside of Eurasia, it could not be otherwise.

The Twenty-First-Century Geopolitical Strategy for Eurasia gives Western institutions such as NATO and the EU—the former seeking to redefine its role in the post-Cold War world and the latter trying to forge a nascent foreign policy—a clear new purpose and geopolitical goal. Of course the utility of both has its limits, and their members must be sensible about what guarantees they extend and avoid giving aspirant and new members the impression that they may conduct their foreign policies with impunity. Yet there are plethora other institutions, including the OSCE, the Council of Europe, the World Trade Organization, and the International Monetary Fund, that have a role to play in the project to grow the West eastwards. The benefits of a forward Eurasian strategy woven into the national fabric of constituent Western states will percolate down, from the grand strategic level through business, education, and culture. Engagement with the smaller Eurasian nations must be a multi-faceted process of indefinite duration. The bright young things of the West are making less of an impact in the world today than their predecessors of Victorian times, and are similarly less aware of how that world operates. In first recognizing the importance of Eurasia for the long-term security of Western values, then determining to pursue a coherent strategy there, Western policy makers can engender a culture of Western involvement on terms mutually beneficial to Western countries and those they expand their institutions into. Kennan's solution of seeking to contain Eurasian powers is the minimal response to the problem of dominance in the World Island, as identified by Mackinder. In the current fluid context of today's Eurasian geopolitics, containment is not sufficient to maintain Western preeminence or to live up to a principled foreign policy of furthering good governance in poorly governed countries. Rather, a strategy of involve-ment as inspired by Pilsudski's Prometheism and alignment of the smaller states, as inspired by his Intermarum idea, are what are needed. In short, the Twenty-First-Century Geopolitical Strategy for Eurasia is a strategy following the logic that offense is the best defense, though applied across a broad range of economic, cultural, and subconflict secu-rity initiatives.

THE NEED FOR WESTERN COHESION

The starting point if a twenty-first-century Western strategy is to be realized is *coherence* among the Western nations. This means coherence about who they are, where they have come from, and what are their immutable shared values. It means coherence in the NATO Atlantic relationship and within the European Union. Since the dissolution of the Soviet Union, Western divisions have encouraged all manner of opportunistic geopolitical point scoring by anti-Western states. The pitfalls of such divisions are most trenchantly represented in the twenty-first-century EU-Russia relationship. Russia exports 90 percent of its gas to Europe. It depends on Europe to keep buying that gas at the high rates it does because it cannot find alternative markets of comparable size. Russian Prime Minister Vladimir Putin has made much of the fact that at no point during the Cold War did Russian gas stop flowing to Europe, not even during the turmoil of 1989 to 1991. However, though admirable in itself, it is also evidence of the slavishness with which Russia must necessarily bow to its obligations under contracts for the supply of gas to its EU customers. EU members should be ever aware of this and deal with Russia in the future on that basis. When the EU has acted coherently, as over Kaliningrad and the 2004 intake of Eastern European members, its solidarity has impressed Moscow, as befits the reality of the EU-Russia trading relationship. By contrast, situations to be avoided are those such as Germany's unilateral agreement to Nord Stream. By frightening the Western Europeans with the prospect of their gas supply being disrupted in the event of future acrimony between Russia and the Eastern European states, the Kremlin's policy of divide and rule has been effective in getting the Western Europeans to countenance a deal whereby Russia has reestablished its historical links with its great friend and enemy, Germany, and at the same time partitioned off Russian energy-dependent Eastern Europe to be menaced alone in the future. It is an important example of why Western coherence is essential if a forward Eurasian strategy in the twenty-first century is to be successful.

That need for cohesion does not stop with Europe. The Atlantic alliance, chiefly but not exclusively encompassed by NATO, should be cherished as a group of states indivisible in their determination to protect and promote Western values. Numerous commentators, as well as some NATO member states themselves, have questioned the degree to which enlargement has benefitted the alliance and whether, in reality, membership has actually enhanced the security of the new members. As examples supporting this view they have cited the continued pressures the New Eastern European members have been subjected to by Russia since joining and the evident refusal of the Kremlin to accept its geopolitical loss. Yet to point to Russia's continuing designs on Eastern Europe and its success in realizing some of them is to identify incidental problems of insufficient

Western support, not the fundamental one of it having been a mistake to grow into the region in the first place. Of course this sort of demurring talk has been more pronounced with respect to the mooted accession of the states of the New Eastern Europe, and with good reason. Yet the basic premise of the plan to grow Western institutions into this region is sound. The sensible approach may well be the one of EU first, NATO later, as the functional economic and governance links best established with the former are more subtle, less provocative, and ultimately higher yielding than their military concomitants, provided that those military guarantees are extant. The plausible extension of existing institutions such as the EU and NATO has its limits, specifically geographically. The OSCE would be an attractive alternative institution were it not for Russia being an obstructive member. For that reason, an effective approach in the New Eastern European and Central Asian states is clearly going to have to be based on developing Western-associated but stand-alone national and multilateral institutions, independent of Russia and China and adopting Western best practice. Coherence among the small Eurasian states, based on their determination to achieve true independence from Russia and remain free from China, will stand them in good stead to rapidly develop and meet their economic potential. Division will invite outside control and retard development. Similarly, where Western designs in Eurasia will fail will be where cracks emerge in the facade of Western cohesion, to be further eroded by the autocratic powers that stand to lose the most if the small states of the New Eastern Europe and Central Asia are allowed to thrive and independently choose their preferred partners.

The Ukraine is genuinely torn between its Russian and Western parts. With the apparently free election of Victor Yanukovich in 2010, some have lamented that Ukraine has been lost. However, this may be an overly pessimistic view. There are in the Ukraine strong signs of fecund democratic sentiment, and the people have shown themselves increasingly willing to publicly protest their grievances over a range of issues. Although indisputably pro-Russian on the big questions that concern Moscow (primarily the Black Sea Fleet's lease at Crimea), at the time of his election Yanukovich indicated that he would pursue a balanced foreign policy—similar to that successfully practiced by Boris Tadic in Serbia—and seek to extract maximum gain from both East and West. In this climate there is ample opportunity to expand functional links from the EU into the Ukraine. Ukraine's historically established Russian population is less hard line in its aversion to Western integration than the more recent Russian arrivals from the Soviet period, in other words, less than those who still enjoy the inherited benefits of the ex-*nomenklatura*. The conspicuous benefits that can be provided by EU investment, most obviously in public infrastructure, may go a long way, given the chronic need for them, to converting some of the older Russian population and marginalizing the newer. That said, the sine qua non for the West is to avoid retrenchment after the electoral setback and remain unanimous in vocally advertising the fact that there is much to be had if Ukraine will change and cease allowing Russia a free hand in exercising its influence in the Black Sea region via its territory.

When speaking of Western cohesion, a specific caution must be made with respect to the risks of anti-Americanism, in the case of the Europeans, and unilateralism in isolation from "Old Europe," in the case of the Americans. The reluctance of the Europeans to support what the Bush administration saw as a unique geopolitical opportunity to legitimately deploy massive power in the wake of the 9/11 bombings was construed by some in the United States as complacency and indifference. In turn, the Bush administration stretched itself strategically by choosing to fight contemporaneously in Afghanistan and Iraq with limited multilateral support. But more significantly, there was a time when that administration's remarks gave succor to any latent sentiment of anti-Americanism that existed in Europe. The fact is that 9/11 did provide a geopolitical opportunity, the potential of which could have been maximized through Western cohesion but which was instead curtailed by division. Cooperation that could have secured the military situation in Afghanistan, as well as capitalized on the color revolutions in Georgia, Ukraine, and Kyrgyzstan by consolidating them and encouraging like in neighboring states, was rejected in favor of hand-wringing over the misadventure in Iraq. The aftermath of 9/11 was a geopolitical opportunity because the pretext of the redundant "Global War on Terror" bore relevance in a number of the small Eurasian countries—but also, crucially, in Russia and China themselves, thereby short-circuiting their reflex objections to Western activity in their Eurasian backyard. The lack of cohesion between Europe and the United States from 2002 onwards meant missed opportunities to address the security and economic needs of the smaller Eurasian actors and thereby position the West as their preferred partner in the Eurasian space.

THE 21CGSE

The Three I's

The Western Twenty-First-Century Geopolitical Strategy for Eurasia can be encapsulated in the "Three I's" of "Independence," "Integration," and "Institutions."

Step One: "Independence"

The first step in the Twenty-First-Century Geopolitical Strategy for Eurasia is "Independence." In the Ukraine, Georgia, and Azerbaijan, Prometheism was a real inspiration for resistance to Soviet rule and for achieving genuine independence after the Soviet dissolution. However, the story is slightly different east of the Caspian. Here, Soviet-era strongmen were not clamoring to declare independence as the union was beginning to disintegrate, and many remained in power for a long time afterward. Some have argued that this means the Central Asian states did not really want to be independent, but while that may be the case for the political and security elites tied to Moscow, it is inaccurate and disingenuous to accept that the Central Asian people themselves did not want independence. In the case of Afghanistan it becomes ridiculous, as the country fought for over a decade against Soviet control. The difference between the Central Asians (except Afghanistan and Tajikistan, where there was civil war that then resulted in an authoritarian regime) and the other CIS states is that Russian-style authoritarian systems remained in place as a legacy of Russian occupation, but also because this was seen as the only way of shoring up sovereignty and state power in a hostile environment surrounded by Russia and China. There was therefore a lack of geopolitical incentive to good governance. The type of good governance that will favor Western integration can only be brought about if all the small Eurasian states, but perhaps especially the Central Asian actors, have their independence enhanced as a defense to Russian and, increasingly for the Central Asians, Chinese encroachment.

The small states of Eurasia have traditionally been dominated by Russia and are increasingly being dominated by China. The West's long-term advantage in its relations with those states lies in facilitating their policy independence. This reduces Russian and Chinese influence, while empowering the smaller states through linking them with the West. Crucially, facilitating the policy independence of the smaller Eurasian states provides a genuine alternative environment. In the abstract it is about maximizing the plurality of foreign relations for the smaller states and is not simply the substitution of one controlling great power for another, because the West is not in a position to be that substitute. In practice, facilitating policy independence means providing for alternative (global) markets; raising the stature of Eurasian states in international forums; encouraging Western investment in those states; stepping up training, education, and aid programs; and encouraging cultural exchanges, whether in education, business, or simply by promoting the relevant states as desirable travel destinations. It also means not undermining Eurasian governments with unconstructive criticism of human rights issues and electoral procedures. To do so is to push them further into the hands of Russia and China, neither of which will criticize those shortcomings because they wish to see them remain. However, the small Eurasian states themselves are sensible of the need for reform and, while not receptive to criticism alone, will respond to concrete offers of advice about how to remedy some of those ills. To do this is to take a long-term view aimed at ensuring Western geopolitical orientation and the sustainable good governance that eventually will come with it.

One way of ensuring the independent action of the smaller Eurasian states is by enhancing their external security vis-à-vis Russia and China. Direct military intervention against either of these powers in the heart of the Heartland would be practically futile and should not form part of any Western strategy in Eurasia. However, by drawing international attention to the machinations of Russia and China in the region, much pressure can be brought to bear economically and diplomatically should those great Eurasian powers be seen to infringe the sovereignty of the small Eurasian states. Bolstering the armed forces of the smaller states would be a tried and tested, but useful, adjunct to the larger program of development proper. A credible deterrent to the more gratuitous liberties often taken by powerful states with the weak would give these smaller states crucial breathing space in which to implement the type of political and economic reform in democratic transparency and commercial efficiency that especially Moscow is loathe to see emerge. In the Caucasian and New Eastern European states NATO expansion is a geopolitically plausible development, especially in the strict geographic sense, assuming that Turkey will eventually join the EU. In this case the inclusion of the Caucasian states to the east furthers the strategic encirclement of the Black Sea while maintaining a contiguous link with existing members. Yet it must be made equally clear to aspirant states that membership is something to be earned and something that can be withdrawn, should it become clear that it is being abused in reckless provocative actions directed with assumed impunity (as Georgia was certainly guilty of in 2008) at neighbors, including Russia. Further east still, although Kazakhstan has a NATO Individual Partnership Action Plan, the organization may yet find that there is high-tide mark beyond which there is a disjuncture that is hard to bridge. Enhancing the external security of the Central Asian states is therefore probably going to have to be undertaken on a bilateral basis but with the broader aim of creating another Intermarum-type association, removed from Eastern Europe (and not between seas), but performing an identical function for Central Asian states grouping together to escape Russia and resist China. This will provide for greater strength and confidence, even if it is decided not to incorporate those states as full NATO members.

Although the manifest need for enhanced external security for the smaller Eurasian states has been evidenced by the Georgian episode, Georgia's provocations notwithstanding, naked aggression does not appear to be Moscow's, much less Beijing's, preferred mode of exercising influence. More commonplace, with respect to Russian interference, is a program of massaging the Soviet-era elites and their descendents and splitting them off from the progressive factions of the various legislatures and political establishments. Moscow has been conspicuously successful in doing this to the extent that what once promised to be a tide of "color" revolutions has now been firmly stemmed and, in the cases of Ukraine and Kyrgyzstan, reversed. Rampant corruption is a governmental ailment familiar and favorable to the Kremlin. Many instrumental people from the smaller Eurasian states can be, and have been, encouraged at little expense to support the Moscow line, while energy contracts are used to tie states and private business interests into long-term dependence. That said, Russia is clearly willing to use naked force to alter regimes it objects to so long as it can find a reasonable pretext, which, in the case of Georgia, while not appearing anywhere near sufficient to excuse Russia's action, was at least pointed to in an EU Council of Europe-sponsored report. China has less contact with the Caucasian and New Eastern European states and is at a disadvantage in the Central Asian arena, where it does not enjoy the same historical links as Russia. Yet what China lacks in a legacy of benefits derived from being the dominant Eurasian power in the past, it makes up for by being widely perceived as the dominant power of the future. For that reason the elites of the Central Asian states are cautiously willing to curry favor with Beijing in so many multivectored foreign policies. In the south, Iran too acts vigorously through clandestine channels to ensure that authoritarian, anti-Western partners are maintained or installed in the governments of its energy-rich neighbors. The reality is thus that foreign-directed coups and revolutions are a very real danger faced by any of the small Eurasian states that display the desire to diverge from the well-worn paths of corruption and authoritarianism.

In this climate much can be achieved by promoting better governance through rule of law and development initiatives. However, more specific measures—such as personal security advice for the leaders of progressive governments and their ministers or support in reorganizing the armed forces and security apparatus hierarchy—are essential if the smaller Eurasian states are to be made more resilient to foreign intervention, such as probably happened in Kyrgyzstan in 2010. Bolstering the internal capacities of fledgling democracies and aspiring ones to resist outside pressure will not necessarily ensure that Western-friendly regimes prevail—Ukraine is the best example demonstrating that. Yet Ukraine and also Belarus are unique in having sizeable Russian populations that genuinely identify more closely with Moscow. In the other small Eurasian states there is greater likelihood that better governance could favor the Western model and Western partnership, should it be seen to be on offer and desired just as strongly by the West itself. It is therefore important that support should be available to those smaller Eurasian states struggling against their more powerful neighbors, especially if the threat is in the form of Russian-Chinese common action, against which these states stand no chance alone.

Despite many of them being energy-rich, the small Eurasian states are still relatively weak economically. Much of the revenue from sale of their resources has gone abroad, principally to Russia but increasingly now to China. In enhancing the degree to which the smaller Eurasian states are able to control their own resources and free their markets from noncommercial, political dominance by the great Eurasian powers, the West will be facilitating these states to enrich themselves through their own means. This is where Western institutions come in as a third way, as opposed to the Russian and Chinese options on the table, and as a strong incentive for better governance, open trade regimes, and regional integration. That is not to try and disguise or distort the strong geopolitical reasons impelling a Western strategy in Eurasia, which concern the West's long-term survival. Rather, it is to highlight the complementary features that come with it and go to ensure its success. It is in this sense that the Prometheism project as begun by Pilsudski provides a viable paradigm, one that must be continued in the form of Western involvement with and empowerment of the smaller Eurasian states, thereby encouraging their voluntary integration into an independent group of modern Eurasian actors. The foregoing points have been made with respect to the smaller Eurasian states in general. However, it is worth discussing at length the individual circumstances and requirements of these states and analyzing how Western, Russian, and Chinese influence can promote, stymie, or detract from their prosperity.

Afghanistan

Afghanistan is not the most geopolitically important of the Eurasian states, but as the West will be committed to the country for years to come, any geopolitical strategy for Eurasia must be concordant with plans for involvement there. Modern Afghanistan represents the rump of the Duranni Empire with many different peripheral centers of gravity that pull at once in different directions. We are unlikely to see a strong central government there in the long term and may well see sporadic periods of serious violence. Under these conditions, the best the West can do is to focus on building the economy and infrastructure to support it, broad spectrum education, and the facilitation of good governance practices where local actors show the desire and aptitude to embrace them. In a more robust sense, it is important to maintain a pervasive human intelligence network to know when to intervene if extremist Islamist rule or conflict between warlords begins to emerge again, as well as to be aware of the machinations of other powers, such as Iran, Pakistan (both government agents and militants), China, Russia, and India. The great Eurasian powers, China and Russia, are not significantly or even substantially involved in Afghanistan. Although there is a sense of unfinished business among some Russian militarists, and Kremlin-sanctioned foreign policy analysts have become more vocal in criticizing NATO, Russian involvement remains unsellable to the Russian people, whose opinion is important, if rarely expressed, to the Kremlin. For China, although Afghanistan does possess some sought-after commodities (the Chinese make substantial investment in copper mining there), its inherent stickiness is enough to tip the cost-benefit analysis well in favor of avoiding anything other than low-level economic penetration, for the time being. Essentially, both powers are content to let the West struggle to achieve a level of stability that they know will benefit them as much as the states putting in the hard work. And struggle the West must. The key in Afghanistan is to remain a determining player among the many other players that, it must be accepted, will continue to operate there. The thing to avoid is weak political explanations to the electorates of constituent Western states about why they are involved in Afghanistan. Those electorates need to be convinced that involvement is necessary to keep the West in Central Asia, as well as to prevent Afghanistan from reverting to being a geopolitical black hole with nothing but drugs and extremism to export to its neighbors and beyond. Only by doing this will the Western states be able to avoid irresistible domestic calls to leave the country altogether and take a back seat in the process of reshaping Afghanistan, in which other countries will inevitably, and probably catastrophically, take upon themselves to participate.

Azerbaijan

Azerbaijan is the most geopolitically important of the small Eurasian states. This is due primarily to its geographical position—because it is located between Russia and Iran, and because it forms the narrow gateway from Europe to the Caspian basin. This is the West's only route to the putative Central Asian partners and the increasingly important energy wealth of the Caspian region, situated between the potentially hostile powers of Russia in the north and Iran in the south. Azerbaijan is therefore a geopolitical "swing state"—if the Azerbaijani gate swings closed, the West has to make a very lengthy detour to get to Central Asia, and even then entry is at the mercy of volatile and nuclear Pakistan. Azerbaijan also constitutes the back door to Iran, both geographically and ethnically (there are more ethnic Azeris in Iran than in Azerbaijan). Western institutions in Azerbaijan would complement and probably add stability to those that are being established in Iraq, thereby further encircling Iran with commercially minded and better governed neighbors. In the event Western relations with Iran grow worse before they get better, and the time comes to decisively resolve the question of a nuclear and belligerent Iran, Azerbaijan would potentially provide a useful complementary staging post to Turkey. Azerbaijan enjoys good relations with Russia, China, and Iran, but it is nevertheless Western orientated and, if afforded reciprocal interest and support to transform itself, may come to represent a model for the other small states of Eurasia. However, the Azerbaijani leadership feels abandoned by the West, which has led to a decline in governance standards and Baku leaning increasingly towards Moscow, as well as exploring options with Beijing. The broad solution is for the West to engage Azerbaijan at a level commensurate with its geopolitical significance. In particular, the West must push for resolution of the Nagorno-Karabakh conflict between Azerbaijan and Armenia. That dispute, not the future of their country as an energy producer and transit corridor, is by far the most important issue for ordinary Azerbaijanis. Impartial international mediation or arbitration to resolve the dispute would be a long overdue move to concentrate Azerbaijani minds on the project of modernizing Azerbaijan proper.

Kazakhstan

Kazakhstan is the regional leader of the smaller Central Asian states (although of course by no means small in terms of area), both economically and as an example of a state with a deliberate multivectored foreign policy. For this reason Kazakhstan must be engaged, and while it is inevitable that Astana will seek beneficial relations with all its neighbors, it should be the West's objective to position itself as the most attractive partner in trade and development. In this respect, competition would be strongest with China. However, because of its geographic proximity to Russia, history, and resultant demographics that include a large number of resident ethnic Russians, Kazakhstan is wont to align more closely with Russia than with China if there appears to be little offered from the West. At the moment, however, Astana is reaching out to the West but staying closer to both Russia and China, and its economic and energy links with China, though comparably weaker than those with Russia, are rapidly developing, being dictated largely on Beijing's terms. Beijing has been pushing hard to secure the massive reserves at the new Tengiz and Kashagan fields for supply through the new China-Central Asia pipeline. Kazakhstan is therefore less of an independent actor than it could be, were it to have an enhanced level of Western involvement. That involvement is currently focused on the international consortium that operates under the North Caspian Sea Production Sharing Agreement. Production at Kashagan has been delayed and there have been many disagreements within the consortium. However, Western policies toward Kazakhstan should not be allowed to be determined by troubles between Astana and Western energy companies. Kazakhstan's known resources are significant but as yet relatively unexploited. It is also likely to have further substantial undiscovered resources. Increasing volumes of Kazakhstan's oil goes west through the Baku-Tbilisi-Ceyhan pipeline, and its uranium deposits are now thought to be the largest in the world. But more than energy, Kazakhstan is important for the geostrategic location it occupies directly between the two great Eurasian powers and for the corridor it forms between the Caspian and democratic Mongolia. It therefore pays to engage with Kazakhstan and geographically split Russia and China— the priority for the Twenty-First-Century Geopolitical Strategy for Eurasia. In 2010 Kazakhstan headed the OSCE and at the time of writing is the only Central Asian state with a NATO Individual Partnership Action Plan. There is therefore great potential for security cooperation between the West and Kazakhstan, but engagement has to be substantive and sustained and also include investment, training, and educational exchanges, not just hard-nosed security- and energy-related measures.

Turkmenistan

Turkmenistan is the Eurasian state with the greatest unexploited potential. It has enormous energy reserves that are only now beginning to be discovered. This means that Turkmenistan has the potential to be a major energy exporter in its own right, as well as an important transit corridor for Caspian energy going east and southeast. Turkmenistan's potential as a transit route for nonenergy, nonlethal supplies to the coalition in Afghanistan has already been partly realized in the form of the Northern Distribution Network() that is discussed in detail later in this chapter. However, Turkmenistan is currently only used as an air transit hub; therefore capacity is limited, so that the majority of supplies have to go through Kazakhstan and Uzbekistan. There is huge scope for enhancing the security, capacity, and efficiency of this route and establishing it as a permanent and primary overland road and rail route to facilitate natural, nonmilitary trade from the Caucasus to Central Asia and South Asia. The bulk of Turkmenistan lies within the Turan Depression, between the southern Kopet Dag Range that borders Iran and the Koytendag Range bordering Uzbekistan; as such Turkmenistan forms a natural gateway between the Caspian and the rest of Central and South Asia and China. Turkmenistan is therefore geostrategically important in terms of its geography and resources. Its relationship with Iran is also of interest to the West and, again, a nonradical, more commercial, better governed Turkmenistan would add to the pressure on the Iranian regime to change before it is toppled, either from within or without. Turkmenistan's historical links are with Russia, from which it has inherited both a Soviet and Czarist legacy. That said, it is increasingly becoming Beijing's most powerful pawn in the Caspian, being as it is the source of the China-Central Asia pipeline. By this avenue Beijing is increasingly able to exercise influence over the broader region's energy reserves and burgeoning trade routes, as well as using the Turkmen corridor for access to Iran, Russia, and Afghanistan. The EU will likely need Turkmen gas to satisfy its energy requirements in the coming years. EU energy security therefore depends on Turkmenistan's vast natural gas resources for diversification away from Russian supplies. Turkmenistan is also integral to the wider security of the Caspian basin, which, together with Azerbaijan, it can interdict, thereby separating Russia and Iran. In general, the best approach for the West to take in Turkmenistan is to facilitate Western companies' building of a trans-Caspian pipeline; also, Turkmenistan should be integrated as a neighbor into the process of building stability in Afghanistan. A more discrete objective would be to facilitate resolution of the Omar/Azeri, Osman/Chirag, and Serdar/Kapaz Caspian oil field disputes between Ashgabat and Baku. Turkmenistan's ever more open government has made it clear that it would like to partner with Western institutions, but if that opportunity is not taken advantage of, Turkmenistan could well become a vassal state of China.

Georgia

Georgia is now in something of a crippled position after the reckless assault on South Ossetia, undertaken on the mistaken assumption that Western security gestures had been sufficient to deter Russia. In the sense that the West did nothing when Russia invaded and seemed to have had no intention of doing anything, then Georgia has been the victim of Western neglect. However, despite its invidious position Georgia is, and will remain, the needle's eye through which the West must pass to reach the Caspian and Central Asia. Georgia is the only country to have formally left the CIS, and despite disappointment with the West, remains the most anti-Russian actor in the Caucasus and, indeed, of all the small Eurasian states. Relations between Georgia and Azerbaijan are critical to maintaining a stable and reliable route from Europe to the Caspian and Central Asia. Both of these small Caucasian states are key Western-orientated partners, but fundamentally ones who also need each other, both geographically and geopolitically. China's interest in Georgia has not yet developed beyond small- to medium-scale business transactions, but that is not to say that more substantial economic overtures will not be made in the future. Moscow is keenly aware of Georgia's gateway function and for that reason tried to cut the connection between the West and the Caspian and Central Asia in the war of 2008. While it is not in the West's interest to directly confront Russia as it annexes northern Georgia, the population of which does appear to have determined in favor of Russia, it must do all it can to keep the current corridor through independent central and southern Georgia open and viable. With the extension of Russia's lease of Ukraine's Crimean naval base, Moscow will be increasingly confident in impressing its will in the Black Sea region, including along the Georgian coast. And while the Montreux Convention governing the movement of warships through the Turkish Straits remains in place, Georgia can expect little substantive help from the West in defending against a rapid Russian amphibious assault. The Montreux Convention is therefore something that Western statesmen ought properly to push for review of, in light of the 2008 invasion. Fewer restrictions on the passage of warships through the straits would ultimately benefit the West, as Western vessels can achieve much more in the Black Sea than Russian ones can achieve in the Mediterranean. A new regime may be possible as a quid pro quo for Turkish EU integration.

Uzbekistan

Uzbekistan is Central Asia's traditional industrial powerhouse and most populous nation. As one of Afghanistan's neighbors it is a key link in the overland and air supply routes for coalition forces there. That route is part of the Northern Distribution Network(), transporting nonlethal supplies from Latvia through Russia, Kazakhstan, and Uzbekistan. Berlin has enjoyed good relations with the Uzbek government. German troops have used the Termez base in southern Uzbekistan since entering Afghanistan in 2002, and are currently playing a vital role in stabilizing the increasingly violent non-Pashtu northern provinces of the country, for which the Uzbek base is essential. Uzbekistan is therefore geopolitically important for the effort in Afghanistan. But more than that, Uzbekistan is integral to any long-term plans for trans-Eurasian trade. The reelection of Uzbek President Islam Karimov in 2007 saw improved relations with the United States, which had deteriorated since U.S. criticism of the Uzbek government's harsh response to protests in the town of Andjian in 2005. Tashkent is now exploring options for reengagement, having concluded that Russian and Chinese domination is the likely and undesirable outcome of estrangement from the West. The West must therefore take advantage of and encourage Uzbekistan's proclivity for independent policy making, as well as facilitate its integration with its neighbors, with whom it has generally had poor relations since the Soviet dissolution. Germany's favored position might mean that Berlin is best placed to lead the engagement effort.

Kyrgyzstan

Kyrgyzstan is strategically important for the effort in Afghanistan, primarily due to the coalition's use of the Manas airbase. However, availability of the base, although guaranteed by the new regime for the

short term, is not certain in the future. In April 2010 the Kyrgyz
opposition came to power in a counterrevolution that saw President
Kurmanbek Bakiyev violently deposed and ethnic clashes ensue. However,
the Manas base notwithstanding, Kyrgyzstan has little geopolitical
significance, which is unfortunate given that it has the most virile
democratic tradition since the Cold War of any of the Central Asian states,
even if Bakiyev failed to live up to the peoples' expectations. The
likelihood, should Western relations with Kyrgyzstan not improve, is that
it will increasingly come under the influence of the Chinese. Beijing is
paranoid about shoring up stability in the non-Han Xinjiang ("New
Territory") Province, which Kyrgyzstan borders and is culturally similar
to. The West must continue to empower democratic reforming trends and
facilitate independent policy making in Kyrgyzstan, but more importantly
it must also encourage and help with integration between Kyrgyzstan and
its richer, more powerful Central Asian neighbors, principally Kazakhstan
and Uzbekistan.

Tajikistan

Tajikistan is the smallest and poorest of the Central Asian states.
Geographically, there is a considerable disjuncture between Tajikistan's
political and cultural boundaries, with many of the people's most
important heritage sites now being in neighboring Uzbekistan. Overall,
it is not as geostrategically important as the foregoing countries in this list,
but its position on the Fergana Valley does make it a significant access
point to Afghanistan and for general transit through the region. Tajikistan
has continued to be politically volatile since the end of the 1992–1997 civil
war. In many ways it is now close to becoming a failed state, with
President Emomali Rhamon struggling to retain control over the main
opposition as well as a pervasive Uzbek Islamic movement. There are
many ethnic Tajiks living in bordering Afghanistan, and the country has
important links to the Northern Alliance. Tajikistan threatens to become
a derelict geopolitical black hole that would suck in Western forces from
Afghanistan, as well as the large Russian security force already stationed
in the country. The Russian 201st division, along with a substantial number of security service troops, is stationed along the Afghan border, ostensibly to protect the Nurek hydroelectric dam and prevent narcotics
leaving Afghanistan. However, the Russian deployment is also part of
Moscow's broader plans to organize its forces in accord with the CSTO
and is clearly designed to retain Tajikistan within what Moscow considers
its sphere of influence. Iran, with whose people the Tajiks share a common
Persian heritage, considers itself to have special rights within the country
and jostles with Russia for influence. Dushanbe has also backed Tehran's
bid to join the SCO as a full member. Tajikistan shares a border with China

and, despite a dispute over that border that is nearing resolution, has been the recipient of a number of Chinese pledges to improve Tajikistan's agricultural, industry, and energy sectors. Many of these agreements have been arrived at around the fringes of SCO summits, at which Tajikistan has supported China's stance on territorial integrity (Taiwan, Tibet, Xinjiang) and civil and human rights. Under these conditions the West needs to position itself as the more attractive of the competing partners. It can do this by extending its expertise in building viable institutions and enhancing human capacity to manage a prosperous country. President Rhamon has shown interest in reaching out to Western actors and breaking the country's historical ties with Russia. However, he has few options available to him to avoid the overbearing advances of both Russia and China. Although it is unlikely that the West would ever want to achieve a significant presence in Tajikistan, integration of the country with its neighbors, including Afghanistan and the reconstruction effort there, should be the West's priority.

Mongolia

Mongolia is a democratic success story in Eurasian terms and contrasts favorably with Russia and China, which it is sandwiched between. Although mineral-rich, Mongolia does not have sought-after energy reserves and has for the most part escaped the attention of Beijing. That said, a large proportion of Mongolia's minerals, produce, and manufactures do go to China, and it is therefore, to a considerable degree, beholden to Chinese markets. China also has historical claims to Mongolia through the Qing dynasty, into which the country was incorporated until 1911. Moscow also continues to exercise considerable leverage over the country since the end of Communist rule through debt and Mongolia's large trade deficit with Russia. Something of a geopolitical backwater now, Mongolia has the potential to become a strategically important Western-oriented outpost in Inner Asia, especially if the grander program of linking the Caucasian and Central Asian states as an associated market-orientated wedge between Russia and China is to be completed.

Armenia

Armenia is a prime example of the dire strategic consequences that result from sparse and misconceived Western involvement with the smaller Eurasian states. Beholden to Russia and Iran militarily, economically, and diplomatically, save for its substantial diaspora, Armenia is isolated from the rest of the world and estranged from its neighbors, with which it has terrible relations, especially with the two most dynamic—Turkey and Azerbaijan. With Azerbaijan Armenia is embroiled in the

Nagorno-Karabakh conflict that it cannot win, but in which Moscow persistently abets it and refuses to allow it to resolve, because as often with the Kremlin, it prefers the stability of instability. In these circumstances the West loses out because Georgia is left as the only gateway from Europe to Central, South, and East Asia. Moreover, the EU and NATO are left with the Nagorno-Karabakh conflict festering on their border. Because of its location Armenia has huge potential to be a vital part of the East-West Transport Corridor through the Caucasus and, by extension, a quickly developing Western-orientated economy. Armenia's large, well-educated, and very successful diaspora is a wasting asset while the country retains its current Russian-Iranian geopolitical orientation. Relations with Turkey have been stalled for nearly a century since the widespread massacre of Armenian subjects by Ottoman troops in 1915. Diplomatic relations have recently been returned to a tentative, if unofficial, state of normalcy, but Armenia insists on Turkish recognition of the massacres as a genocide as a prerequisite for proper interaction. Turkey is understandably loathe to make a concession that might further prejudice its prospects for overcoming French and Austrian opposition to its bid for membership of the EU, in return for improved relations with a weak, disgruntled, but largely nonproblematic neighbor. The situation is unfortunate because with the potential that exists for wholesome Georgian, Azerbaijani, and Turkish integration, Armenia remains as the black sheep of the Caucasian family. The West's priority in Armenia should be to demonstrate the desirability of realignment away from the Moscow-Tehran axis and toward the type of development in train in Turkey and Azerbaijan.

Ukraine

When talking about Western expansion into Eurasia, Ukraine is usually at the top of most strategists' priority lists. Here, however, it is towards the bottom. In this sense the Twenty-First-Century Geopolitical Strategy for Eurasia updates Mackinder and Pilsudski, who both considered Ukraine a strategic priority and determinant of successful expansion. While a wholly "converted" Ukraine would indubitably be a major coup, in the same way that the symbolism of Belarus casting its lot with the EU would represent a miraculous sea change away from the old tale of accepted Russian imperialism, it is for the same reason that Ukrainian conversion is unlikely to happen in this generation—it is simply too much to expect. The reality is that Ukraine will always hold more significance for Russia than for any Western actor. Russia has its historical origins in Muscovy, which in turn has its in Kievan Rus. As Zbigniew Brzezinski famously remarked in *The Grand Chessboard*, without Ukraine Russia becomes a purely Asian empire. For these reasons Moscow will not give up Ukraine without a fight, a real fight, and not a fight the West wants to be drawn into, because it will lose. The corresponding reality is that Ukraine is not essential for Western integration to continue in Eurasia. A strategy that advocates bypassing Ukraine to focus on the far more strategically important Caucasus-Central Asia region is not just a viable but a more appropriate one. Ukraine should not be seen as a barometer of the West's success in expanding eastwards. Its competitive democracy should be encouraged and the door to EU membership and investment held open, but unless the Russian-speaking half of the population performs a volte-face and shifts its cultural and political orientation, and unless the Russian Black Sea Fleet is given a date of departure from its Crimean base, then the West is at a strategic disadvantage that it will have to accept and adapt to. Low-yield fumbling in Ukraine, such as the West has been engaged in for the past decade, fritters away the opportunity to engage in a truly Eurasian strategy, not just a Black Sea strategy.

Moldova

Moldova is not of great geopolitical significance. The Russian-sponsored black hole of Transdinistria is a major source of transnational threats, including arms smuggling, human trafficking, drug running, and money laundering, and it constitutes a direct threat to EU and NATO members. However, for reasons similar to those which dictate its actions in Armenia, Russia will discourage Moldovan integration of Transdinistria, instead seeking to maintain the status quo and keep control of the Soviet-era arsenal in the region. It is likely that Moldova will eventually be naturally integrated into the EU, but for now it is not worth the confrontation with Russia to aggressively expedite that process. That said, Western actors with the biggest stakes, such as Poland, Romania, and Turkey, should take the lead in resolving the Transdinistria question as best they can.

Belarus

While President Alexander Lukashenko has shown signs of pulling away from Moscow and reaching out to the EU, Belarus will not achieve truly independent policies, much less Western integration, with the current regime and its proximity to and dependence on Moscow. Moreover, even when there have been moves away from Moscow, they have not always been in the direction of the EU but also towards China, therefore placing Belarus closer to the SCO partnership (in the spring of 2010 Chinese President Hu Jintao was in Minsk signing trade deals). However, for the time being Belarus serves the role of buffer between Russia and the EU and NATO. The priority should be to prevent full incorporation into Russia, which could perhaps become a real possibility during a tumultuous transition period after Lukashenko. Although Putin himself has been deprecating when Lukashenko has previously made overtures for Belarus to become part of the Russian Federation, the fact that Belarus has so little national consciousness and that Belarusians identify so closely with Russia proper means that Moscow could yet attempt to take advantage in a moment of political disarray. The implications of this are that many Eastern European EU members may react unpredictably if Russia suddenly appears once more on their doorsteps. The benefits of Belarus as a buffer, if not a member, for the EU are therefore plain.

Turkey

Turkey does not appear here in any order of importance. Although it should not be considered among the small states of Eurasia, its significance means that it requires mention. There is much to rue in the possible "loss" of Turkey as it departs from its staunchly pro-Western stance of the Cold War. However, this is to a large extent inevitable and simply signifies the growth of Turkey as a major power in Eurasia, something that is ultimately to the West's advantage if not mishandled through historical or racial prejudice. In a strategy that "bypasses" Ukraine, Turkey's role becomes crucial as a bridge to the Caucasus and Central Asia but also as an independent, powerful actor in the Black Sea-Caspian region. The West should not attempt to stifle Turkey's independence but rather work with Ankara to better integrate Turkey into the West, in achieving which there are three main components. The first is to intensify energy and transport integration, using the vehicles of the Energy Community, the Nabucco pipeline, and the Marmara Tunnel. The second is EU membership for Turkey. France, Germany, and Austria are the main opponents of this process, but Europe-wide there needs to be greater recognition of the reality that Europe is at grave geopolitical risk should Turkey become a Middle Eastern- or Russia-Iran-orientated power. Europeans must do their part in keeping Turkey as part of the West. The third is an agreement from Turkey to open the Turkish Straits to NATO, EU, and U.S. warships. That means reforming the Montreux Convention as discussed above. This is the only way to counter Russian dominance of the Black Sea after the recent extension of the fleet's lease at Crimea. A welcome concomitant of this is that Ukraine becomes less necessary geopolitically, as the Black Sea itself can become a corridor for Western influence, and the possibility of Russia "closing off" the Black Sea, as Mackinder warned about, ceases to be a danger.

Step Two: "Integration"

The second step of "Integration" can be achieved primarily through facilitating transcontinental trade by using one well-established institution and two newer initiatives. The roles of the EU, the Northern Distribution Network (NDN), and the Modern Silk Road (MSR) are discussed here.

The EU

The EU has a highly dynamic role to play in integrating the smaller Eurasian states, both among themselves and with the West. The EU is one of the existing institutions best placed to do this because, despite its evolving military and security identity, it remains primarily a free trade association, and a model one at that. Aside from the wider geopolitical significance of promoting the West's agenda on the World Island, the EU's interest in facilitating the integration of the smaller Eurasian states lies in enhancing its own energy security. Much more than the United States the EU is at the mercy of capricious energy supply conditions in the Caucasus and Central Asian region. One of the priorities for the EU must therefore be the rehabilitation of INOGATE, discussed previously, and Transport Corridor Europe-Caucasus-Asia (TRACECA). The TRACECA initiative was agreed upon in 1998 between the European Commission and most of the Caucasus and Central Asian states, as well as Iran, Turkey, Romania, and Moldova, with the object of establishing a comprehensive road, rail, air, and sea transport corridor from Europe via the Caucasus to Central Asia and beyond. The project had a propitious beginning but has become stagnant in recent years, not least because of the deterioration in relations between the EU and Iran. However, Iran, although desirable, is not a make-or-break link in the chain as envisaged. The other Caspian states are sufficient for that vision to be realized and it should therefore be pushed ahead.

The East-West Transport Corridor is a separate but complementary concept originally intended to link the EU-Turkey-Central Asia-China and South Asia—essentially the key East-West link within the TRACECA network. The Baku-Tbilisi-Ceyhan pipeline was central to the East-West Transport Corridor but with the potential to link up with TRACECA and INOGATE and the emerging markets in the Black Sea region, Central Asia, and the Far East. The Eastern Partnership program(), also sponsored by the European Commission, is another ongoing initiative to better incorporate Armenia, Azerbaijan, Moldova, Belarus, and Ukraine into the existing EU trade and cultural framework. Although the limits to Belarusian and Ukrainian partnership are readily apparent, as discussed above, the scheme nonetheless takes the right approach and should be encouraged, especially where it has the potential to complement TRACECA, INOGATE, and the East-West Transport Corridor. There is huge potential within these initiatives to boost transit capabilities with new pipelines, roads, railways, and air and sea ports. However, the security of the regions concerned has been historically fickle and Western countries, but especially the EU, will have to take the lead among the various partners to ensure stability.

Another priority must be the success of the Nabucco pipeline, intended to bring up to 10 billion cubic meters of natural gas annually from the Caspian (primarily Azerbaijan and Turkmenistan) to Europe. There have been some doubts about the viability of supply for the proposed pipeline and even the suggestion that it be integrated with its strategic rival, Russia's South Stream, to guarantee that supply. However, Nabucco does not need South Stream in order to succeed. The Nabucco consortium has defined a route taking in Turkey, Bulgaria, Romania, Hungary, and Austria, and at the time of writing engineering work has already begun. Moreover, the Russian monopoly on Turkmen gas that existed until 2009 has now been sundered in favor of open competition, in which Western contenders ought to have the edge. Security and infrastructure investment from the EU is also going to be essential to ensure that Kazakhstan's oil pumped through the Baku-Tbilisi-Ceyhan pipeline reaches its European customers. Similarly, the EU must recognize the strategic contest that it is now engaged in with China for access to Turkmenistan's enormous gas reserves, as discussed earlier. Azerbaijan and Turkmenistan will therefore need to be brought within a broader security umbrella. If this is not done through NATO then the EU will have to play a leading role in forging bilateral security agreements with Azerbaijan and Turkmenistan.

The Northern Distribution Network (NDN)

The Northern Distribution Network represents a policy of diversification for the supply of coalition forces in Afghanistan, as named by the U.S. Transportation Command. Developed in the first half of 2009, the NDN now sees supplies that arrive by ship in Riga, Latvia being taken by road and rail through Russia, Georgia, Azerbaijan, Kazakhstan, Tajikistan, and finally from Uzbekistan, via the German-controlled Termez airbase, to forces in Afghanistan. That Russia features as one of the partners may come as a surprise until one remembers that only nonlethal supplies are sent along the route, and, more importantly, Russian companies are enjoying a lucrative enterprise in providing services, especially with heavy lift capabilities. The whole project is based on a series of commercial arrangements between local companies and provides an alternative to the Karachi-Kandahar road through Pakistan into Afghanistan. Many of these routes include infrastructure built in the 1980s by the Soviets and used as the principal arteries for their forces during their war in Afghanistan. Shipborne supplies to the Pakistani port of Karachi are still the primary means of supply, however. Supply via the NDN has the advantage of not requiring supplies originating in the United States or

Europe to transit the Suez Canal. Ultimately, however, the advantage of the NDN is enhanced security through diversification away from reliance on the volatile Pakistani route from Karachi that must necessarily go through Taliban-controlled territory.

The NDN properly consists of three distinct routes: NDN North, NDN South, and KKT. The NDN South route transits the Caucasus, bypassing Russia. The route originates at the Georgian port of Poti on the Black Sea and crosses Azerbaijan on the way to Baku. The goods are then loaded onto ferries for the journey across the Caspian Sea. The supplies arrive at Kazakhstan's west coast port of Aktau before being moved to Uzbekistan and finally on to Afghanistan. If the United States is able to secure a transit agreement from Turkmenistan, the port of Turkmenbashi could also be a reception point for goods arriving from Baku by ferry. The KKT route takes in Kazakhstan, Kyrgyzstan, and Tajikistan. KKT is an alternative to the Uzbek border crossing at the Termez base. Because of bad stretches of road in Tajikistan fewer units of goods can travel along KKT and can only do so at higher cost. Developing the Pakistani port of Gwadar would allow Kandahar to be opened to long-distance truck traffic, in turn further opening up the Afghan economy and giving Afghans "their best hope of generating legal income through long-distance trade ... [and giving] ... Central Asians a southern alternative to shipping everything to market through distant Russia."[2]

The three routes of the NDN have a valuable role to play in facilitating the reconstruction effort in Afghanistan, as was originally envisaged. Yet its potential as a permanent East-West transit route is much more significant. However, the problems of melding together the route are multitudinous, with one of the overarching difficulties being the obsession with "regime preservation," as well as plethora logistical inefficiencies among the many Caucasian and Central Asian partners. Recognizing the threat from disputes within Central Asia is another essential requirement for the project to prosper. These disputes include those over water use, payment for natural gas and electricity, militant incursions, the status of ethnic minorities, and espionage, all of which have strained relations to the detriment of multilateral cooperation. The results are often border closures, which represent the bête noire of such an ambitious transport project. Suspicion of U.S. and European intentions is also fueled by Russian and Chinese activity. Nonetheless, the NDN has the potential to make a profound and long-lasting impact on the geopolitical landscape of Eurasia.

If expansion of the West into Eurasia is the skeleton and outline around which a geopolitical strategy for Eurasia is to be built, then the NDN and its sister project, the MSR, which will be discussed following, represent the flesh and detail. Consolidation of the NDN as an alternative supply route to Afghanistan and its transformation into a permanent transit corridor for Eurasian trade should therefore be a long-term geoeconomic priority for the West.

The Modern Silk Road (MSR)

From the discrete aim of developing an alternative supply route for the coalition forces in Afghanistan, it soon became apparent that the solution—the NDN—had the potential to be a trans-Eurasian trade and transit corridor of much greater proportions and longevity beyond the anticipated Western military presence in Afghanistan. The parallels with the ancient Silk Road were obvious, and it was not long before the NDN and its intended expansion began to acquire the epithet of the "Modern Silk Road." In reality, the ancient Silk Road was not a single route but a cobweb of routes stretched out as a network across Eurasia. Much of it covered what is now a blank swath of underdeveloped land—the only part in the Northern Hemisphere—lying roughly between the eastern Black Sea region and the western provinces of China, which is now referred to as the "modern activity gap." The West must realize this modern trade network and plug the activity gap to ensure the manifest benefits it promises to bring to all the constituent Western states and the smaller Eurasian states themselves. It is understandable that the U.S. government at least believes that the countries in the region that stand to benefit most directly, such as China, India, Iran, and Pakistan, should bear the lion's share of the funding, but realistically a lot of the initial funding will have to come from Western sources. The starting point might simply be to address the "Eurasian customs challenge," which states that, new infrastructure aside, the greatest current obstacles to increased trans-Eurasian trade are the draconian customs and tariff regimes that prevail throughout Eurasia east of the EU. The most immediate challenge is to convince Eurasian states that the benefits of increased trade from abolishing these regimes massively outweigh the revenue from imposing them in the first place. The West's role should be to catalyze the project, starting with customs abolishment. Inevitably, funding some of the infrastructural development and forums for exchange will be necessary and costly, but in the long run, the West will be the major beneficiary geopolitically.

In their report for the Center for Strategic and International Studies, with a forward by S. Frederick Starr, author of *The New Silk Roads: Transport and Trade in Greater Central Asia*, Andrew C. Kuchins, Thomas M. Sanderson, and David A. Gordon detail the benefits the NDN and MSR can bring. An overland route running from Lianyungang, China to Rotterdam via Xinjiang and Central Asia, they say, would reduce transport time between China and Europe from 20–40 days to 11 days. Costs, they argue, would also be reduced from a figure of $167 to $111 per ton. According to the report the Asian Development Bank() believes that overall trade

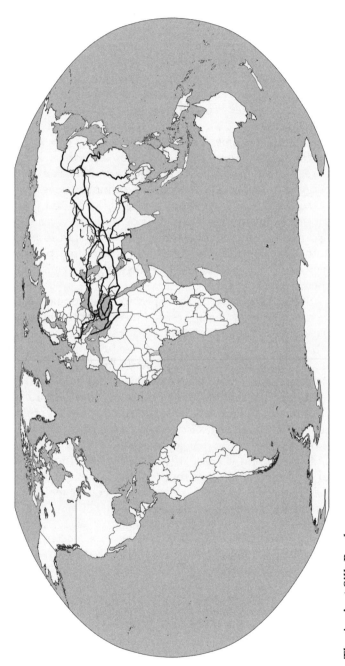

The Ancient Silk Road

could be increased by up to 80 percent, should rudimentary improvements be made to the transport infrastructure connecting Central Asia to Afghanistan. The Asian Development Bank has similarly predicted huge knock on benefits to Afghanistan's bilateral trade with neighbors, as well as transit trade through the country, thereby boosting imports and exports by a significant proportion. A UN study put the figure of GDP growth up by 50 percent throughout Central Asia within a decade, should trade cooperation be prioritized between constituent states. Creation of the MSR, the report argues, would give a boost to oil, gas, and electricity producers in Central Asia at the same time as undermining Russia's export monopoly and allowing for access to new markets in China, India, and Pakistan. Moreover, there is a demonstrable link between proliferation in nonenergy trade and energy cooperation. The authors cite examples suggestive of this: the Central Asia-South Asia power supply project, where Kyrgyzstan and Tajikistan are the main suppliers to countries such as Afghanistan and Pakistan; also the Turkmenistan-Afghanistan-Pakistan-India natural gas pipeline to rival the Iran-Pakistan-India natural gas pipeline; and cross-border power, specifically aimed at addressing Afghanistan's power importation needs with its neighbors.

S. Frederick Starr explains that "the prospect of transforming Afghanistan and the entire region of which it is the heart, into a zone of secure sovereignties and viable market economies . . . can roll back the forces that give rise to extremism and enhance continental security." The MSR project therefore has the potential to promote security and prosperity throughout Central Asia, providing conspicuous alternatives to extremism and helping to stabilize the region. In the short term the development would help to stabilize Afghanistan by "providing economic alternatives to insurgency and generating an indigenous revenue stream for the Afghan government."[3] So what can the West do to expedite the development of the NDN and creation of the MSR? Aside from improving security and infrastructure, the Center for Strategic and International Studies report authors identify eight specific actions they argue the U.S. government ought to focus on, which we might apply more broadly to Western governments in general:

1. Identify and embrace the strategic implications of the Modern Silk Road.
2. Create an immediate strategy for the Modern Silk Road's development.
3. Promote the Modern Silk Road concept and U.S. strategy for its implementation.
4. Identify and empower a lead U.S. government entity.
5. Stimulate alternative corridors.
6. Focus resources on the key obstacles to the Modern Silk Road.
7. Give Afghanistan the tools to harness the Modern Silk Road.
8. Recognize that the Modern Silk Road will benefit all of Eurasia.[4]

But more than just governments, there is a whole host of Western institutions that need to become involved in this project to partner and develop the smaller states of Eurasia.

Step Three: "Institutions"

Growing Western Institutions Eastward

It is a common feature of Russian foreign policy analysis to make the criticism that Western efforts since the dissolution of the Soviet Union have focused too much on spreading the influence of Western institutions instead of creating structures for a new world order, presumably meaning ones such as Medvedev's new European security initiative. But this begs the question, already asked here, of what does Russia and, for that matter, China, have to offer in any new system? It must be remembered that unlike Russian or Chinese nationalism many Western institutions, the EU and NATO foremost among them, stand for a set of values. The West's greatest strength in Eurasia is not military intervention, nor organized investment to match that of China, but rather its own values, institutions, and conspicuous success that make it the most attractive option for partnership for the small states of Eurasia. That is why utilizing the full spectrum of functional links to spread Western institutions is a sensible strategy by which Western actors can engage the smaller states of Eurasia. Perhaps the ultimate Western institution is representative government. Its propagation is also perhaps the most controversial. However, one does not need to be a so-called neoconservative to support the agenda of democracy promotion—it is right to advocate what is simply the best system of government available. The spread of democracy is a positive trend and should form one of the principles on which the West conducts its foreign policy, because democratic regimes are likely, though not assuredly so, to favor an expanded Western presence in Eurasia and generally a more peaceful and prosperous world. This is because of the opportunity to achieve that prosperity and cultural modernization that free people typically aspire to. However, spreading democracy to nations with no history of it is a lengthy, incremental process and not one that should be doted upon to the detriment of spreading trade and other aspects of good governance.

Good governance is a more appropriate base from which to begin, and it is more accurate in encompassing the scope of Western integration, from safety standards through trading normalcy and finally to representative government. For example, it includes encouraging the small states of Eurasia to embrace market reforms. This, however, can also sensibly include the great powers of Eurasia. For the same reasons that the West is benefited by the inclusion of the small Eurasian states in institutions such as the World Trade Organization, Russian membership would be a good thing too, because it would force Moscow to adhere to certain rules of practice, or, in other words, good governance. Ultimately this favors Western actors who are more dynamic on a level playing field. In this way the Twenty-First-Century Geopolitical Strategy for Eurasia is firmly anchored in realist logic and should not be confused with the tenets of liberal internationalism. The democracy aspect is secondary to the primary aim of growing the West eastwards, but it is complementary, because it will facilitate trade and ultimately cement Western influence once better established in Eurasia. Western institutions must neither seek to convert the unwilling nor deny the fruits of the West to those willing and, more importantly, ready to join its ranks. The real strength of Western institutions has always been and should always remain (in fundamental contrast to Russian and Chinese modes of action in Eurasia) their voluntary nature. They do not represent unwilling empires or reticent hegemons but are, in fact, clubs. This is the West's great advantage in Eurasia and why it should seek to bolster and not restrain the independent action of the smaller states and integrate them through trade, which will of course include Russia and China. But clubs that are too exclusive become staid and wither, which does not mean that entrance qualifications must be slackened but rather that all good clubs must welcome new blood, as long as it qualifies, and over time they require new blood to stay vital. The comity and cooperation of Western institutions is a strategic strength in Eurasia vis-à-vis the dominance of Russia and China.

The West's Twenty-First-Century Geopolitical Strategy for Eurasia must be one that uses the methodical and determined spread of good governance as that value set's greatest defense. This will be best accomplished through the functional links that come with the expansion of Western institutions. Only if those institutions penetrate to the heart of the World Island can the West prevent its eclipse by autocratic powers in the struggle for Eurasia. Yet there is much room for improvement within those Western institutions. Foremost, they must be reformed for greater efficacy. NATO-EU compatibility needs enhancing, as those are the two most instrumental organizations. The OSCE and Council of Europe would work better if they adopted majority decision making and short-circuited the ability of Russia to wreck initiatives. The addition of coercive powers to bring along recalcitrant members would also improve efficiency. Peacekeeping forces need mandates as well as rapid-reaction and humanitarian assistance teams. All these institutions need their scopes expanded and to be given a primary new purpose—that of focusing on Eurasia. It is now essential that greater integration is not put paid to by the challenge of the 2010 Eurozone crisis. Real benefits come from stability and camaraderie among the Western states. They must now refocus on those most successful aspects and expand that comity and stability eastward.

Promoting good governance through institutional links is best achieved not through criticism of human rights or electoral procedures but rather through the gradual process of growing functional links with and institution-building in Eurasian states. The full spectrum of functional links includes security, trade, good governance, rule of law, education, civil and human rights, the social contract, and investment. Security, trade, and good governance have been covered at length. Assistance in enabling Eurasian states to adopt the rule of law is another functional link that undoubtedly benefits local populaces while facilitating Western engagement on terms that Western actors, both at the state and substate level, are familiar with. Rule of law is clearly a derivative of good governance, but is one of the most crucial devices for ensuring a degree of normalcy that is otherwise missing when disparate actors suddenly enter into more intimate trade and legal relationships. States that respect the various processes of rule of law systems are attractive to investors because of the level of certainty that those investors can expect to surround their business relationships and transactions. Education is another key lower-level form of engagement that has huge scope in many of the smaller Eurasian states, not only to provide assistance in rudimentary teaching and learning techniques, but more generally to inculcate a better understanding of Western values. Through reciprocal educational schemes such as those well-established between Europe and the United States, hopefully a greater degree of affinity can be engendered between emerging leaders in both regions. Investment not directly related to any of the major infrastructural projects discussed above can also have a profound effect in countries where a little in Western terms goes a long way on the ground. It is when the jobs and opportunities provided by local businesses are missing that young men, especially, turn to destructive outlets to vent their frustration. This is often the underlying factor ensuring a recruiting pool for religious extremists and need not be the case with a little input into promising and/or necessary local enterprises.

The West must therefore retain as one of its prime objectives the spread of good governance and its derivatives throughout Eurasia in order to consolidate Western influence, but it must do so in a way that looks towards the long term. Eurasian partners must not be badgered but incentivized. They must not be spoken down to but given advice, shown the overall desirability of good governance practices, and given strict benchmarks. This does not necessarily mean "going at their own pace"—often a euphemism for foot-dragging and backsliding—but it does mean focusing on the rudiments of good governance first, not the final triumphs. In practice this means facilitating meritocratic educational systems, implementing tax codes and a small but efficient bureaucracy for collecting taxes due, and ensuring the independence of judges before expecting free and fair elections and reduced state-sanctioned corruption. The only proven way of

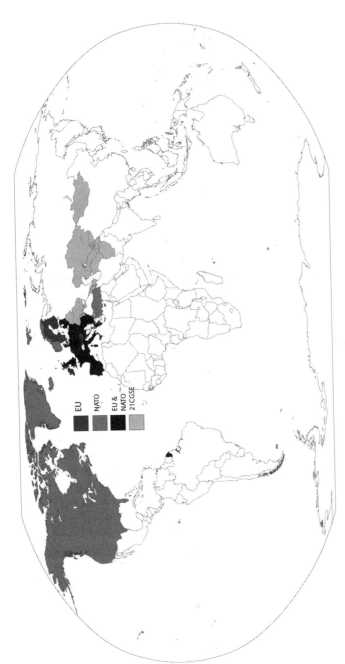

The Twenty-First-Century Geopolitical Strategy for Eurasia

ensuring good governance is through integration with Western institutions. Spain, Portugal, and Greece are all examples of formerly poor dictatorships which, by their own volition, began adopting, in their case, northern European political and financial institutions and progressed rapidly to political transparency and prosperity. Although now in the midst of an existential crisis in the Eurozone, of which they are at the center, none of those states is currently thinking of a radical change of government that would depart from the type promoted in these pages. The former Eastern bloc states that have joined the EU have similarly moved from dictatorship to democracy, good governance, and historical prosperity within a very short period. These examples must be regarded with confidence when contemplating the Twenty-First-Century Geopolitical Strategy for Eurasia.

Growing the West into Eurasia

The argument that the Eurasian countries cannot be linked and integrated with the West because they are fundamentally different does not hold. Integration of apparently opposed political and economic systems has been achieved before. The Twenty-First-Century Geopolitical Strategy for Eurasia is not new in that sense. Germany, a great Eurasian power, was integrated into the West by force after the Second World War; so too was Japan. Historically, both states had less participatory governance systems and much more state-controlled economies than their Western counterparts. Central and Eastern Europe and the Balkans had suffered under radically different systems, with completely opaque political apparatus and state-controlled economies. In the case of the Balkans, that is a region ravaged by conflict, both inter- and intrastate, and with significant destabilizing influence from Russia, which is now firmly within the geopolitical zone of the West and, Bosnia excepted, is composed of states progressing toward full EU membership and all the benefits that brings. Balkan integration will only be reversed if Western power on the World Island greatly diminishes and the impetus comes to lie with the great autocratic powers of Eurasia. If those powers see the opportunity to turn the tide of Western integration, which they see as such a threat to their opaque regimes, and propagate new concentrations of autocratic power that they understand and can deal with, then they will. Although it would be a long time before the core Western states themselves were under direct threat from such a regression, the more recently integrated and transitional states would be highly susceptible to power being recovered by the corrupt authoritarian elements that remain in those countries and rue their lost privileges. If the West is without a strategy for Eurasia this is not only a possibility but a likelihood, and if it begins to happen, the West will be on the back foot strategically as it was in the 1940s and 1950s.

There is of course the question of how far Western actors must be prepared to go in furtherance of the agenda to grow the West eastwards. One lesson of Georgia 2008 was that, in certain places and in certain circumstances, Moscow is prepared to use naked aggression to achieve what it cannot politically. We must also assume this to be the case for China, and that the U.S. Seventh Fleet remains in the Taiwan Straits is testament to that fear. Even if there had been a preparedness in the West to intervene in Georgia, however, it would not have been sensible to have been drawn into what was a desperate attempt by Georgia to hold on to an almost inevitably lost part of its territory. The West must not allow itself to be drawn into small Eurasian conflicts with little greater strategic bearing. However, it also must not relive a humiliation and strategic loss like that of Georgia in 2008. The best way to ensure that the West will not be faced with this choice is to resolve lingering conflicts through active involvement in conflict resolution, the fostering of intra-Eurasian integration, and the expansion of Western institutions to provide the incentive to a stable and prosperous future for Eurasian states. Many will of course say that it was the expansion of Western institutions itself that provoked the Georgia conflict. Moscow may well see that expansion as threatening, but a Eurasian geopolitical environment in which Russia or China try to assert dominance over the small states of Eurasia would see much more conflict, as governments and forces within the small states would eventually resist Russia's unscrupulous hegemony and China's plundering. A Western strategy that focuses on the underlying problems of poor governance and economic opportunity is therefore the one to follow if Western actors are to avoid having to make decisions about military action.

The Twenty-First-Century Geopolitical Strategy for Eurasia accomplishes Pilsudski's Prometheism and Intermarum on a grand scale, by empowering all the small states of Eurasia from Georgia to Mongolia and seeking to integrate them and bring them closer by propagating Western institutions in an Intermarum-type Western-oriented grouping—not between Germany and Russia, but between the great Eurasian powers of the twenty-first century: Russia and China. While the fundamentals of this strategy are not new, they form a unique overall approach to the current challenges facing Western policy makers. The Twenty-First-Century Geopolitical Strategy for Eurasia advocates for greater Western involvement in Eurasia than ever before. It argues that Western involvement and integration is not only possible but strategically imperative, not just in the Black Sea region, but also around the Caspian and Central/Inner Asia. The strategy departs from the traditional emphasis placed on the future of Ukraine and its schismatic domestic politics. Rather, it links Western efforts in Europe, Russia, Afghanistan, China, and Iran into a strategic whole to form an overarching purpose for Western institutions and governments. It is neither hopelessly isolationist nor vaingloriously imperialistic. It is aggressively realistic, informed by geographic constants and the urgent need for the West to renew itself in its own defense. In short, it is a wise strategy—something sorely lacking in the Western attitude towards Eurasia today.

CHAPTER 7

Conclusion: New, Old, or Enduring Geopolitics?

In the fifth century nomadic Hunnic tribes descended like a plague of injurious locusts on the settled peoples of northern Europe and the Roman Empire. Although evincing an inclination to move west for up to a century before, the conspicuous strength of the Roman Empire made it unthinkable that a migratory tendency would transform into invasion. But internal division over identity, organization, and purpose sowed the seeds of decay that stimulated the appetite of the invaders and gave them the confidence to tip the balance in favor of a countermovement to finally reverse the tradition of eastwardly conquest that had characterized the Empire's ascent. The result was that the Germanic tribes to the north of the Empire, who while hostile had nevertheless begun to be incorporated and civilized, were suddenly afforded the opportunity to give free reign to their violence and smite the Empire as they had for centuries desired. Revisionist history aside, the fall of the Roman Empire has traditionally, and with good reason, been heralded as the beginning of a dark age for Europe, a dark age in the relative sense of it being a regression from the fallible but ultimately progressive project of the Pax Romana. The eastern Roman Empire survived as Byzantium, only to suffer a similar fate almost a thousand years later. This time the nomadic Mongols swept westward, causing fresh migratory panic in the settled farmlands of Asia Minor and Europe. Under these conditions the Turks seized the opportunity to topple what was left of Rome in the east. The Hunnic invasions forced great hardships upon the Western population and stifled its development, although contributing to its emergent identity. The Mongol and Turkic invasions in large measure forced the European sea voyages of the fifteenth century, which, although pioneering, were nonetheless first undertaken in order to discover an alternative to the more efficient trade routes to East Asia through the Turk- and Arab-controlled Caucasus and Central Asia. These were the great geopolitical stories of the known world until the fruit of those sea voyages opened up the theater of imperial competition to a greater extent still.

Coinciding with the early spread of Western European empire over the seas, Russia finally ejected the Mongols and began its own impressive aggrandizement through much of Eurasia. For two centuries, however, that growth was checked in the west by the Polish-Lithuanian Commonwealth, which finally came to grief at the hands of the Russian and Germanic (we can include Austria here) organizers in the eighteenth century. Thereafter Russia's bid to organize the resources of the World Island was tempered only by its inability to make its will felt beyond the great natural border of the Himalayan and Persian mountains and press itself on the littoral zones controlled by the Turks and the British. When he delivered the Pivot paper Mackinder seemed to view Russia as the more threatening of the Eurasian powers, although this was before Russia had become the first white power to be defeated by nonwhites when it lost to the Japanese in the war of 1904–1905. By the time of *Democratic Ideals and Reality* Mackinder believed the principal threat to Western values and institutions derived from Germany, which he considered at that time a non-Western Eurasian power. Germany's ambitions, Mackinder believed, extended to domination of the World Island. That assertion looks debatable, as it is likely Germany would have been satisfied with an overseas empire to match those of Britain and France. However, Germany's next expansion under Hitler certainly was directed at that end, as Hitler evinced little if any interest in traditional overseas colonies. Indeed, his strategy, got by way of Rudolph Hess and Karl Haushofer, was much more in tune with what Mackinder had assumed were German intentions during the First World War.

War weariness, suspicions within the Alliance, and miscalculation at the close of the Second World War meant that the victorious Western powers missed the opportunity to forestall Russian encroachment into the heart of Europe. Much to everyone's surprise Russia emerged as the more potent organizer of Eurasian resources. The process of decolonization that followed the peace, although admirable in its object of self-determination for European colonial subjects, was a strategic calamity in its execution. The British Colonial Office for one had been conscious of not just the inevitability but the desirability of decolonization for decades. Indeed, the prevailing attitude there was that the British Empire was too large and more of a burden than a boon, the retention of which was becoming increasingly unrealistic as the strain of modernity—chiefly technology transfer—made itself felt. Yet the pace at which the pullout

occurred, strongly abetted by the United States, prevented the propagation of Western institutions in the countries their true benefits had been
withheld from. That they were withheld was readily understandable for
the purposes of maintaining imperial control. Nonetheless, the pragmatic
view once the untenability of the imperial position had been realized was
to co-opt these former colonies as so many Western-orientated offspring
for partnership in the future. The pace of change precluded this process,
not least because it created a vacuum into which Russia, principally, was
able to step. The British pullout from east of Suez in 1968 saw the error
of this process writ large. Nearly everywhere the British left, the Russians
moved in. The Russian navy was massively expanded and began to make
its presence felt in waters in which it had hitherto been unknown. Anglo-
American influence in Persia and Iraq was reduced, with revolutions
eventually expelling them from both. Russia threatened China, ingrati-
ated itself on India, and eventually invaded Afghanistan.

The physical geography of the land that impelled, impeded, and bore
upon it these great structural events has not changed in any significant
sense up through today. Although man has mastered the skills and crafts
to prevail over some of its insouciance, this is only in the narrow instances
of unearthing some of its buried wealth, bridging some of its truculent
rivers, and penetrating between some of its high mountains. The overbearing influence of its geography remains undiminished and from this
emerges the land's timeless politics. Mackinder, Kennan, and Pilsudski
all drew on that fundamental understanding to put forward their respective theses on how to manage the prevailing problems of their day. Today,
the geopolitical challenge that confronts the West wears the habiliments of
a modern world, yet remains in its essentials what it was in the early
twentieth century and, indeed, in antiquity. It now becomes us in the
twenty-first century to revisit Mackinder's warning together with Kennan
and Pilsudski's diverging solutions and with those ideas fashion a coherent strategy for the West in Eurasia.

Halford Mackinder, the British geographer and politician, surveyed the
historical pattern of conquest over the Eurasian continent and gained a
lively appreciation of the manner in which power waxed and waned
among the polities that held sway there. Although drawing on an established tradition of geopolitical understanding known to the great
Eurasian states themselves, Mackinder was to do more than pour old
wine into new bottles, much more. He was the first to identify and
describe the specific loci at which power hinged on the continent. He
described the Heartland as that area of land stretching from the broad
isthmus between the Black and Baltic seas eastward to Siberia, north to
the wending belt of taiga forest, and south to the deserts of Arabia and
the Persian mountains. He described how mobility over this area allowed
access to the more productive but more vulnerable littoral zones, Western

Europe, the Arab and Persian lands, the monsoon lands of India, and finally the ancient civilization of China. The great tale of Eurasian history, contended Mackinder, was that of migration, whether peacefully or belligerently, through this space. The corresponding tale of non-Eurasian history had at the kernel of its development the voyages of the Western Europeans over the great oceans. Yet for all their supposed superiority, the great seapowers could not penetrate into the hinterland of Eurasia. Thus Mackinder described the pivotal area of world politics—that area of Eastern Europe and the Caucasus where the Heartland begins, where seapower exhausts its potency and landpower begins its. In this way Mackinder employed geography to express the fundamentals of world politics, as distinct from the incidental described in history.

Mackinder's descriptive analysis was suffused with an instructive warning. Landpower, as encompassed by the Eurasian states, Mackinder argued, was inherently superior to seapower, as represented by the Islanders, and would ultimately prevail over it. Such assertions apparently placed Mackinder in direct opposition to another of the nineteenth century's principal strategists, Alfred T. Mahan. Yet Mahan's seapower-centric theory, stressing the superiority of seapower over land, was not alien but integral to Mackinder's theory. At some point the question stole across Mackinder's mind of what might happen were a mighty Eurasian landpower to secure the entire continent and turn its prodigious resources to securing control of the oceans. The result, Mackinder believed, would be for this new landpower organizer to eclipse the seapowers in their own strategic environs. Mackinder therefore went beyond Mahan's assumptions of a seapower-landpower struggle that focused merely on control of the littoral zones or, as Mahan termed them, the "debated and debatable" zones. Mackinder envisaged a dominant Eurasian power strategically immune in its remote fortress, inaccessible to the ships of the Islanders but from which it could descend at will upon the production centers of the littoral, and where eventually it too would put to sea in irresistible numbers and set upon the lands of the Islanders, including the Americas.

Although a Member of Parliament in Britain, Mackinder's strategic influence on his own generation was slight. It was not until the Second World War, when Mackinder was at an advanced age, that interest in his thesis revived, though for primarily negative reasons. A link was supposed between Mackinder's Heartland theory and Nazi grand strategy before and during the war. In particular, careful observers pointed to Mackinder's emphasis on an organizer of Eurasian resources emerging to dominate the World Island before turning its attention to the oceans. It is true that Nazi policy adopted the mantra of lebensraum as promoted by a professor of geopolitik at Munich University, Karl Haushofer. And indeed, Hitler had shown himself little interested in overseas colonies, even when they had been on offer during the appeasement years. Rather, Nazi strategy evinced a strong intention to penetrate as comprehensively as possible into the Eurasian interior where the living space, both in terms of land and resources, was to be found. In this way Mackinder's work garnered criticism by association with a ruthless aggressor. Yet others took a less jaundiced view to appreciate the value of Mackinder's message. One of those was the Dutch-American geostrategist Nicholas Spykman, who in many ways provides the conceptual link between Mackinder's Heartland theory and George Kennan's containment strategy. But it was Mackinder who provided a truly global analysis where previously there had been only strategic myopia. The essential geography of the world remains today what it was in antiquity. And for that reason Mackinder's analysis and warning are as relevant now as ever.

George Kennan's long-term position at the U.S. embassy in Moscow in the lead-up to the Second World War and during it afforded him an intimate knowledge of one of the great states of Eurasia. During those years Kennan formed a firm opinion of Soviet intentions and capabilities and a corresponding strategy to be the basis of Western interaction with Russia. In 1946 Kennan communicated his views to a largely ambivalent State Department in what came to be popularly known as the Long Telegram. A year later Kennan followed up the Long Telegram with a piece in *Foreign Affairs* magazine entitled "The Sources of Soviet Conduct," which he signed "X" and which came to be known as the X Article. From these writings Kennan might understandably be accused of according too much weight to what he saw as the peculiar character of the Soviet government. In geopolitical terms, the Soviet Union was little more than a more efficient and ruthless version of Czarist Russia. Although talk of international communism abounded, in the areas of Central and Western Eurasia where the rhetoric (sincere rhetoric) had the greatest impact, it was not difficult to discern behind the facade the thinly veiled face of Russian nationalism. Kennan was aware of this continuity in tradition, yet seemed to ascribe especial importance to the Soviet mindset as distinct from the Russian. Nevertheless, Kennan appreciated the supervening threat from a state that, unlike Germany, was not surrounded by powers intent on and with the collective capabilities to keep her down. Kennan's didactic response was to advocate the formation of a primarily political and economic cordon sanitaire, backed and made credible from a position of military strength. The object, argued Kennan, was to ensure that Russian encroachment into non-Russian lands as it stood at the end of the Second World War would represent a high-tide mark, not to be bettered by the Soviets, but nor forcefully made to recede by the West.

This meant acknowledging but monitoring Russia's position in Eastern Europe while simultaneously reinvigorating Western European, particularly German, economic and military strength. It is instructive that

Kennan was able to take such an unpopular view over reunifying and revitalizing a state that the West had so recently defeated, something opposed by many other Americans, not to mention the victorious Europeans. Kennan was only able to do this because Western penetration of the German heartland and actual occupation meant that the once-feared state was already in the process of being integrated into the West. Kennan's strategy also meant bolstering India, Pakistan, and Japan as respective southern and eastern bulwarks against the Soviet expansionist proclivity. China was weak and racked by civil war when Kennan was writing the Long Telegram and X Article, yet he saw in that ancient country the potential for resurgence and therefore viewed it as an important potential partner for the West in its strategic encirclement of Russia. In the event, China became Communist, together with North Korea, with the logical concomitant that their power had to be contained too. In Kennan's thesis, once thus contained, the Soviet Union would decay from within. To be confident in championing this strategy Kennan had an immovable belief in the superiority of the Western system—this belief hardened during his time in Moscow before the war, in the very years when others in the West were flirting with the supposed virtues of international socialism. Once surrounding the Eurasian continent, Western institutions would then come to the fore simply by advertising their conspicuous success to the isolated Soviet world. The Western world would thus be able to repose in an attitude of aloof superiority, confident that Soviet power could only contract and not expand, and in the process dissipate among the many contradictions that Kennan asserted suffused the Soviet system, just as Marxism argued would be the downfall of the capitalist.

However, although Kennan's seminal and well-timed telegram ensured that he was plucked from policy-making obscurity and given a central role as director of the Policy Planning Staff, the thrust of his argument was lost on some of the minds it impressed in Washington. Beginning positively, Kennan's thesis provided the intellectual foundation for and was instrumental in engendering the Marshall Plan announced in 1947. This saw the necessary funds apportioned to realize the first prerequisite of his containment strategy—the revitalization of Western Europe and West Germany. However, what followed was an escalation in militarization between the emergent blocs, the creation of which was implicit in Kennan's strategy for sectioning off the non-Communist periphery of Eurasia. The 1948 Truman Doctrine was the final expression of the implacable relations that had emerged and made military force a much more prominent tool for ensuring containment than Kennan had ever envisaged. Thus it was that the political and economic measures that proved so effective in reintegrating Western Europe into its traditional democratic, market-orientated guise were not extended to the Communist world itself, where threatened use of force was preferred instead. Containment therefore performed a useful function in the atmosphere of heightened tension in the early Cold War years, but is not sufficient to press home Western interests in the more fluid reality of twenty-first-century Eurasian politics. Containment is the minimal default position for any Western strategy for Eurasia, which today will necessarily require a less prominent military aspect and more conspicuous growth and success of reformed Western institutions.

Josef Pilsudski, the Polish interwar leader, was at the head of a Eurasian state in the heart of the pivot, as identified by Mackinder. There is no evidence that Pilsudski was influenced by Mackinder's thesis; more likely, Pilsudski shared his geopolitical understanding with Bismarck, who had famously said that Bohemia was the key to control of Europe. However, Pilsudski and Mackinder were contemporaries, and it was not long after the latter's seminal 1904 paper that his ideas were being imported to the continent by the nascent German school of geopolitik pioneered by Friedrich Ratzel and developed by Karl Haushofer. In any event, Pilsudski came to advocate two complementary strategies that essentially suggested solutions to the problem of Eurasian dominance in the form of Russian authoritarianism. The first and most important of his ideas was Prometheism. In it Pilsudski advocated a strategy of denuding Russia of its non-Russian peoples and lands. This meant a large proportion of the Russian Empire of the late nineteenth and early twentieth centuries. Pilsudski knew that ever since its earliest days under the yoke of the Mongol Hordes Russia had sought security in depth, and as she became more powerful, that depth was increasingly achieved at the expense of her European, Caucasian, and Central Asian neighbors. Without those extraterritorial gains Russia would be insecure and meek and cease to be a threat to her neighbors. Pilsudski therefore championed a strategy of empowering the minority peoples of the Russian empire through propaganda and clandestine means, thereby giving them the succor to rise up against their imperial masters.

The Prometheist movement was a pan-Eastern European enterprise that enjoyed considerable support at times between the wars. Prometheism was a real inspiration for many Caucasian countries seeking to escape Russian dominance, and even now there can be found a Prometheism statue in Tbilisi. However, it had only tacit and token backing from the Western powers, which limited its efficacy. With Pilsudski's death in 1936 the dynamic impetus behind the project was lost, although its legacy did live on for a while under the stewardship of some of Pilsudski's talented disciples, such as Edmund Charaszkiewicz. That said, the Soviet Union was not affected in any significant way. In fact, the remit of Soviet power in Eastern Europe became more pervasive after Stalin had consolidated his own power at home. The result was that Poland once more found itself the unsupported

(French security guarantees having become increasingly meaningless during the 1930s) buffer state between the great Eurasian powers of Russia and Germany. Pilsudski's second concept was his Intermarum or "between the seas" federation of the states of Eastern Europe plus Finland, stretching between the Black and Baltic seas at the gateway to the Heartland. The idea was to ally all these states in an anti-Russian-orientated bloc that would provide strength in numbers and complement the Prometheist strategy. Poland was to be at the head of this alliance, and indeed it bore more than a passing resemblance to the seventeenth- and eighteenth-century Polish-Lithuanian Commonwealth. It was in part for that reason that the Intermarum concept was never taken up by its putative members, nor did it gain even outline support from the great powers of the West—the latter to which Pilsudski ascribed its ultimate failure.

The failure of Prometheism and Intermarum in Pilsudski's lifetime meant for Poland a fourth partition between Germany and Russia, both competing to be the final organizer of Eurasia. Russia was victorious but did not manage to integrate Germany into its system; rather that was achieved by the West, to its great advantage. Ironically, it was only after Pilsudski's death and Poland's defeat that his strategies began to be adopted, even if unconsciously, by the powers that possessed the capabilities to see them prevail. The Soviet dissolution of 1989–1991 saw Prometheism partly realized. However, the process was largely self-initiating and more limited than Pilsudski had envisaged. Russia's minorities deserted it en masse until the Russian state itself, in its Soviet guise, became so weak that it too collapsed, fated to spend a decade in ignominy. Yet it was only the Eastern European states that managed to capitalize on the change and consolidate their independence. The states of the Caucasus and Central Asia gained independence only in the abstract; tellingly, they immediately joined the cobbled-together CIS in response to being cast strategically adrift. These smaller Eurasian states now need empowering because their strength vis-à-vis Russia and China is the West's too. Similarly, the European Union, as it has come to be constituted since the addition of the Eastern European states, looked to all the world to be the final act in the completion of Pilsudski's Intermarum alliance. But again the concept remains incomplete, as a revanchist Russia is continually able to exert precisely the sort of pressure on its neighbors that the Intermarum was designed to deter. Today, Western policy makers must therefore reacquaint themselves with Pilsudski's concepts, especially that of Prometheism, in order to move beyond a containment strategy and make the strategic inroads to Eurasia that will prevent that critical region from coming under the sway of authoritarian organizers, about which Mackinder warned.

The condition of geopolitics in Eurasia today is marked by increasing instability. Russia's grip on the smaller states of Eurasia remains strong despite the strife and ostensible decline of the 1990s. Yet Beijing is increasingly active in courting these states for access to the resources they possess. In this climate the Caucasian and Central Asian states themselves are increasingly minded to explore nontraditional forms of partnership, which typically means a choice between China and the West. China is poised to exploit any economic and soft-power opening, while the West is occupied with Afghanistan, just one small part of Eurasia, to the neglect of other, more strategically important areas. The West's capacity for dynamic involvement in Eurasia is being curtailed by a general perception of Western decline. Brazil, Russia, India, and China are spoken of in the same breath as the major developing economies set to reorder the global balance of power along more multipolar lines. The inclusion of India and China in that list is indicative of the broader Asian ascendency that contrasts with a decrease in Western numbers, productivity, and power. Although Russia ought properly to be excluded from that list, as it suffers from many of the problems the West faces and has little of the dynamism of the other three, the grouping is nevertheless representative of a genuine potential shift in the balance of power. It is tempting for the West to respond with an act of retrenchment. Yet the wise course is in fact quite the opposite. First, Western policy makers need to be aware of the fundamental trends playing out in Eurasia.

Russia is as dysfunctional as it has ever been. Yet simply by virtue of the huge space it occupies on the map, it is the most resource-rich country in the world, with the potential to sustain a large and productive population. Russia's harsh climate and relative inaccessibility as described by Mackinder place quite strict limits upon its development. Yet it is the country's poor political and economic organization that truly retards the sort of development many much smaller and less well-endowed states have nonetheless been able to achieve. Russia's inability to sustain productive manufacturing without brutal state control has led to the economy as a whole relying on commodity exports, just like many in the Third World. While commodity prices are high there is therefore little real incentive to diversify and develop a knowledge-based economy to compete with the West and Asia. It is for that reason that Russia is in exalted company when its economy is grouped together with those of Brazil, India, and China. However, catastrophic is the mistake of writing off Russia. The parts of its manufacturing economy that do remain intact primarily include weapons and nuclear technology. In its quest to reenergize its historical predominance in Eurasia Russia has advantages in the substantial markets that exist for these products there. Then there is the energy factor. Energy is the central plank not just of Russia's economy but also its foreign policy and geostrategy. With it, Russia has been able to exert enormous influence over its neighbors, especially in Eastern Europe, but also China and the small states of Eurasia, even to the extent of dividing the European Union partners. But more than that, Russia demonstrates a ruthlessness and unpredictability in its foreign relations that means it in many ways punches above its actual weight. In the case of the Caucasian and Central Asian states, with few exceptions, Russian involvement retains an imperial air that is accepted by the elites still tied to Moscow, for whom it is indeed their sustenance.

Further east, China is the rising dragon that many believe will emerge as the peril of folklore. China's economy is now the second largest in the world and is poised to take over the United States at some point in the middle of the twenty-first century. Shocking though it appears for many in the West, for the Chinese this trajectory represents no more than a reversion to the historical norm. But what of the fact that one great power is set to be replaced by another—is it not, after all, the way of things for great powers to rise and fall? It must be remembered that China is an authoritarian, antidemocratic, and in many ways mercantilist state that has little love for the Western model of government or even benevolent empire. These are traits it shares with the other great Eurasian power, Russia, and China is increasingly enhancing its presence among the smaller Eurasian states where Russia once held sway, but is now desperately trying to cling onto its former colonies and satellites. In Central Asia in particular, China has been busy buying influence in virtually every major new energy project going. Chinese investment in infrastructure and energy production now means that Beijing exercises a level of influence in Central Asia that neither Russia nor the West can hope to match by financial means alone. Although for many decades pursuing a foreign policy that has stressed the innocuous nature of Chinese prosperity, the Chinese Communist leadership has made a quiet but consistent effort to modernize, expand, and diversify the country's armed forces. Where once China's extraterritorial ambitions seemed to stop at Taiwan, more recently China has begun putting to sea. A string of Chinese naval bases has sprung up, stretching as far as the Persian Gulf. This propitiously places China for a strategic takeover of the Indian Ocean and leverage over Middle East oil exports. But more resonantly, it represents the graduation by a great Eurasian organizer from landpower to seapower that Mackinder foretold.

More disconcertingly still, there is a confluence of Russian and Chinese interests despite their ostensible competition. This is represented most conspicuously in the Shanghai Cooperation Organization (SCO). The organization also includes many of the former Soviet satellites in Central Asia and was originally formed to provide a forum for dispatching with border issues lingering from the Soviet dissolution. The body dealt efficiently with almost all of those disputes and then broadened its remit to include cooperation on issues as diverse as security, trade, separatism, terrorism, and extremism. The SCO has variously been described as the most dangerous organisation Americans have never heard of, as well as OPEC with [nuclear] bombs. Indeed, between them SCO members control an enormous proportion of the world's known energy reserves and nuclear weapons, yet the body remains little discussed in mainstream Western media. Careful analysts have correctly assessed that the SCO is riddled with tensions, primarily between its two great power members, Russia and China, but also between those states and the smaller ones, the latter wary of exchanging one form of tutelage for another. Indeed, China is the driving force of the organization, while Russia displays greater caution in a body that has its geographic focus in an area where China has everything to gain and Russia much to lose. However, the crucial point is that China and Russia evidently prioritize cooperation over their known, if not acknowledged, mutual suspicions. That cooperation is directed toward eliminating the West from Eurasia, beginning with its military manifestations, and preserving their smaller neighbors for their own exploitation.

Russo-Chinese designs on the smaller states of Eurasia will do nothing to raise the geoeconomic standard of the region and everything to retard its development. Moscow is seeking to preserve the dependence of the smaller Eurasian states on Russian technologies, markets, and investment. China is seeking to plunder as much energy and other resources as it can from the same peoples, while cultivating its direct neighbors so as to shore up sovereignty in its restive western provinces. There is clearly, therefore, much over which Moscow and Beijing could come into conflict. Yet the evidence indicating the intentions of the two great powers points in the opposite direction. The key issue around which the SCO alliance coagulates is the stated determination to stamp out terrorism, separatism, and extremism. This is simply to disguise a commitment to authoritarianism with diplomatic camouflage. First and foremost Russia and China want to preserve their regimes and their way of doing business, both in the literal and figurative sense. The preeminent threat to that happening is Western involvement in Eurasia. The sort of market reforms and good governance the West should seek to promote among the smaller states of Eurasia is anathema to the Moscow and Beijing elites' way of life. If not condominium, then, at least an agreement is evident in the Russo-Chinese partnership to partition Eurasia east of Europe for the prolongation of authoritarianism and mercantilism. In this climate the Western powers are proving increasingly ignorant of what stands to be lost and indeed gained by their strategy in Eurasia. If the West can engage the smaller states of the continent, economic benefits can be mutually conferred while sectioning off Russia and China from one another and from the weaker states of the littoral zone. Alternatively, if the Islanders remain adrift and without a clear forward policy for Eurasia, they are likely to find themselves divided and on the back foot strategically around the globe.

What is then needed, if the West is to maintain its preeminence globally and capacity to be instrumental in the World Island, is a coherent twenty-first-century strategy for Eurasia. This strategy must be founded on an acute understanding of Mackinder's warning. It must adopt containment as the baseline beneath which Western action becomes negligent. And it must take up and update Pilsudski's Promethean and Intermarum concepts for use in the twenty-first century and beyond. Western actors need to engage with the people and progressive politicians of the critical smaller Eurasian states, who are crying out for an alternative to a revanchist Russia and an expanding China. They need to strengthen the independent action, sovereignty, and governance of the states of Eurasia and tie them to Western institutions through functional and other links, and promote open trade regimes to facilitate the transcontinental trade that is potentially more efficient than maritime. Although there is a place for military strength and the extension of security guarantees, this task must be completed primarily by growing nonmilitary Western institutions eastwards and reforming them where necessary. Superiority of institutions is the Western difference. Any argument that Eurasian states cannot be linked and integrated into the West because they are fundamentally different does not hold. It has been done before in the cases of Germany and Japan and can be done again in the Caucasus and Central Asia. The keys to this process are the strategic steps of Independence, Integration, and Institutions. In nurturing these facets, Western actors can facilitate transcontinental trade that will empower the smaller states and allow them to escape Russia's control and emerge from China's shadow through development of their own resources and enterprise. Growing the West into Eurasia by establishing lasting functional links is a sensible strategy that achieves Western goals without a military focus while benefiting the subjects of its attention. Crucially it will employ the benign spread of Western institutions to divide Russo-Chinese partnership and prevent the emergence of a single Eurasian organizer to consolidate power and threaten the Islanders.

The bipolar character of the Cold War rapidly gave way to a brief period of unipolarity in the decade that followed its end. The first decade of the twenty-first century has in turn seen a move towards more multipolar and, one might argue, more traditionally balanced world politics. Yet in this prospective new multipolar world there is a real likelihood that the West will be less well represented than it was in the last multipolar one of the nineteenth century, when Great Britain was first amongst equals and the United States and France close behind. Old orthodoxies are being thrown out with the bathwater as negotiation increasingly takes the place of the demands the hegemonic United States was once able to gratuitously make. As ever, the coming multipolar world will be marked by a global struggle for resources. The World Island will be the strategic focus of that struggle, and the danger for the West is that it becomes eclipsed as a serious player there. A world in which Eurasia is dominated by the great authoritarian powers will be one where the United States and

Europe find themselves in a fresh struggle with Brazil for influence in the Atlantic. Brazil is populous and has had one of the best performing economies of the first decade of the twenty-first century. There are popular calls for the country to join the G8 and be given a permanent seat on the UN Security Council. That status is backed up by the widespread knowledge that Brazil is nuclear-capable, if not actually a nuclear weapons state. The country is also modernizing at a rapid pace and is continually discovering more of its own natural resources, especially in offshore oil. To this there is a military concomitant, as Brazil naturally seeks to consolidate its emerging great power status by equipping itself with suitably large and modern armed forces. As Brazil strives to sustain its expanding industry and satisfy its growing middle class, it will inevitably come into greater competition, even if limited to the commercial sphere, with the United States and Europe for access to the rest of Latin America, as well as Africa, in both of which China already has considerable influence. In this way the West may well find that, should it be ejected from Eurasia, it will be unable to simply recover and set out anew but will rather be forced into an immediate struggle to hold on to predominance in the Atlantic. The fate of the West's global influence, in Latin America, Africa, and beyond, lies in involvement in the Pivot Area of the World Island.

The prospect of nuclear proliferation among otherwise respectable members of the international community brings into focus the argument that geopolitics no longer matters now that nuclear weapons can be deployed almost instantly anywhere across the globe. Yet however unlikely actual conflict between great powers seems, there will always be geopolitical jockeying through institutional, political, and economic influence, as well as through small wars such as Afghanistan and Georgia. This is the format for great power relations even in peacetime. Just because Washington and Beijing are unlikely to come to major blows in the immediate future does not mean that they will cease to compete geopolitically, especially across Eurasia. Moreover, that this struggle goes on in peacetime does not mean that its results cannot have profound consequences for the future of all engaged in it.

Avoiding eclipse and ejection from Eurasia will require more than a coherent program to expand Western institutions. It will also require reform of many of them. The EU offers the starkest example of a great multilateral achievement stagnating and failing to achieve its potential in the world. The progressive political arrangement that once looked formidable in not just its statistics, but its sheer modernity, has been called into question and found wanting on some of the issues that matter most to its people, people who still define themselves along national lines. In 2010 the EU faced a financial crisis that exposed the more profound existential question of how it would have to redefine its internal relations should the powerful states refuse to underwrite the weak. The process of addressing those questions is still in train, but whatever the outcome, the future of Europe is less easy to discern than it was just a few years before. Germany is the pivotal state in the European project, and may decide that its import-export interests are better served by disentanglement from the institutional framework it has been integrated into and the adoption of a more unilateral world role. Alternatively it may even move closer to its great friend and enemy, Russia, and bring into sharp relief the fears Mackinder had in 1904. That said, a more likely scenario will be that the strong states of Europe do rescue the weak this time, though with the proviso that top-down reform be implemented to avoid a repeat in the future. If that happens there will be an opportunity for Europe to rediscover its shared values and collective strength, which should, given the numbers, knowledge, and history, be the composite superlative of any region in the world. A reformed and revivified EU, with a coherent vision for its internal and external development and with suitable teeth, is central to a forward Western strategy for Eurasia.

It is in Eurasia that the West's level of involvement will determine its geopolitical prowess and eventual survival. Russia and China will inevitably compete there as their histories suggest, but will fundamentally prioritize ejecting Western actors and reign in their mutual distrust for that purpose. Of the two, China is by far the greater global threat and is determined not to become democratic or any more Western-orientated. Beijing's analysis of the Soviet collapse points to the acceptance of Western ideals as the primary reason that bore an empire in need of restructuring, economically, past the point of terminal decline, politically. Yet in the central theater of Eurasia both Russia and China need to be countered by Western actors. For that purpose a strategy closer to Pilsudski's Prometheism is now more relevant than Kennan's containment. Containment must remain the minimal or default position of the West in Eurasia, but more important is a forward strategy to secure the partnership of Russia's former satellites, before China does the same on terms much more disadvantageous for the West and those small states themselves. Previous strategies for Eurasia have focused on the "taking" of Ukraine and possibly Belarus, and indeed, were the EU to integrate those countries, it would certainly look very tidy on the map. However, to concentrate on those goals is to set horizons little further than the Black Sea region. Western geopolitical control of the Black Sea region, as far as it means the improvement in governance of the region's states and an open trade regime there, should certainly be an objective. However, there exist other, more subtle ways of achieving the same end, primarily by properly integrating Turkey into the EU. More to the point, these are less painful ways and some that, if skillfully exploited, offer broader opportunities for growth beyond the Black Sea. The preoccupation with Ukraine in particular is a recipe for frustration and little gain. That will remain the case until there is a sea change in the attitudes of the Russian part of the population or else a rupture between east and west. A more sensible strategy is one that does not ignore but is realistic about Western prospects vis-à-vis Ukraine and concentrates instead on the Caucasus and Central Asia.

Azerbaijan is often referred to as the cork in the bottle of Caspian riches. Western engagement with the country, however, does not reflect much sincerity in that belief. Azerbaijan is indeed the gateway to the Asian part of Eurasia. With Russia in control to the north and Iran to the south, Azerbaijan sits at the point where Central Asian energy and trade goods must flow westward and Western investment, education, and governance must flow eastward. Only in this way can the smaller states of Eurasia be empowered and co-opted into the task of splitting the authoritarian states and preventing condominium in Eurasia. Rather than campaigning on a platform of "saving" the smaller states of Eurasia from direct Russian and Chinese control, the West needs to demonstrate that it can provide an alternative to the Russo-Chinese system of authoritarian government as a way of ensuring sovereignty. This is where Western institutions come in. Good governance has a life of its own if based upon certain accepted principles and protected from molestation in its infancy. The United States and the Monroe Doctrine is a case in point. After accepting its loss Great Britain quickly accommodated itself to the new regime precisely because it was borne of its own values. The Royal Navy guaranteed the Monroe Doctrine, which allowed Anglo-American institutions to flourish unmolested by the other European powers. The result was a boom in trade and an enduring, if at times difficult, partnership between the two countries. A Monroe Doctrine for the smaller states of Eurasia is clearly not possible in the military sense. Yet much can be done to provide that crucial breathing space that will allow the potent devices of good government, open society, and liberal trade to take their course. After all, it is much easier to justify on whatever spurious grounds putting pressure on an authoritarian state than it is on a market-democracy.

It must be stressed that the 21CGSE is not an assault on Russia or China but rather a response to a sober assessment that their current modes of governance are detrimental to the future of Eurasia and, by extension, the Western world. It is the Russia-China diplomatic axis that protects international pariah states like Iran, North Korea, and Burma and under-mines concerted international efforts to deal with the problems those regimes present, which in the case of Iran go beyond its nuclear ambitions and extend to Afghanistan, Israel, Palestine, Syria, and Lebanon. However, the 21CGSE will not cut connections in Eurasia between Russia and China, just the potential for geopolitical dominance. Western involvement in Eurasia will allow for the flourishing of trade routes across the mega-continent, albeit with much of it under the informal aegis of the West—just as with maritime trade today. As has already been discussed, there is much evidence that transcontinental, as opposed to transoceanic, trade is more cost effective and has the potential to get products to consumers quicker. The great Eurasian powers will actually benefit from this arrangement economically, though they will fear it politically. China especially has huge markets in Europe that would be better reached overland than by sea. The chief obstacles are draconian tariff regimes and poor infrastructure, either as a result of Russian obstinacy or Caucasian and Central Asian underdevelopment. Whether Russia and China choose to buy into these new arrangements will be a matter of heads over hearts.

Mackinder's warning rings true a century after it was written because the fundamentals of his thesis remain valid. While for the time being the Western and Eastern great powers may not engage in armed conflict across Eurasia, their geopolitical jostling over resources, markets, and influence will become increasingly intense. At the moment, Western efforts are the weakest in this struggle. If the autocratic powers are given the space to carve up Eurasia, it will not be long before their irresistible influence extends to the weaker states of Europe. Iran will be preserved as an authoritarian regional hegemon in the south of the continent, and India too is at risk of being left as an isolated democracy to be pressured on three fronts. Alternatively, Russia's unpredictability and weak-link status in the Moscow-Beijing partnership mean it might spasm at any moment, leaving a geopolitical void which the West needs to be prepared to fill before China does. Broader Asian development is not proving inimical to Western interests, as the majority of major Asian states are developing along democratic market-orientated lines and identify more closely with Western political and economic values than with their Chinese equivalents. An undramatic but focused and consistent Western strategy in Eurasia will provide the balance in the Eastern Hemisphere that is needed to counteract and ameliorate Chinese growth, thereby reassuring the other Asian players and reducing the danger of one or more of them precipitating a crisis by reacting against the Chinese threat.

The multiplicity of reasons pointing to the pivotal nature of Eurasian geopolitics is overwhelming. In Mackinder we have a paradigm by which to understand the mechanisms at work there. In Kennan and Pilsudski we have two twentieth-century solutions, which in combination are instructive for forming a coherent forward strategy for the twenty-first. Mackinder's vision, Kennan's emphasis on patience, and Pilsudski's fervor are key to the implementation of the Twenty-First-Century Geopolitical Strategy for Eurasia. The fate of the West has been and will be determined by events on the World Island. Western governments, peoples, and institutions must therefore organize their still-preponderant energies and resources to engage vigorously and with long-lasting determination in the geopolitics of Eurasia.

Notes

CHAPTER 2

1. Sir Eyre Crowe, "Memorandum on the Present State of British Relations with France and Germany," *British Documents on the Origins of War 1898–1914*, edited by G. P. Gooch and Harold Temperley, Vol. III (London: H.M.S.O., 1928), 402.

2. Brian W. Blouet, *Mackinder: A Biography* (College Station, TX: Texas A&M University Press, 1987), 145.

3. See Niall Ferguson, *Empire: How Britain Built the Modern World*, comparing the peace of the Roman and British empires.

4. Halford John Mackinder, "The Geographical Pivot of History," *The Geographical Journal* 23, no. 4 (1904), 434.

5. Halford John Mackinder, *Democratic Ideals and Reality: A Study in the Politics of Reconstruction* (London: Constable, 1919), 80.

6. Mahan, *The Influence of Seapower upon History*, 35.

7. Mackinder, *Democratic Ideals and Reality*, 88.

8. Mackinder, "Geographical Pivot," 436.

9. Halford John Mackinder, "The Round World and the Winning of the Peace," *Foreign Affairs* 21, no. 4 (1943): 601.

10. Mackinder, *Democratic Ideals and Reality*, 46.

11. Mackinder, *Democratic Ideals and Reality*, 49.

12. Mackinder, *Democratic Ideals and Reality*, 99.

13. Mackinder, *Democratic Ideals and Reality*, 80.

14. Mackinder, *Democratic Ideals and Reality*, 110.

15. Curzon had recently taken up the post of foreign secretary and, being an Oxford contemporary of Mackinder's and a known empathizer with his geostrategy, it is a moot point whether his influence was instrumental in the appointment. Alfred

Milner, former high commissioner to South Africa and highly influential member of Lloyd George's government, was Mackinder's other patron at the top circle.

16. Brian W. Blouet, "Sir Halford Mackinder as British High Commissioner to South Russia, 1919–1920," *The Geographical Journal* 142, no. 2 (1976): 230.

17. Blouet, "High Commissioner," 235.

18. Blouet, *Mackinder: A Biography*, 178.

19. Colin S. Gray, "In Defence of the Heartland: Sir Halford Mackinder and His Critics a Hundred Years On (2003)," in *Contemporary Essays* (London: Strategic and Combat Studies Institute, 2004), 34.

20. Blouet, *Mackinder: A Biography*, 179.

21. Blouet, *Mackinder: A Biography*, 122.

22. Gray, "In Defence of the Heartland," 25.

23. Blouet, *Mackinder: A Biography*, 178.

24. Mackinder, *Democratic Ideals and Reality*, 16.

25. Mackinder, "Round World," 604.

26. Blouet, *Mackinder: A Biography*, 109.

27. Blouet, *Mackinder: A Biography*, 113.

28. Blouet, *Mackinder: A Biography*, 114.

29. Blouet, *Mackinder: A Biography*, 109.

30. Mackinder, "Round World," 202.

31. Mackinder, "Geographical Pivot," 192.

32. Mackinder, "Geographical Pivot," 177.

33. Mackinder, *Democratic Ideals and Reality*, 120.

34. Mackinder, *Democratic Ideals and Reality*, 120.

35. Mackinder, *Democratic Ideals and Reality*, 146.

36. Gray, "In Defence of the Heartland," 29.

37. Mackinder, *Democratic Ideals and Reality*, 51.

CHAPTER 3

1. The influential theater critic Justin Brooks Atkinson.

2. Henry Kissinger, *White House Years* (Boston: Little Brown and Co., 1979), 135.

3. George F. Kennan, "America and the Russian Future," *Foreign Affairs* 29, no.3 (1951): 130.

4. George F. Kennan, *The Realities of American Foreign Policy* (London: Geoffrey Cumberlege for Oxford University Press, 1954), 73.

5. Sean Greenwood, "Frank Roberts and the 'Other' Long Telegram: The View from the British Embassy in Moscow, March 1946," *Journal of Contemporary History* 25, no.1 (1990): 111.

6. Kennan, *The Realities of American Foreign Policy*, 66.

7. George F. Kennan, *Memoirs 1925–1950* (London: Hutchinson and Co., Ltd., 1968), 74.

8. Kennan, *Memoirs 1925–1950*, 70.

9. Kennan, *Memoirs 1925–1950*, 57.

10. Kennan, *The Realities of American Foreign Policy*, 27.

11. Greenwood, "Frank Roberts and the 'Other' Long Telegram," 112.

12. Kennan, "America and the Russian Future," 130.

13. Kennan, *The Realities of American Foreign Policy,* 21.

14. Kennan, "America and the Russian Future," 131.

15. Kennan, *The Realities of American Foreign Policy,* 39.

16. Kennan, *The Realities of American Foreign Policy,* 36.

17. Kennan, "America and the Russian Future," 136.

18. George F. Kennan, *American Diplomacy 1900–1950* (London: Secker and Warburg, 1952), 120.

19. Kennan, *The Realities of American Foreign Policy,* 99.

20. Kennan, "America and the Russian Future," 145.

21. Kennan, *Memoirs 1925–1950,* 364.

22. Wilson D. Miscamble, *George F. Kennan and the Making of American Foreign Policy 1947–1950* (Princeton, NJ: Princeton University Press, 1992), 6.

23. Kennan, *Memoirs 1925–1950,* 74.

24. John Lewis Gaddis, *Strategies of Containment: A Critical Appraisal of American National Security Policy during the Cold War* (New York: Oxford University Press, 1982), 25.

25. Kennan, *Memoirs 1925–1950,* 367.

26. Terry H. Anderson, *The United States, Great Britain and the Cold War, 1944–1947* (Columbia, MO: University of Missouri Press, 1981), xiv.

27. Kennan, *Memoirs 1925–1950,* 353.

CHAPTER 4

1. Churchill's remark at the end of the First World War that "when the war of the giants is over, the wars of the pygmies will begin."

2. W. F. Reddaway, et al, eds., *The Cambridge History of Poland, from Augustus II to Piłsudski, 1697–1935* (Cambridge: Cambridge University Press, 1941), 593.

3. Richard Woytak, "The Promethean Movement in Interwar Poland," *East European Quarterly* 13, no. 3 (1984): 275.

4. Edmund Charaszkiewicz, *Zbiór dokumentów ppłk. Edmunda Charaszkiewicza, opracowanie, wstęp i przypisy* (*A Collection of Documents by Lt. Col., edited, with introduction and notes by* Andrzej Grzywacz, Marcin Kwiecień, Grzegorz Mazur), Biblioteka Centrum Dokumentacji Czynu Niepodległościowego, tom [vol.] 9 (Kraków: Księgarnia Akademicka, 2000), 56.

5. Woytak, "The Promethean Movement," 275.

6. Woytak, "The Promethean Movement," 273.

7. Woytak, "The Promethean Movement," 274.

8. Miron Rezun, "The Soviet Union and Iran: Soviet Policy in Iran from the Beginnings of the Pahlavi Dynasty until the Soviet Invasion in 1941," *Russian Review* 49, no. 1 (1990): 101.

9. Woytak, "The Promethean Movement," 273.

10. Zygmunt J. Gasiorowski, "Did Piłsudski Attempt to Initiate a Preventive War in 1933?" *The Journal of Modern History* 27, no. 2 (1955): 145.

11. Woytak, "The Promethean Movement," 273.

12. Rezun, "The Soviet Union and Iran," 101.

13. Norman Davies, "Sir Maurice Hankey and the Inter-Allied Mission to Poland, July–August 1920," *The Historical Journal* 15, no. 3 (1972): 38.

14. Davies, "Sir Maurice Hankey," 26.

15. Davies, "Sir Maurice Hankey," 43.

16. Jacob Kipp, ed., *Central European Security Concerns: Bridge, Buffer, or Barrier?* (London, Portland. 1993), 95.

17. Gasiorowski, "Did Piłsudski Attempt to Initiate," 139.

18. Woytak, "The Promethean Movement," 277.

19. Alex Pravda, ed., *Yearbook of Soviet Foreign Relations, 1991 Edition* (London: I.B. Taurus, 1991).

20. Alex Pravda, ed., *Yearbook of Soviet Foreign Relations, 1991 Edition* (London: I.B. Taurus, 1991).

21. Alex Pravda, ed., *Yearbook of Soviet Foreign Relations, 1991 Edition* (London: I.B. Taurus, 1991).

22. Alex Pravda, ed., *Yearbook of Soviet Foreign Relations, 1991 Edition* (London: I.B. Taurus, 1991).

23. Alex Pravda, ed., *Yearbook of Soviet Foreign Relations, 1991 Edition* (London: I.B. Taurus, 1991).

24. Alex Pravda, ed., *Yearbook of Soviet Foreign Relations, 1991 Edition* (London: I.B. Taurus, 1991).

25. Alex Pravda, ed., *Yearbook of Soviet Foreign Relations, 1991 Edition* (London: I.B. Taurus, 1991).

26. Blouet, *Mackinder: A Biography,* 160.

27. *Marian Kamil* Dziewanowski, "Polski pionier zjednoczonej Europy" ("A Polish Pioneer of a United Europe"), *Gwiazda Polarna* (*Pole Star*), Sept. 17, 2005, 10.

28. J. Szapiro, "Poland and Piłsudski," *Journal of the Royal Institute of International Affairs* 8, no. 4 (1929): 380.

29. Davies, "Sir Maurice Hankey," 560.

30. Gasiorowski, "Did Piłsudski Attempt to Initiate," 137.

31. Stefan Litauer, "The Role of Poland between Germany and Russia," *International Affairs* 14, no. 5 (1935): 658.

32. Blouet, "High Commissioner," 233.

33. Blouet, "High Commissioner," 233.

34. Blouet, "High Commissioner," 235.

35. Zbigniew Brzezinski, *The Grand Chessboard: American Primacy and Its Geostrategic Imperatives* (Basic Books, 1998), 46.

CHAPTER 5

1. http://www.niallferguson.com/site/FERG/Templates/ArticleItem.aspx?pageid=138

2. http://www.niallferguson.com/site/FERG/Templates/ArticleItem.aspx?pageid=138 (23.03.2010)

3. Bobo Lo, *Axis of Convenience: Moscow, Beijing and the New Geopolitics* (Washington, DC: Brookings, 2008) 150–151.

4. http://adm.rt.com/Politics/2010-02-26/fm-sergey-lavrov-interview.html (26.02.2010)

5. http://adm.rt.com/Politics/2010-02-26/fm-sergey-lavrov-interview.html (26.02.2010)

6. http://www.cacianalyst.org/?q=node/5286 (17.03.2010)

7. Kennan, "America and the Russian Future," 130.

8. http://www.telegraph.co.uk/finance/comment/ambroseevans_pritchard/7442926/Is-Chinas-Politburo-spoiling-for-a-showdown-with-America.html (15.03.10)

9. http://www.telegraph.co.uk/finance/comment/ambroseevans_pritchard/7442926/Is-Chinas-Politburo-spoiling-for-a-showdown-with-America.html (15.03.10)

10. http://www.telegraph.co.uk/finance/comment/ambroseevans_pritchard/7442926/Is-Chinas-Politburo-spoiling-for-a-showdown-with-America.html (15.03.10)

11. Mackinder, "Geographical Pivot," 437.

12. Brzezinski, *Grand Chessboard*, 31.

13. http://www.cfr.org/publication/10883/

14. Kennan, *Realities of American Foreign Policy*, 33.

15. The Russian population has fallen from around 158 million at the end of the Soviet Union to under 140 million in 2010—https://www.cia.gov/library/publications/the-world-factbook/geos/rs.html

16. http://www.jamestown.org/single/?tx_ttnews[tt_news]=34654&

17. http://eng.globalaffairs.ru/engsmi/1325.html

18. http://www.worldsecuritynetwork.com/showArticle3.cfm?article_id=18249&topicID=31

19. Brzezinski, *Grand Chessboard*, 195.

20. Krasnaya Zvezda, March 5

21. Krasnaya Zvezda, March 5

22. Krasnaya Zvezda, March 5

23. http://www.wilsoncenter.org/index.cfm?fuseaction=wq.essay&essay_id=545818 (Summer 2009 *Wilson Quarterly*)

24. Brzezinski, *Grand Chesboard*, 46.

25. Brzezinski, *Grand Chessboard*, 46.

26. http://rt.com/Politics/2010-03-18/crimea-black-sea-fleet.html (22.03.2010)

27. http://eng.globalaffairs.ru/engsmi/1326.html (19.03.2010)

28. http://www.jamestown.org/programs/recentreports/single/?tx_ttnews[swords]=8fd5893941d69d0be3f378576261ae3e&tx_ttnews[any_of_the_words]=schneller&tx_ttnews[tt_news]=34654&tx_ttnews[backPid]=7&cHash=e7fdda93df

29. http://www.jamestown.org/single/?no_cache=1&tx_ttnews[tt_news]=36171&tx_ttnews[backPid]=13&cHash=189d3b8f04

30. http://www.cacianalyst.org/?q=node/5288 (23.03.2010)

31. http://www.cacianalyst.org/?q=node/5288 (23.03.2010)

32. http://www.niallferguson.com/site/FERG/Templates/ArticleItem.aspx?pageid=138 (23.03.2010)

33. Mackinder, *Democratic Ideals and Reality*, 17.

34. http://www.globalpolicy.org/component/content/article/155/26019.html

35. http://www.foreignpolicy.com/articles/2010/03/11/what_the_neocons_got_right?page=full

36. Mackinder, *Democratic Ideals and Reality*, 148.

CHAPTER 6

1. http://www.foreignpolicy.com/articles/2010/01/04/123000000000000?page=

2. http://csis.org/files/publication/091217_Kuchins_NorthernDistNet_Web.pdf (Dec 2009)

3. http://csis.org/publication/northern-distribution-network-and-modern-silk-road

4. http://csis.org/program/northern-distribution-network-ndn (25.03.2010)

Selected Bibliography

Anderson, Terry H. *The United States, Great Britain and the Cold War, 1944–1947.* Columbia, MO: University of Missouri Press, 1981.

Blouet, Brian W. *Mackinder: A Biography.* College Station, TX: Texas A&M University Press, 1987.

Blouet, Brian W. "Sir Halford Mackinder as British High Commissioner to South Russia, 1919–1920." *The Geographical Journal* 142, no. 2 (1976).

Brzezinski, Zbigniew. *The Grand Chessboard: American Primacy and Its Geostrategic Imperatives.* New York: Basic Books, 1998.

Charaszkiewicz, Edmund. *Zbiór dokumentów ppłk. Edmunda Charaszkiewicza, opracowanie, wstęp i przypisy (A Collection of Documents by Lt. Col., edited, with introduction and notes by* Andrzej Grzywacz, Marcin Kwiecień, Grzegorz Mazur). Biblioteka Centrum Dokumentacji Czynu Niepodległościowego, tom [vol.] 9. Kraków: Księgarnia Akademicka, 2000, 56.

Crowe, Sir Eyre. "Memorandum on the Present State of British Relations with France and Germany." *British Documents on the Origins of War 1898–1914.* Edited by G. P. Gooch and Harold Temperley. Vol. III. London: H.M.S.O., 1928, 402.

Davies, Norman. "Sir Maurice Hankey and the Inter-Allied Mission to Poland, July–August 1920." *The Historical Journal* 15, no. 3 (1972).

Dziewanowski, Marian Kamil. "Polski pionier zjednoczonej Europy" ("A Polish Pioneer of a United Europe"). *Gwiazda Polarna (Pole Star)*, Sept. 17, 2005, 10–11.

Gaddis, John Lewis. *Strategies of Containment: A Critical Appraisal of American National Security Policy during the Cold War.* New York: Oxford University Press, 1982.

Gasiorowski, Zygmunt J. "Did Piłsudski Attempt to Initiate a Preventive War in 1933?" *The Journal of Modern History* 27, no. 2 (1955).

Gray, Colin S. "In Defence of the Heartland: Sir Halford Mackinder and His Critics a Hundred Years On (2003)." In *Contemporary Essays*. London: Strategic and Combat Studies Institute, 2004.

Greenwood, Sean. "Frank Roberts and the 'Other' Long Telegram: The View from the British Embassy in Moscow, March 1946." *Journal of Contemporary History* 25, no.1 (1990):103–122.

Kennan, George F. "America and the Russian Future." *Foreign Affairs* 29, no.3 (1951): 351–370.

Kennan, George F. *American Diplomacy 1900–1950*. London: Secker and Warburg, 1952.

Kennan, George F. *At a Century's Ending*. New York, London: W.W. Norton, 1996.

Kennan, George F. *Memoirs 1925–1950*. London: Hutchinson and Co., Ltd., 1968.

Kennan, George F. *Memoirs 1950–1963*. London: Hutchinson and Co., Ltd., 1973.

Kennan, George F. *The Nuclear Delusion: Soviet-American Relations in the Atomic Age*. New York: Pantheon Books, 1982.

Kennan, George F. *The Realities of American Foreign Policy*. London: Geoffrey Cumberlege for Oxford University Press, 1954.

Kennan, George F. "The Sources of Soviet Conduct." *Foreign Affairs* 25, no. 4 (1947): 566–582.

Kennan, George F. Text of Long Telegram, 861.00/2—2246. Telegram. "The Charge in the Soviet Union (Kennan) to the Secretary of State," SECRET, Moscow. February 22, 1946—9:00 p.m. [Received February 22—3:52 p.m.] 511. Answer to Dept.'s 284, Feb 3 [13].

Kennan, George F., Charles Gati, Richard H. Ullman. "Interview with George F. Kennan." *Foreign Policy* no. 7 (1972): 5–21.

Kipp, Jacob, ed. *Central European Security Concerns: Bridge, Buffer, or Barrier?* London: Routledge. 1993.

Kissinger, Henry. *White House Years*. Boston: Little Brown and Co., 1979.

Lippmann, Walter. *The Cold War*. 1947.

Litauer, Stefan. "The Role of Poland between Germany and Russia." *International Affairs* 14, no. 5 (1935).

Lo, Bobo. *Axis of Convenience: Moscow, Beijing and the New Geopolitics*. Washington, DC: Brookings, 2008.

Mahan, Alfred Thayer. The Influence of Sea Power Upon History 1660–1783. Boston: Little Brown and Co, 1894.

Mackinder, Halford John. *Democratic Ideals and Reality: A Study in the Politics of Reconstruction*. London: Constable, 1919.

Mackinder, Halford John. "The Geographical Pivot of History." *The Geographical Journal* 23, no. 4 (1904).

Mackinder, Halford John. "The Round World and the Winning of the Peace." *Foreign Affairs* 21, no. 4 (1943): 597.

Miscamble, Wilson D. *George F. Kennan and the Making of American Foreign Policy 1947–1950*. Princeton, NJ: Princeton University Press, 1992.

Pravda, Alex, ed. *Yearbook of Soviet Foreign Relations, 1991 Edition*. London: I.B. Taurus, 1991.

Reddaway, W. F., et al, eds. *The Cambridge History of Poland, from Augustus II to Piłsudski, 1697–1935*. Cambridge: Cambridge University Press, 1941.

Rezun, Miron. "The Soviet Union and Iran: Soviet Policy in Iran from the Beginnings of the Pahlavi Dynasty until the Soviet Invasion in 1941." *Russian Review* 49, no. 1 (1990).

Spykman, Nicholas. *America's Strategy in World Politics*. Transaction, 2007

Spykman, Nicholas. *The Geography of the Peace*. Harcourt, Brace and Co., 1944.

Szapiro, J. "Poland and Piłsudski." *Journal of the Royal Institute of International Affairs* 8, no. 4 (1929).

Woytak, Richard. "The Promethean Movement in Interwar Poland." *East European Quarterly* 13, no. 3 (1984): 273.

Index

Page numbers in italics refer to map.

About the Author

ALEXANDROS PETERSEN is Director of Research at the Henry Jackson Society: Project for Democratic Geopolitics. An internationally recognized scholar of grand strategy and energy geopolitics, he also serves as Non-resident Senior Fellow with the Eurasia Center at the Atlantic Council, Washington DC. Prior to his current position, Petersen was Fellow for Transatlantic Energy Security and Associate Director of the Eurasia Center. He came to the Council from the Woodrow Wilson International Center for Scholars, where he was Southeast Europe Policy Scholar and the Center for Strategic and International Studies, where he was an Adjunct Fellow with the Russia and Eurasia Program. Previously, he served as Program Director of the Caspian Europe Center in Brussels and Senior Researcher at the International Institute for Strategic Studies in London. In 2006, he was a Visiting Scholar at the Georgian Foundation for Strategic and International Studies in Tbilisi. He has also provided research for the U.S. National Petroleum Council's Geopolitics and Policy Task Group and the Council on Foreign Relations Task Force on Russian-American Relations.

Petersen regularly provides analysis for publications such as the *Economist*, *Wall Street Journal*, *New York Times*, *International Herald Tribune*, *Boston Globe* and *Washington Times*, among many others. He is also a frequent contributor to journals and magazines including *Foreign Affairs*, *Foreign Policy* and the *National Interest*. Petersen has appeared on the BBC, Sky News, CTV and NPR. He serves on the board of Young Professionals in Foreign Policy and the editorial board of *Millennium: Journal of International Studies*. Petersen received a BA in War Studies with First Class Honors from King's College London and an MSc in International Relations from the London School of Economics.